HOLY RUS'

Holy Rus'

The Rebirth of Orthodoxy in the New Russia

JOHN P. BURGESS

Yale

UNIVERSITY PRESS

NEW HAVEN AND LONDON

Published with assistance from the Mary Cady Tew Memorial Fund.

Yale University Press books may be purchased in quantity for educational, business, or promotional use. For information, please e-mail sales.press@yale.edu (U.S. office) or sales@yaleup.co.uk (U.K. office).

Set in Electra type by IDS Infotech, Ltd.
Printed in the United States of America.

Library of Congress Control Number: 2016948024
ISBN 978-0-300-22224-1 (hardcover: alk. paper)

A catalogue record for this book is available from the British Library.

This paper meets the requirements of ANSI/NISO Z39.48-1992 (Permanence of Paper).

10 9 8 7 6 5 4 3 2 1

For my daughters Hannah, Luisa, and Rachel

CONTENTS

Acknowledgments   ix
Note on Transliteration   xii

Introduction   1

ONE

Envisioning Holy Rus'   8

TWO

The Rebirth of Orthodoxy   24

THREE

Religious Education   51

FOUR

Social Ministry   91

FIVE

The New Martyrs   122

SIX

Parish Life   164

SEVEN

The Future   194

Notes   225
Index   253

ACKNOWLEDGMENTS

I have incurred many debts in writing this book, so many, in fact, that my expressions of gratitude will necessarily and regretfully be incomplete. I begin with thanks to those institutions whose financial support over the past decade has allowed me to live in Russia for extended periods and immerse myself in the worship and life of the Russian Orthodox Church. Pittsburgh Theological Seminary graciously granted me sabbaticals in 2004–5 and 2011–12. I am especially thankful to Dr. Barry Jackson, former academic dean, for his consistent encouragement and support. A Fulbright Fellowship in the fall of 2011 and a Luce Foundation grant for Fellows in Theology in 2012 allowed me to extend my sabbatical time and complete the bulk of my research.

As every scholar knows, getting around to actually writing is another thing. I am therefore deeply grateful for the invitation that I received to be a fellow at the Center of Theological Inquiry in Princeton, New Jersey, in 2014–15, where I completed a first draft of my manuscript. My colleagues in a year-long colloquy on law and religious freedom were among the first scholars with whom I shared my research, and their comments helped me shape the book. I am especially thankful to Dr. William Storrar, director of the center, and to Dr. Robin Lovin, its research director. Dr. Storrar made it possible for me to invite two groups of scholars to daylong colloquies in Princeton to reflect on issues of Orthodoxy and politics. Dr. Lovin, from early on, saw the significance of my project and opened up opportunities for me to develop and share it.

Dr. William Gleason, for many years head of the Russia–Eurasian Studies Program of the State Department's Foreign Service Institute, has been another trusted friend and advocate. He invited me to Washington many times over the course of these years to share my research, and he read and commented on the entire manuscript. Father Leonid Kishkovsky, head of the Department of External Church Relations of the Orthodox Church in America, also reviewed the manuscript in its entirety and offered insightful suggestions. I am equally indebted to the anonymous reviewer for Yale University Press who saved me from numerous historical errors in the first draft and pushed me to clarify that I was writing as a theologian rather than a historian. But of the revising and correcting of book manuscripts there is no end, and any errors that remain are my own.

Other scholars have been extremely generous with their time in reviewing particular chapters of the book. I wish to thank in particular Dr. Nadieszda Kizenko, University of Albany–SUNY; Dr. Scott Kenworthy, Miami University of Ohio; Dr. Michael Bourdeaux, Keston Institute; Dr. Roy Robson, Penn State Abington; Dr. Aristotle Papanikolaou, Fordham University; Dr. George Parsenios, Princeton Theological Seminary; and Dr. Josh Mauldin, Center of Theological Inquiry. I am also grateful to Dr. Nigel Biggar, Christ Church, Oxford University, and Dr. Kenworthy for invitations to speak about my work at their institutions. I have been blessed by their hospitality and friendship.

Colleagues in the American Academy of Religion, the Society of Christian Ethics, and the American Theological Society helpfully critiqued work that I presented at their annual conferences. Dr. Regina Smyth, Indiana University–Bloomington, has been an important and supportive conversation partner ever since we met on the Fulbright Program in Moscow. Richard Brown, director of Georgetown University Press, has also offered steady encouragement. At a time when I was unsure how to frame the book, he persuaded me that it could be of value not only to scholars but also to a wider intellectual audience seeking to understand post-Communist Russia. I was delighted when Yale University Press recognized these possibilities and agreed to publish the book. My editor, Jennifer Banks, has enthusiastically promoted my work and offered wise counsel. I have also benefited from the excellent work of Heather Gold, Susan Laity, and Robin DuBlanc.

Needless to say, this book could not have been written without the assistance of dozens of Russian friends and conversation partners. I have identified some by first and last name in the chapters that follow; in other cases, I have changed or deleted names in order to respect people's privacy. Together, these people have done more for me than I will ever be able to give in return. Not only have they been my most important teachers about Russia and Russian Orthodoxy, but they have also welcomed me into their homes, introduced me to parishes and monasteries, offered me food and accommodation, been patient with my imperfect Russian-language skills, and arranged for me to meet their friends and acquaintances in order further to assist my research. Because of their love and care, Russia and Russian Orthodoxy have come to feel like a second home to me, even though I remain an outsider who also raises hard questions. I wish to offer a special word of thanks to Father Vladimir Volgin and Father (now Bishop) Mefodii (Kondrat'ev) for providing me broad access to their parishes, and to St. Tikhon's Orthodox Humanitarian University in Moscow, which hosted me as a research scholar in 2011–12 and made it possible for me to return for several shorter stays. It goes without saying that I alone am responsible for the observations and opinions in the following pages.

Last but in no way least, my wife, Deb, has been my partner in exploring Russia. She has sacrificed considerable time and comfort to support my research and writing. She has read and reread every chapter of this book and assisted with notes and transliteration. The end product will appear under my name alone, but her love and insight have made all the difference to its completion. I have no words to express my gratitude.

In general I have followed the standard (modified Library of Congress) system for transliterating Cyrillic. However, in the case of names of people or places well known in the West—such as Leo Tolstoy—I have retained the anglicized forms. In the endnotes, I have translated the names of major university publishers in Russia, such as Moscow State University. But I have not been rigidly consistent with the names of other publishers. Scholars who wish to track down my sources on the Internet will, ironically, have to work their way back from my transliterations to the original Cyrillic.

HOLY RUS'

Introduction

Father Vladimir Volgin is one of Moscow's most prominent priests. I first attended his parish in 2009, and ever since he has blessed me with time and attention. But we belong to two very different worlds. I am a cosmopolitan American; he is a patriotic Russian. I make my living as a Protestant theologian; he is an Orthodox priest who invites me into his home for dinner but is forbidden by Church canons from serving me the Eucharist in his parish. I have a small, unimpressive mustache, but his large bushy gray beard tickles when he offers me a three-part, Russian-style kiss. And while I speak Russian haltingly and with a heavy accent, his Russian is so beautiful that people hang on every word. When he asked me to accompany him to Ostankino, I jumped at the chance.

Ostankino is a Moscow suburb where the Soviets built a massive television and communications center in the 1960s. Today, several dozen state and private broadcasting companies have their studios here. More than fifteen thousand people work in the complex; another five thousand visit it daily. As we pass through a security checkpoint and a maze of hallways, I suddenly have an eerie feeling. I realize that I am stepping into what had once been the very heart of the Soviet propaganda machine. This place represented everything that I had feared about Russia as I grew up during the Cold War. But the world has changed. I, an American, am here, and Ostankino now broadcasts diaper and detergent commercials for Western companies doing business in Russia—and also the Putin-friendly evening news.

Father Vladimir has a different take on Ostankino. "You see," he tells me, "Russia needs spiritual renewal." He leads me around the corner to the room that for him represents the heart of the complex. The hustle and bustle of twenty-four-hour, seven-day-a-week television programming suddenly gives way to the ancient, seemingly unchanging rhythms that have defined Russia for more than a thousand years. Slender candles flicker before huge icons of Mary, the Mother of God, and Jesus, the World Ruler. A male quartet is intoning the soaring melodies of Orthodox prayer. People are entering a space of worship, crossing themselves, and finding a place to stand. We have come to the place that Orthodox believers call heaven on earth. At the heart of Ostankino—at the heart of the new Russia—is the Orthodox Church.

This book is about the religious vision that guides Russia and the Orthodox Church today. I describe a nation that longs for Holy Rus', that elusive ideal of a people and place transformed by the holy. Russians have suffered immense deprivation and hardship over the ages—and again in the twentieth century, with the October Revolution, the gulags, and Stalingrad—but they have also reported glimpsing an intense, otherworldly beauty that has enabled them to endure and even to know joy. Today, the Orthodox Church is calling Russians to reclaim their heritage. Gold and silver onion domes again stand against the horizon, church interiors with precious icons and frescoes draw worshippers into an alternative, spiritual realm, and Russia's magnificent lakes and springs invite pilgrims to drink and bathe in their holy waters. Holy Rus' seems to promise Russians a world different from, and a world better than, the technical efficiency and competitive rat race of what we have come to call "postmodernity," which now governs their everyday lives as much as anywhere in the West.

Westerners, of course, have always projected their own longings for a different and better kind of world onto Russia. I remember asking my friend Aleksandr, an admirer of Russia's Old Believers, who rejected Peter the Great's modernizing reforms in the eighteenth century, whether he ever had mystical experiences in church. He laughed and replied, "No, and sometimes I'm even bored." But another friend, Irina, told me that she once saw a priest levitate during the liturgy: "He just kept rising higher and higher in the air, and his face kept glowing brighter and brighter before he came back to earth." Irina cleans her parish church every Friday morning and says that she talks to the icons—and they answer. No, Holy Rus' is more than just one more Western imposition on the East. Holy Rus' belongs to Russians' own aspirations of what makes Russia most truly "Russia."

This world of miracles and holy things, of weeping icons and healing waters, has intrigued yet confused me. I am a North American Calvinist who traces his roots to Buchanans and McLaughlins in Scotland. We are a no-nonsense, hardworking kind of people, committed to the principle, completely unbiblical, that "God helps those who help themselves." And not only am I a Presbyterian, I am also a professor of Calvinist, or so-called Reformed, theology. I make my living thinking about ultimate questions of life and death, and I know how to do so only by drawing on my Reformation heritage and putting it into conversation with modern science and contemporary philosophical and social movements. Priests do not levitate in my religion.

Nevertheless, we Calvinists are a curious lot, always asking how the One whom we call God may be at work in a speck of dust or the glance of a stranger. So in 2004–5, when I received my first sabbatical, my wife and I took our three school-age daughters with us to St. Petersburg, Russia. I already knew a good deal about Western Protestantism and Catholicism; now it was time to learn about Eastern Orthodoxy. Besides, I had read that religion was coming back to life in this part of the world. I wanted to understand why, especially because mainline Protestant bodies and my own Presbyterian Church were steadily declining in the United States and the future of Christianity seemed to lie elsewhere.

So my family and I immersed ourselves in Orthodox life. Every Sunday we attended an Orthodox parish—in fact, we were among its most regular worshippers. My daughters participated in the parish Sunday school, and the priest often invited us to lunch in the parish house after the liturgy. As an academic theologian, I had come to Russia with the intention of sitting in libraries and studying scholarly literature about religion and society, but within days after our arrival I realized that my Russian was still too poor—I had my first lessons at age forty-eight, as we prepared for the trip—and besides I knew too little about Orthodoxy. My research plan "evolved." I put away the books and began instead to visit parishes and monasteries. By the end of the year, I had attended dozens of Orthodox liturgies, youth clubs, and academic conferences; gotten to know deacons and priests, monks and nuns; joined ordinary believers in making pilgrimage to Russian Orthodoxy's most holy sites; venerated miracle-working icons and relics; and observed the Church calendar, including the eight-week Great Lent in which believers remove all animal products—meat, cheese, eggs, and fish—from their diets.

Little by little Russia's religious vision drew me in until suddenly I, too, an exhausted American Protestant in a foreign land, arrived at Easter morning and stood on what seemed to me a mountain of transfiguration from which I could glimpse Holy Rus'. I momentarily stepped out of my

Author with monks, pilgrims, and rehabilitants, St. George's Parish, Ivanovo Region (with permission of St. George's Parish)

self-centered worries and anxieties into a place where the holy had perme-
ated the everyday. I was perhaps experiencing "heaven"—the promise of
genuine, intimate communion with divinity and humanity. Ever since,
doors have kept opening for me to meet Russians and enter more fully into
Orthodox life. In 2011–12, I spent a second sabbatical in Russia, this time in
Moscow. And many shorter trips before and after have taken me from the
Solovetskii Islands in the White Sea in Russia's far north to the Crimean
peninsula along the Black Sea in the far south.

More than a decade of getting to know Russia has taught me that how a
person recounts past and present events is at the same time a way of
expressing his or her hopes for the future. My academic training is not in
history or political science, but I nevertheless dare in this book to tell a story
about Russia past and present in order to project a vision of what it may yet
become. No doubt my definition of Holy Rus' is personal and idiosyncratic.
But it is not fanciful or arbitrary. I am seeking to delineate the contours of a
religious understanding of society that I have glimpsed in the efforts of
Russians, especially Orthodox Russians, to build a new nation. What I am
offering is more than a journalistic report. It is an interpretive essay about
the contribution that Orthodox Christianity is making—or, as I understand
it, could be making—to national identity in the new Russia. I am capturing
a moment in time, synthesizing impressions gained from many years of
putting my ear to the ground; more important to me than official Church
position papers or patriarchal pronouncements has been the "lived theology"
of the parishes and monasteries, priests and laypeople, professors and
pilgrims who have invited me into their lives. It is on the basis of these many
personal encounters that I make my case, namely, that the Orthodox
Church in Russia today is seeking to re-create the Holy Rus' I glimpsed on
that Easter morning in St. Petersburg.

The Orthodox tradition uses such terms as *transfiguration, deification,*
and *eternity breaking into time* to speak of the divine presence in history and
human lives. In Russia, these notions have sometimes been conjoined with
that of Holy Rus', a people and nation chosen by God to be transformed by
divine beauty. I believe that current Church social initiatives can be

understood as contributing to realization of this religious vision. And the Church can also be judged by whether its actions and activities ultimately fulfill or violate the promise of this Holy Rus'.

I recognize the dangers with this approach. I will not always be able to present the hard evidence that historians, political scientists, and sociologists demand, although I do support my case as much as possible not only from personal conversations and observations but also from books and journal articles. My experience is limited to 2004–16; new events will have occurred by the time this book appears. Moreover, I will not be able fully to explicate and evaluate the many alternative ways of interpreting Church, society, and state in Russia today, although I will often refer to how they challenge and complicate my interpretation of events. And it goes without saying that Russia and its Church are not monolithic entities; Russians relate to religion in many different ways. There is no single "Church" but rather a variety of "Orthodoxies." Holy Rus' is itself an imprecise term, and not everyone will agree with my definition. When one of my Russian friends first heard the title of my book, he protested, "But Holy Rus' just means a Church and state that work together to dominate the rest of us." While his concern is legitimate, I nevertheless wish to propose a different way of defining the Russian Church today—how out of the diversity and complexity of Russian Orthodox life I also discern a unity of purpose to make Russian society truly better and freer.

My interpretation of the Church's vision of society is not necessarily that of its hierarchy, and I do not seek to represent a particular political faction, either liberal or conservative, within the Church. Rather, I am sketching an "ideal type" in the spirit of the twentieth-century German sociologist Max Weber and his university colleague, theologian Ernst Troeltsch. An ideal type heightens key features of a social movement in order to highlight what makes it distinctive. No social movement is reducible to an ideal type, but ideal types, at their best, deepen our ability to understand people who are different from ourselves, and that is my goal: to help us in the West better understand the remarkable rebirth of Orthodox Christianity in contemporary Russia.

Father Volgin claims that the Orthodox chapel in Ostankino is already radiating spiritual values into Russian broadcasting. "There is less pornography

and violence, and the major channels have become friendlier to the Church."
I do not ask him for evidence, and I wonder whether he is merely projecting
his own hopes. But I am a theologian: I know that hope is what humans live
by, and Holy Rus', even if not always named in that way, seems to me to
capture the aspirations of today's Orthodox Church. A religious vision of the
future is touching millions of Russians. Anyone who wants to understand the
new Russia has reason to pay attention.

Envisioning Holy Rus'

Whenever I arrive, I ask myself, "Where am I really?" Blurry-eyed from the overnight plane ride, I pick up my baggage, make my way through passport control and customs, grab a taxi, and stare out the window. The long ride into the city center takes me past shopping malls, dilapidated industrial zones, and endless rows of sparkling new banks, offices, and fitness centers. Eventually, Soviet-era apartment blocks become more prominent. Then the towers of the Kremlin loom in the distance, and traffic grinds to a stop.

Moscow is again a great European capital—a world-class, cosmopolitan city—that rivals London or Paris. But I am quickly reminded that I am not in western Europe. An inexpensive plastic icon of St. Nicholas is affixed to the dashboard of the taxi. As traffic lurches ahead, we pass a massive church whose silver onion domes are ablaze in the intense morning sunlight. An elderly woman has paused on the sidewalk and is crossing herself and bowing toward the church. Farther down the road, a giant billboard announces an Orthodox festival at the city's main exhibition grounds: "Consecrated honey from monasteries, water from holy wells and springs, presentations by leading Church personalities."

We arrive at my friends' flat just south of the Moscow River, and I pay the cabbie. Church bells are ringing. As I step out of the car, I dodge to avoid a procession of dark-bearded priests in glistening, golden vestments. They are chanting Church hymns as they carry a huge icon of Mary, the Mother of

God, down the sidewalk. Several dozen women in brightly colored head scarves and men with neatly pressed white shirts follow close behind, while young people in dapper suits or tight jeans pay no attention and hustle by on their way to work. Music blares out from a nearby bar: Frank Sinatra crooning "New York, New York." And in the doorway, a half-naked woman calls out in Russian, "Welcome to Moscow."

A bold experiment is taking place in this new, still developing Russia. After a century of being scarred first by militant atheistic Communism and then Wild West capitalism, the Orthodox Church has become Russia's largest and most significant nongovernmental organization, and as it has returned to life, it has pursued a vision of "re-Christianizing" Russian society. The Church does not want the global marketplace to have the last word. Rather, it wishes to ensure that wherever Russians go today, they will encounter and learn to venerate Orthodox symbols, narratives, and rituals. After the 1917 Revolution, the Bolsheviks tried to eliminate the Church as a public institution—and came very close to succeeding. By 1939, a nation that had once prided itself on being thoroughly Orthodox had only a few hundred churches left in operation. And these were nothing more than Potemkin villages, a way to assure the occasional Western diplomat or tourist that the Soviet Union respected freedom of religion. In the meantime, hundreds of thousands of believers had perished in labor camps, and hundreds of thousands more were hiding their faith from public view. Today a dramatic reversal has taken place. The Church has been reborn, and it asks Russians once again to regard Orthodox Christianity as an essential part of their national identity.

The Church, at least by institutional measures, seems well on its way to success. Since the collapse of Communism, the number of parishes (the Church's canonical territory includes not only Russia but also other areas of the former Soviet Union) has grown from seven thousand to thirty-three thousand. The number of men's and women's monasteries—in the 1990s, fewer than thirty—now exceeds eight hundred. Chapels have been established not only in the central television center in Ostankino but also in airports, train stations, and state universities. As many as 70–80 percent of Russians call themselves Orthodox. And political leaders such as Vladimir

Putin and Dmitrii Medvedev profess to be Orthodox and cross themselves in public. Russia has "got" religion.

To be sure, Russia resembles western Europe in regard to religion, with high rates of affiliation and low rates of participation. But because so many Russians call themselves Orthodox again, the official Church believes that it has a remarkable opportunity to make them active members. The slogan for its mission is, translated literally, "in-churching"—that is, turning nominal Orthodox Russians into true believers by incorporating them into the Church's life of prayer, worship, sacraments, and service.[1]

In-churching is not only a matter of church attendance. In a way that Westerners sometimes call mystical, Orthodox Christianity envisions the in-churching of all of society, indeed the whole of creation. And for the Orthodox Church, Russia is the place to begin. As I have watched events unfold, I have sometimes wondered: could contemporary Russia, despite all of its complexities and contradictions, point again, however faintly, to Holy Rus', that mythical yet historical homeland of the eastern Slavic peoples . . . that foretaste of the perfect justice, peace, harmony, and beauty for which Christians and other spiritual traditions long . . . that elusive ideal of a divinely transfigured nation that persuaded Prince Vladimir to accept Orthodox baptism in Crimea in AD 988? Many Westerners—and some Russians—may be skeptical, even cynical, about a Church that seems hopelessly compromised by worldly wealth and political manipulations. But the story has another side that many of us do not yet know.

In trying to understand Communist and now post-Communist Russia, Western observers often focus on its political leaders. In recent years, all eyes have been on President Vladimir Putin—his KGB background, his political ambitions under and since President Boris Yeltsin, his cozy relations with the new oligarchs, his corrupt amassing of immense personal wealth, and his ruthless elimination of political opponents.[2] Obsession with Putin, however, has diverted our attention from key social and cultural factors that help explain his widespread popularity among Russians.

At the height of East-West tension after Ukraine's revolution on the Maidan in 2014, Princeton historian Stephen Kotkin noted that Putin had brilliantly responded to an almost desperate need among Russians for reassurance that their country remains great and continues to have a unique mission among the nations of the world after the collapse of the Soviet Union.[3] What Kotkin and so many other historians and political scientists have neglected, however, is the religious dimension to this search for national identity. The Orthodox Church has offered Russians—and Vladimir Putin himself—a compelling narrative of national greatness and uniqueness.[4]

When Communism collapsed, Western observers typically regarded the new Russia as an important but second-tier power. While it still possessed an impressive arsenal of nuclear weapons, it seemed to have enough problems at home that it would necessarily relinquish any global political ambitions. Russia, the thinking went, would quietly integrate itself into Western-dominated economic and political structures. Cooperation with the West would ensure Russia's prosperity and stability.

The West, however, failed to understand that Russians, while eager to achieve a Western standard of living, did not now think of themselves as mere "junior Europeans," poorer cousins to the Germans, French, or other "Euro" peoples. Rather, Russians wanted to know more than ever what made Russia uniquely "Russia." Orthodoxy has offered an answer. It has told Russians that their worldview is fundamentally different from the West's—as different as Orthodox onion domes from Catholic and Protestant steeples, as different as Andrei Rublev's Trinity icon from Michelangelo's *Last Supper.*

Not long after the Maidan, Sergei Lavrov, the Russian Federation's eloquent foreign minister, declared that Russia and the West had become estranged from each other because of deep differences in their fundamental civilizational values. While Western societies are "ever more detached from their own Christian roots," "the new Russia is returning to its traditional values, which are rooted in Orthodoxy."[5] In such statements, Holy Rus' finds articulate expression not only as Church doctrine but also as political ideology.

Few Western political scientists studying Russia today mention the Russian Orthodox Church. And if they do, it is almost always to assert that the

Church has made a devil's pact with Putin. According to common Western interpretations of events, the Russian state guarantees the Orthodox Church social privilege and material wealth in exchange for political loyalty.[6] President Putin and Patriarch Kirill are in cahoots.

But when we examine the Russian Orthodox Church only in terms of its compromises with and subservience to the state, we miss the extraordinary religious renaissance that is taking place on the ground far away from official meetings between the patriarch and the president. Major initiatives in education, social ministry, historical commemoration, and parish life are helping the Church reach deeply into Russian society. Whatever the Church's faults and failures—and they are real—I have seen how Russia is the better for the Church's efforts to bring its values into society.

The Church's educational efforts are helping Russians take pride again in a Russia whose history goes back more than a thousand years before 1917. The Church today reminds Russians of the remarkable achievements of Russian culture, music, literature, and the arts, and how Orthodoxy decisively shaped them. The Church has vigorously promoted social outreach to society's weak and vulnerable. Its initiatives in drug rehabilitation, hospice, and care of autistic children have cutting-edge significance in a society whose social safety net still has not been fully repaired since it ripped apart as Communism fell. The Church has reminded Russians of the immensity of the Bolshevik crimes against the nation and the need for national repentance and renewal. And as the Church has reestablished parishes and monasteries, people gather for worship, experience intimate community and mutual care, and commit themselves to deeds of mercy and compassion.

Underlying all of these initiatives has been a steady confidence that Russia is somehow essentially Orthodox. Orthodox values and ways of thinking have embedded themselves so deeply in Russian culture and Russians' psyche that Russia cannot be truly "Russia" without Orthodoxy. As Patriarch Kirill has famously remarked about the Soviet period, "The Gospel was proclaimed primarily not by priests, missionaries, or Church literature. It was proclaimed by the culture. . . . Literally everything that had been created during centuries of cultural development—literature, poetry, architecture, art, and music—made a witness to Christ. . . . A Christian worldview, the Church's wisdom, and biblical aphorisms lived on in the people's consciousness."⁷ When Russians said "Sunday" (*voskresen'e*), they were witnessing, however unintentionally or unconsciously, to Christ's resurrection (*voskresenie*). When they said "thank you" (*spasibo*), they were declaring, "May God save you" (*spasi Bog*).

In this way of thinking, Orthodoxy's vision of "heaven on earth" has always shaped Russia. The Church today, with its program of re-Christianization, is only making explicit what is already implicit in the Russian consciousness. And those who think this way go on to conclude that the perfect peace, justice, and interpersonal mutuality that characterize heaven can find provisional expression on earth. Church and state can work together to shape a society that is rightly ordered, a nation in which people treat each other with respect and care, and honor the sacred authority of both Church and state.

From this perspective, a Russian does not have to become an Orthodox believer to commit him- or herself to Holy Rus', but a Russia in which the Orthodox Church is vital will better help Russians protect their distinctive national identity. And while I as a Christian theologian believe that the ultimate purpose of the Church is to point people to life beyond death and this world, I can see the Orthodox case for making in-churching key to national identity. Those who actively participate in Church life may begin to embody even now the values and way of life that make Russia most truly Russia. This kind of re-Christianization would mean the renewal of both Church and nation.

Despite talk of re-Christianization, the term is potentially misleading.⁸ A sociologist of religion in a small university in Russia's south told me that Russia was never "de-Christianized." Orthodoxy remained an essential dimension of Russian national identity even during the worst years of Communist oppression. "People kept icons in their homes," he insisted, "and they baptized their children." But a professor of church history in Moscow warned me that my project was doomed from the outset. Russia could not be re-Christianized because it had never really been

Christianized. To her, a "Christian Russia" has always been an exaggerated ambition, never an on-the-ground reality.

This ambiguity also suggests the complex, contradictory place of religion in contemporary Russia, where Orthodoxy seems to explain everything about Russian national aspirations and yet really elucidates very little. Orthodoxy has indeed come back to life, but often in ways that defy observation and measurement. Russians are religious—or not—in many different ways. Re-Christianization is not the only way to think about what is happening. Suspicion, ignorance, indifference, detached curiosity, and sympathetic disinterest—these, too, accurately describe Russians' attitude toward the Orthodox Church.

Nevertheless, I believe that many Church initiatives, whether beginning from the patriarch above or parishes and monasteries below, today take as a given that Orthodoxy can help Russians understand how they are different from, and even superior to, the West. The implicit line of argumentation goes something like this: in the early sixteenth century, the Russian monk Philotheus asserted that Moscow was a "Third Rome" uniquely entrusted with protecting Christian civilization. The first Rome had fallen to the barbarians in the fifth century and then to Catholic and Protestant heresy in the Middle Ages and the Reformation. The second Rome, Constantinople, had fallen to the Turks and Islam in 1453. In the twentieth century, Communism inherited the notion that Russia had a unique mission to save the world. But the Bolsheviks saw Marxist-Leninist ideology, not Orthodox Christianity, as the future. Since the fall of Communism, the Orthodox Church may not be rebuilding the Third Rome, but it can again cultivate Russia's distinctiveness and greatness over and against a West that, in its view, has lost its moral foundations.

To be sure, I have often heard Orthodox priests lament that the Russian nation has never fully lived up to its religious legacy—Russians have regularly failed to be true to the Orthodoxy that they confess. But if Patriarch Kirill is right, even seventy-four years of Communism could not drive Orthodox symbols, narratives, and rituals totally out of people's consciousness. And so, when I put the pieces together, I see a Church that has come to the following conclusion: because Russia, often in spite of itself, has preserved Orthodoxy through the ages, the nation and its Church now have a special responsibility to demonstrate what is good and true not only for Russia but also for humanity as a whole. Russia's greatness lies in preserving this vision of heaven on earth and offering it to the world.

Perhaps no other church in the world today thinks about re-Christianizing its society. Churches in historically Christian western Europe and North America have experienced declining numbers and waning social influence. Their societies increasingly define themselves as secular in their public institutions and pluralistic in their religious composition. These churches sometimes see themselves as beleaguered minorities, "resident aliens" in a world that has become "post-Christian."[9] Even where Christian churches continue to exercise social influence, they can no longer take their authority for granted. Some of them find themselves in places that sociologists judge to be more secularized than anywhere else in the world, such as eastern Germany and the Czech Republic.

In parts of Africa and Asia, Christian churches are growing rapidly, but in societies whose religious heritage is non-Christian. Christianity represents an alternative to the past, an option for a more Western and more personal and experiential way of believing—or freedom from an oppressive political past. In South Korea, Protestant Christianity has achieved social prominence because of its contributions to national independence, industrialization, and economic prosperity. In China, the Communist Party is tolerating and even encouraging the growth of Christianity; the churches' moral values seem to correspond to the nation's Confucian past. In sub-Saharan Africa, Pentecostal Christianity has helped people negotiate social stresses related to modernization. What is taking place in all of these places is perhaps Christianization but not re-Christianization.

In the Middle East, Christianity is in full retreat. Long-established Christian communities in Iraq, Iran, Syria, and Palestine are suffering under discrimination and persecution by radical forms of Islam; thousands of Christians have fled to the West. De-Christianization is occurring. And in other parts of the world, the relation of church to society is best described as "non-Christianization." Despite a historical presence for several centuries,

Christianity has never really taken hold in such places as Japan, where it remains the religion of a tiny minority.

The rebirth of religion in Russia has defied predictions by some sociologists that religious identities, especially in historically Christian societies, will irreversibly decline.[10] The Russian situation challenges us to consider why and how traditional religious symbols, narratives, and rituals remain deeply embedded in societies even after they become "secularized" and religiously pluralistic. What is happening in Russia today attests to the surprising resilience of religion in the modern world. And these religious symbols, narratives, and rituals become sites of vigorous negotiation of meaning. The institutional Church is not the only actor. Many social and ecclesiastical interests compete to interpret the contours of what I am calling Holy Rus'.[11] Priests and laypeople, bishops and politicians, men and women, social liberals and conservatives—all have their particular take on what an Orthodox Russia should or should not be.

The sustained efforts of the Orthodox Church to bring its values into post-Communist Russian society raise significant sociological, political, and theological questions. At stake for those of us who observe these developments is not only how to describe them but also how to evaluate them. Is re-Christianization actually taking place, and if so, just what difference does it make—or not make—for people's lives individually and as a nation? Again, different perspectives yield different insights.

The sociologist has the challenge of identifying and measuring religiosity. Just what constitutes re-Christianization? Although Russia is one of the few countries in the traditionally Christian world in which people report that religion is becoming more, not less, important to them, few Russians understand basic Church doctrine or observe the Church's most important rituals. By some measures, no more than 3–5 percent of Russians regularly attend the Sunday liturgy, and even fewer strictly keep the Lenten fast.[12] To many observers, these statistics suggest that Orthodoxy is more a matter of cultural identity ("I'm Russian, so I'm Orthodox") than genuine religious faith.[13] Nevertheless, if re-Christianization is defined in other terms—for example, affirmation of Orthodox moral values or respect for the patriarch as a public leader—percentages fall in a middle range (40–60 percent).[14] And all of these statistics are further complicated by the fact that sociologists can measure only outward behavior or self-reported attitudes; they cannot say what is going on in a person's heart.

As a political phenomenon, the resurgence of Orthodoxy is equally complex. Some observers, noting how Church and state in Russia cooperate in guaranteeing religious education in the public schools or acquisition of property for new parishes in crowded urban districts, assert that the Church has returned to ancient Byzantine notions of *symphonia*, according to which Church and state, though distinct in their responsibilities, work together for the sake of the nation's good. At the same time, the Russian Constitution provides for freedom of conscience and disallows government establishment of religion, and recent scholarly studies have demonstrated that the Church pursues its own political agenda largely apart from state support.[15] Moreover, state legislation is rarely influenced directly by Church interests.[16] Russian politics, many observers have persuasively argued, is driven by internal social and economic dynamics, not by religious ideology.[17]

The theological questions are the most vexing of all. Is religious faith best understood as a matter of individual conscience and freedom of choice? And if so, to choose what? To believe select doctrines, participate in particular rituals, embrace specific moral norms, or affirm the authority of certain religious leaders or institutions (such as the Church hierarchy)?

Can a person be latently religious, perhaps living a religious life without being consciously aware of it? Or can one be regarded as a believer if one observes religious norms or practices (such as lighting candles in front of an icon in one's kitchen) without Church oversight? What constitutes faithfulness to a religious tradition and who makes that determination? The Russian situation makes me as a theologian wonder again about the very character of religion in today's world.

Since the collapse of Communism, the Orthodox Church has, as I see it, implicitly proposed an answer to these conundrums. Holy Rus' would develop along two parallel trajectories. The Church would strive above all to invite Russians into a personal faith and moral transformation—or, in

Orthodox terms, communion with the divine. But the Church would also give Russians a sense of national distinctiveness and destiny. It would replace Communism with Orthodoxy.

Stalin tried to create the "new Soviet man" who would be thoroughly indoctrinated in Marxist-Leninist ideology and unquestioningly loyal to the Party. As one Party leader exclaimed in 1928, "We [Bolsheviks] are not like other people. We are a party of people who make the impossible possible. . . . And if the Party demands it, if it is necessary or important for the Party, we will be able by an act of will to expel from our brains in twenty-four hours ideas that we have held for years. . . . Yes, I will see black where I thought I saw white, or may still see it, because there is no life for me outside of the Party."[18]

But by the 1970s, Soviet ideology had faltered, and with the collapse of Communism, Russians suffered a mass identity crisis. They struggled to know where they fit in the world, what they could take pride in. Orthodoxy has offered them what sociologist Robert Bellah once called civil religion: symbols, narratives, and rituals that unite a people and offer them a sense of transcendent value and purpose.[19] Bellah has helped me understand why something deep stirs within me when I climb the 145 steps to the chamber of the Lincoln Memorial in Washington, D.C. I remember the assassination of John F. Kennedy, the Vietnam War protests, and Martin Luther King's "I Have a Dream" speech. I ponder again the nation's highest calling and deepest failures. And my Russian friend Oleg tells me that something similar happens to him when he stands at one of Russian Orthodoxy's most photographed sites, the Church of the Protective Veil, a strikingly plain yet magnificent twelfth-century white-walled edifice on the banks of the quiet Nerl River near the town of Vladimir. "I'm not a religious person, at most an agnostic," he tells me, "but I was surprised at how deeply moved I was when I first saw the church with my own eyes. Somehow I suddenly understood what makes Russia 'Russia'—the glorious beauty that is possible even amid the ugliness of our people's mistakes and wrongdoing."

The relationship between these two dimensions of religious expression— Orthodoxy as personal spiritual and moral transformation and Orthodoxy as civil religion—has both promise and peril. The growing establishment of

Orthodoxy as Russian civil religion could give the Church access to people's deeper religious loyalties. If Russians were to regard Orthodoxy as an essential part of their national identity, they might take the next step and actively participate in Church life.[20] But the historical experience of churches in the West as well as recent events in Russia demonstrate that civil religion does not necessarily lead to religious faith and can even get in its way. Many Russians, such as my friend Oleg, are content to be Orthodox in name alone. Or they think of themselves as Orthodox apart from the Church, perhaps observing some of its rituals but not caring about the beliefs that underlie Church practice. They may ask for baptism for themselves or their children, but they resist catechization. They receive the Eucharist but fail to understand that it asks them to commit themselves to life in Christian community. Orthodoxy apparently gives them a sense of national or cultural identity but does not draw them into a religious way of life that claims to offer "heaven on earth."

Similar issues arise in relation to Church-state relations. How should religious people and institutions think about secular government, and how should the state treat matters of religious faith? Will religious and political interests always diverge, or will they sometimes converge? In recent decades, some Western Protestant theologians have strongly criticized "Constantinian Christianity" or "Christendom," that long historical era in the West during which identification with the church was virtually synonymous with imperial or national identity. These theologians have argued that state or cultural establishment of Christianity has inevitably undermined rather than supported Christian faith. The disestablishment of Christianity has been good because it has freed the church to live by its deepest theological principles rather than in servitude to the state.[21] At the same time, many Western churches that have strongly affirmed political disestablishment of religion have nevertheless sought to participate in the formulation of public policy. These churches believe that Christian values should help shape society, even if not all members of that society will be or need to be Christian. Christianity can demonstrate to a secular society just what it means to be truly human and therefore what constitutes genuine justice and human rights.[22]

A similar and equally vigorous debate about religious faith and political order is taking place in the Russian Orthodox Church, although with a different vocabulary and accent. On the one hand, Orthodox leaders sometimes argue that their nation's constitutional principles of separation of Church and state are theologically warranted. Not only do these principles respect the genuine religious pluralism of contemporary Russian society, they also free the Church from state control. Too often in the Russian past, say these thinkers, the Church was reduced to almost a department of state in which the Church traded away spiritual freedom for institutional survival. And, they add, a Church that depends on state patronage or cultural establishment inevitably turns faith into something coerced rather than freely chosen, and therefore it is not truly faith. Only a strong commitment to legal guarantees of religious freedom will allow the Church to make a vital Christian witness to its society.[23]

On the other hand, because Russia has been so deeply shaped by the Orthodox tradition, Church leaders have also argued that the state should guarantee the Church a privileged social position in relation to other religions or ideologies. These clergy and theologians have called on the state to protect the Church from blasphemous attack and sectarian proselytism, and to affirm the unique historical contributions of the Orthodox Church to uniting Russians into a great nation.[24]

Whether a cultural and perhaps legal privileging of Orthodoxy by the state can be squared with a vigorous affirmation of religious freedom remains unclear. Smaller religious, especially Christian, groups—Protestant, Catholic, and dissident Orthodox—often feel marginalized by "Orthodoxy resurgent."[25] And some Russian Orthodox leaders worry that the Church will go astray if it focuses on shaping a post-Communist national identity rather than on its principal task of calling people to Christian discipleship and Christian ways of self-giving love for God and neighbor.[26] As one priest complained to me, "I spend so much time promoting the Church's institutional interests that I run out of time for doing what really matters: helping my people know God and each other."

Lack of clarity about the difference between Orthodoxy as civil religion and Orthodoxy as personal religious faith too often leads Russian Orthodox leaders to overestimate the Church's influence in society. Re-Christianization takes place in a Russia that has been deeply secularized by seven decades of militantly atheistic Communism. Sociological surveys demonstrate that the Church's efforts have not yet resulted in significantly higher levels of Church participation, ritual practice, or doctrinal knowledge. And Orthodox civil religion competes with—or sometimes merges with—other national symbols, narratives, and rituals, such as those associated with the Great Patriotic War (World War II) and the victory over fascist Germany.[27] The Church itself seems ambivalent about Russian identity. Patriarch Kirill has both condemned Stalin's crimes and praised his successes in transforming Russia into a world power.[28]

Moreover, a globalized popular culture and consumer ethic arguably shapes Russia today more profoundly than ancient Christian ideals. Young Russians are more apt to know the biographical details of their favorite pop singers or sports stars than the life of Jesus the Christ or Mary, the one whom Orthodox believers call the Mother of God. The Church aspires to be a comprehensive presence in Russian society but often finds itself nothing more than another lifestyle niche in a country that may be as religiously and ideologically pluralistic as the Western societies from which it wishes to differentiate itself.

A day of public reckoning may come sooner than the Russian Church ever anticipated. After more than twenty years of successfully reestablishing its claims on Russian society, the Church is encountering significant social resistance to its authority. In recent years, the term *anticlericalism* has become part of everyday Russian vocabulary. For many Russians, the problem is not so much the Church's hierarchical structure but rather its hierarchs' unwillingness to speak out against obvious social injustices and the political machinations of the Putin government. A deep cleft now runs through Russian society. On one side are those Russians who seek a more democratic and liberal political order; on the other, the official Orthodox Church and its leaders. To the pro-democracy movement, the Church's unwavering support of President Putin and "traditional social values" appears only to justify both the Church's and the state's authoritarian posture in society.

Nevertheless, I would never count religion "out" as a reforming, perhaps even democratizing, social factor. Just as Orthodoxy gave thousands of Russians the strength to resist Bolshevik domination even to the point of martyrdom, what is happening on the ground in parishes and monasteries today has the potential, I believe, to shape a different kind of Russia. The Church's holy things and places point Russians to a transcendent beauty that represents ultimate justice and truth. Even when Church or state authorities ignore or misuse this vision of "heaven on earth," history has again and again demonstrated that religious symbols, narratives, and rituals retain a potential to help people see beyond the status quo and to dream new dreams.[29] And as the Church reaches into society through initiatives in religious education, social ministry, commemoration of the twentieth-century martyrs, and parish life, it offers Russians a "free space" for civil society—those voluntary associations in which people organize their life apart from the state.

Religion and society interact in complex and unpredictable ways, and none of us can know exactly where Russia and its Church are headed. Nevertheless, it is clear to me that Holy Rus' cannot be reduced to a political ideology, even if some Church and state leaders use it that way. And Russia's Church cannot be limited to the latest social or political posturing of any specific group of hierarchs, no matter how much prominence they enjoy.[30] My way of interpreting Church and society is, to be sure, as much religious vision as sociological description: a proposal for how Orthodox Christianity today might point Russians to ultimate spiritual realities beyond this world as well as commit them to a more just and vigorous order within it. Whether this vision will come to realization is not at all clear. But I and my Russian friends do sometimes catch glimpses of something remarkable—perhaps even "holy"—stirring in the air . . .

. . . such as the sound of church bells, no longer silent as in the Soviet era. Several years ago, Church authorities in the Siberian city of Novosibirsk began visiting sixteen nearby prison colonies and training interested prisoners to ring a portable set of bells. The Church wanted, in part, to give the men a skill that they could use after their release; skilled church bell ringers are in short supply. But for the Church the bells also have immediate spiritual significance. Father Vladimir Sokolov, director of the program, believes that under the harsh conditions of the camps, the bells awaken repentance and promise healing: "You never get tired of hearing the bells. They purify and protect your soul." Aleksei Talashkin, his assistant, adds, "Their sound is a clear, perceptible manifestation of God's love for the men." And one of the prisoners, Vitalii, speaks of the indescribable joy that he experiences when he plays the bells. All three men believe that church bells sooner or later lead a person to God.[31]

TWO

The Rebirth of Orthodoxy

Just south of the Moscow River, a simple archway invites me to step away from the city's noisy streets into a quiet courtyard. A cobblestone walk leads to a modest, single-domed, stone church, the Church of the Protective Veil of the Mother of God. At one end of the exterior, the Mother of God and her Child look down at me from an icon constructed out of brightly colored tiles; at the other end, the penetrating eyes of Christ the Pantocrator (World Ruler) meet mine. Well-tended gardens stretch out behind the church, and opposite them are the recently restored buildings of the Martha and Mary Monastery.

For more than a decade, I have often come here to meditate on Russia and its Church, for the monastery tells the story of Russian Orthodoxy in the twentieth century—a story of Holy Rus', that elusive Orthodox vision of an ideal Russian nation whose very landscape and people become transparent to the divine. The twentieth century began and ended with the Church— and the Martha and Mary Monastery—appealing to Russians to return to this sacred mission. In between, the Communists imposed their own program for a just and equal society. They were determined to eliminate religion because it was the opiate of the people. The founder and abbess of the monastery, Elizabeth Fedorovna Romanova, was arrested, imprisoned, and martyred, and the monastery was closed.

An institutional Church that once knew worldly power and glory was soon reduced to a few smoldering embers. But the state's harsh repression of Orthodox Christianity never entirely destroyed Russians' vision of Holy Rus'. Even in the worst years of Soviet persecution, millions of people quietly continued to perform religious rituals that had deeply embedded themselves into the rhythms of their lives, as when they anticipated the first snow cover (*pokrov*) every year on October 1 (Julian Calendar), the day on which the Church commemorates the Virgin's Protective Veil (*pokrov*). Believing that the Mother of God was watching and waiting, peasants cleared their fields and gardens of the autumn's last fruits and moved from their summer to winter quarters. Unmarried young women lit candles in church, praying for the Mother of God to grant them husbands. Married women prepared *bliny*, thin Russian pancakes, and placed them beneath the household icons to "feed" the ancestors and entreat their protection.[1]

In 1991, the unthinkable occurred. Communism fell, and the Soviet Union was dissolved. Religion no longer had to hide underground. Today, the institutional Church openly prays that its vision of Holy Rus' will again define the Russian nation. And as the Church prays, it actively reaches into Russian society. To be sure, there is no official patriarchal program of reconstituting Holy Rus'. But I discern a cohesive religious vision that, I believe, implicitly guides the Church's new initiatives in religious education, social ministry, historical commemoration, and parish life. I see an Orthodoxy that is striving to make its society better, even as I am aware of the diversity and even contradictions within the Church and Russian religious life. Some observers will accuse me of constructing a fantasy. I would rather call it a hope for what Russia is and can be.

Across the courtyard from the Church of the Protective Veil, the living quarters of Elizabeth have been turned into a museum. Here one learns that Elizabeth moved easily in circles of Church and state power. She was the sister of Alexandra, the last tsarina, and like her sister, she married into the Romanov family. But after her husband's assassination in 1905, she abandoned the life of royalty and founded the Martha and Mary Monastery, a new and unique venture for Russian Orthodoxy. The monastery combined social outreach (the active service associated with the biblical Martha) with monastic prayer (associated with Martha's more contemplative sister Mary).[2]

The monastery was also groundbreaking in including both sisters who lived at the monastery and laywomen in the city who belonged to a sisterhood. Moreover, the sisters, though living by a rule that Elizabeth composed, were not tonsured. Rather than the typical black robes of the Orthodox monastic tradition, Elizabeth and her nuns wore white habits, indicating their commitment to serve in the world rather than retreat into a cloister. These Sisters of Mercy ministered to Moscow's poorest and neediest.

Elizabeth played an active role in planning the Church of the Protective Veil, for which the cornerstone was laid in 1908. The architect, Aleksei Shchusev, combined elements of art nouveau with ancient Russian Orthodox motifs associated with the Novgorodian architectural tradition. While Shchusev went on to design major monumental secular buildings in Moscow, including the Kazan Railway Station and Lenin's mausoleum on Red Square, the Church of the Protective Veil impresses the visitor by its

Martha and Mary Monastery, Moscow (WikiCommons, Valeri965)

simple yet elegant beauty. The thick exterior walls, painted white, are punctuated by stonework with elaborately carved crosses, plants and vines, and fanciful animals.[3]

Elizabeth commissioned the well-known Russian artist Mikhail Nesterov to design and execute the interior murals and iconostasis. Nesterov, like Shchusev, would remain a creative force after the rise of Communism, although he would no longer address religious themes. At the time of his work on the Church of the Protective Veil, however, Nesterov was obsessed with the idea of Holy Rus'. For Nesterov, Christ had revealed himself in a special way to Russia and would inaugurate his heavenly kingdom there.

Fifteen years earlier, Nesterov had executed a series of famous paintings devoted to St. Sergius of Radonezh, the fourteenth-century founder of the Holy Trinity–St. Sergius Lavra, perhaps Russia's most important monastery. During these and subsequent years, Nesterov also depicted monastic life amid the glorious fields, forests, hills, rivers, and lakes of Russia's far north. This creative energy reached its climax in several large canvases in which Nesterov showed the Russian people encountering the resurrected Jesus in their midst.

In *Holy Rus'* (1905), Nesterov depicts a group of peasants in a cold winter landscape. Christ, muscular and manly, has mysteriously appeared to them. Behind him stand three saints especially venerated in Russia — St. Sergius of Radonezh, St. Nicholas the Wonderworker, and St. George the Victory Bearer. Men and women, adults and children, monks and simple believers — all come to Christ. One man falls to his knees; another seems filled with mystical wonder. A woman overcome by the vision clutches her face. Other peasants react with disbelief or confusion.[4]

In 1910–11, Nesterov executed a version of *Holy Rus'* (*The Way to Christ*) for the Martha and Mary Monastery. As in his 1905 painting, a beautiful landscape serves as the backdrop, but now the season is early summer. As evening falls, the calm waters of a nearby lake have taken on a shimmering rose color; a green meadow studded with yellow and purple wildflowers leads down to the water's shores. Perhaps Nesterov was recalling Psalm 23: "He maketh me to lie down in green pastures; he leadeth me beside the still waters." On the other side of the lake rises the spire of a church belonging to a small monastic, semi-hermetical community (skete). Father Mitrofan Srebrianskii, spiritual father to Elizabeth and the sisters of the monastery (in the *Icon of the New Martyrs and Confessors*, he stands next to Elizabeth and her assistant Barbara), later wrote of Nesterov's painting: "Here, namely, close to a skete, in the midst of the green of nature and the quieting evening song of birds, Christ appears to the Russian soul, which with special vitality senses God. . . . Especially the Russian soul so tenderly loves every little bird, blade of grass, flower."[5]

Nearby, the transfigured Christ, filled with light and dressed in radiant white garments, has appeared at the edge of a birch forest. In comparison to the Christ of Nesterov's *Holy Rus'* of 1905, his physique is slight. And he expresses humble compassion rather than heroic assertiveness, as though gently calling out, "Come unto me, all ye that labour and are heavy laden, and I will give you rest" (Matt. 11:28). Nesterov depicts people of many different backgrounds and conditions who do indeed draw close to this loving Christ: men and women with contrasting facial features and skin tones representing ethnic groups from different parts of Russia, a soldier maimed by war and hobbling on crutches, a sick child too weak to walk, grieving women, schoolchildren dressed in their best clothes, a great schema monk, simple peasants, and well-to-do city people. Three women fall down before him; he grasps the hands of one. All are in great need, and the Sisters of Mercy of the Martha and Mary Monastery accompany them, carrying the sick, supporting the lame, and comforting the distressed.

In early 1918, Elizabeth and Barbara were arrested and transported to the Ural Mountains. On July 18, one day after the execution of the royal family, Elizabeth's persecutors threw them and several other members of royalty alive into a mine shaft, where they died. Soon afterward, the Bolsheviks began appropriating the buildings of the Martha and Mary Monastery and then in 1926 sent the last sisters into exile. Under the Soviets, the monastery complex suffered damage and neglect; for a time, the church served as a movie theater. Later it was sealed shut, and Nesterov's mural remained hidden from public view.

In 1992, the year of Elizabeth's canonization, the state returned the Martha and Mary Monastery to the Church. A new community of sisters was organized, and the Church of the Protective Veil and the monastery buildings were carefully restored. Today, when visitors step into Elizabeth's church, they again stand beneath Nesterov's *Holy Rus'*. Like the figures in his mural, they come with their worldly cares and concerns. In Orthodox understanding, they will meet the living Christ as they participate in the liturgy, receive the Eucharist, experience the healing touch of doctors and nurses at the monastery, venerate St. Elizabeth's relics, and walk in the gardens.[6] A larger-than-life-size statue of St. Elizabeth stands nearby, as does a small wooden chapel in which visitors may pause and pray. Holy Rus' again beckons.

In the summer of 2006, I visited a skete in Russia's far north that could have been Nesterov's. This skete, like the Martha and Mary Monastery, represents the history of Holy Rus' in the twentieth century. It too has experienced death and rebirth, and again draws pilgrims. But in contrast to the monastery, modern-day visitors to the skete will glimpse its wonders only briefly before they return to the workaday world of contemporary Russia; no one besides the monks and their guests may stay there overnight.

The Golgotha-Crucifixion Skete is located on the island of Anzer, part of the Solovetskii Archipelago in the White Sea and only sixty miles south of the Arctic Circle. The main Solovetskii island is famous for its monastery, whose tall, thick rock walls seem to rise right out of the deep blue waters. The trip to the site, also known as Solovki, has always been demanding, and while today it is possible to come by seaplane, pilgrims have traditionally traveled hundreds of miles—once on foot; later by train—to the village of Kem'. From there, they have come across the open sea, but only from July to September. The remainder of the year, strong winds and icy waters cut off Solovki's monastery and sketes from the rest of the world.

This isolation has made Solovki a magical place. Even in a globalized, consumer-driven world—the main monastery attracts more than thirty thousand visitors each year—Solovki remains a place of unspoiled natural beauty. Otters and seagulls follow pilgrims across the sea. When visitors step on shore, they encounter an otherworldly landscape of tundra, brush, low forests, and small lakes and streams. Anzer seems especially remote. The monks have only one motor vehicle, a truck that they use to bring in supplies that boats deliver to the shore; and the island has no electricity. When evening falls, the silence is deafening.

By the end of the nineteenth century, the Golgotha-Crucifixion Skete had become the spiritual heart of Solovki. The monks were renowned for their uninterrupted reading of the Psalter in commemoration of the community's living and deceased benefactors. But in the 1920s, this heaven on earth turned into hell. The main monastery was transformed into the Soviet Union's first gulag, and the skete on Anzer became a "hospital"—a holding pen—for prisoners with typhoid. Many of them had been arrested for their faith; others were political opponents or simple criminals. The men slept on the bare wooden floors, packed together like sardines. The guards would wake them up several times during the night and order them to roll over all at the same time. Some were beaten; many died from medical neglect or the harsh climate. In the 1930s, the Communists abandoned Anzer, and the skete was left to deteriorate in the raw elements. Sixty years later, a solitary monk arrived on the island to reestablish a monastic community. The skete and its churches were in ruin, with walls stripped down to the lath. Blood had stained the floorboards. A mass grave lay nearby. Anzer represented death and devastation.

One of the panels of the Russian Orthodox *Icon of the New Martyrs and Confessors* commemorates this tragic history. On Solovki's main island, prisoners look out from their prison cells beneath the monastery walls as a soldier aims his rifle at a group of believers on the shoreline, who respond with a sign of blessing. The panel also includes Anzer and its Church of the Crucifixion. And if you look closely, you will see an unusual sight on the island: a tree in the shape of a cross.

When monks returned to Anzer after the fall of Communism, they found just such a tree. On the side of the island's one steep hill, not far from the Church of the Crucifixion on the hill's summit, a birch tree had grown to maturity over the seventy-four years of Communism. Birch trees figure prominently in Russian mythology; their white bark seems to cast a heavenly light into the dark forest. This tree on Anzer called forth additional wonder because its trunk had grown straight up, while the tree's two most prominent branches jutted out at a ninety-degree angle opposite each other.

Today, pilgrims to Anzer climb the hill to venerate the "miracle" tree cross. It represents to them God's abiding presence with the Church through

Suffering and resurrection at Solovki: panel from the *Icon of the New Martyrs and Confessors* (author's photograph)

the darkest days of Communism. The Church of the Crucifixion, once a place of unspeakable horrors, again gathers the monks for daily prayer. As I joined them for prayers that lasted from 10 p.m. to 4 a.m., the summer light of the far north softened but never darkened. In that place of speechless tragedy, I nevertheless sensed a presence from beyond.

Religiosity is a hard thing to define and measure. Christians, as well as adherents of other religions, have debated throughout history the connection between outward religious observance and inward religious conviction. All that we can say with certainty is that, no matter what was happening in people's hearts, the Russian Orthodox Church had a dominating presence in Russian society on the verge of the 1917 October Revolution. Ninety percent of the country's population participated, even if only once a year, in the Church's sacraments of confession and Communion.[7] Fifty thousand parishes, twenty-five thousand chapels, one thousand monasteries, sixty seminaries, and four theological academies covered the land. The tsar was revered as the Church's chief benefactor and protector. Orthodoxy was an integral part of Russian culture.[8]

What happened after the revolution was unprecedented in Christian history. While the statistical evidence is imprecise and sometimes hotly debated, there is no question that the Church suffered persecution on a scale not previously known. By the end of Stalin's Great Terror in 1939, the Bolshevik state had almost completely eliminated the institutional Church. Every Russian Orthodox monastery and theological school had been closed. Only four bishops remained in office, and perhaps no more than three hundred parishes were still open—and even for these few churches, clergy were not always available to celebrate the liturgy. Eighty-five percent or more of clerics and monastics had been arrested; few would survive internal exile or the prison camps. As many as 200,000–350,000 people died because of their association with the Church; in comparison, Roman persecutions of the early Church claimed perhaps 3,000 victims.[9]

Nevertheless, the state's secret census of 1937 demonstrated the tenacity of religious belief. Despite two decades of repressing the institutional Church, the Communists found that two-thirds of the rural population, which still constituted the vast majority of Soviet citizens, and one-third of urban dwellers designated themselves as Orthodox.[10] In the Russian Republic, the heartland of Bolshevik rule, 57.1 percent of people said that they believed in God.[11] The real numbers were likely much higher, given that people had every reason to fear confessing religious allegiance.

In one of the great ironies of history, the German invasion of the Soviet Union in 1941 saved the institutional Church from complete annihilation. The Nazis were no friends of religion and had their own plans to eliminate Christianity, but as they advanced eastward, their generals sought to win popular support by allowing existing parishes to continue to operate and parishes that had been closed to reopen. Stalin felt his hand forced. He began to allow churches and monasteries to reopen in areas that he still controlled. By 1943, he was asking Church leaders to call a council of bishops to elect a patriarch. All was to be done with great dispatch; he even provided airplanes to transport the handful of hierarchs to Moscow.

For their part, Church leaders were genuinely eager to bless the war cause and demonstrate their loyalty to the nation. Today, visitors to Moscow encounter historic tanks on the grounds of the Donskoi Monastery. The tanks memorialize a famous armored unit for which the Church raised funds. As in olden days, Church leaders organized processions with famous icons around the outskirts of cities that were threatened by Nazi attack. By the end of the war, the Church had fifteen thousand parishes, one hundred monasteries (including the great Holy Trinity–St. Sergius Lavra, to which the patriarch moved his residence from Moscow), eight seminaries, and two theological academies, although the vast majority of these religious institutions were in western territories that the Germans had occupied or that the Soviet Union had acquired after 1939, such as western Ukraine. Most regions within Russia proper still had only two to four churches.[12]

Nevertheless, the years of the most brutal persecution had passed. With the death of Stalin and rise of Khrushchev, few people would be executed just because of their Church affiliation. But the Khrushchev years brought new pressures on the Church. State efforts to promote a scientific-atheistic education became more intensive. People who asked the Church to baptize a child could expect to encounter practical difficulties with the government, which might prohibit them or their children from receiving a higher education or advancing professionally. Believers hesitated to attend the same church every week, as they did not want to draw the attention of KGB informants who might be watching. Schoolchildren were taught that religion was sheer superstition. By the end of the Khrushchev era, the Church had been reduced again: to seven thousand parishes, sixteen monasteries, three seminaries, and two theological academies.

During the following years of Soviet "stagnation," this basic religious infrastructure remained in place, sometimes expanding slightly, sometimes contracting. The state continued to forbid parishes and monasteries from conducting educational activities or social ministries. Few priests were able to receive a basic seminary education.[13] Candidates for the priesthood had to be vetted by the KGB, which also determined appointments to parishes and bishoprics. In many parishes, especially those that attracted a following among younger, educated Russians, informants regularly reported on priests' preaching and activities.

Despite this limited free space, the Church enjoyed a unique status. It was the only social institution able to offer an alternative vision of reality to that of Marxist-Leninist ideology. In the Orthodox liturgy, people could glimpse a transcendent power that called for their ultimate loyalty and devotion and therefore implicitly brought into question the exclusive ideological claims of the Communist Party. For its part, the state increasingly regarded religion as a social factor that would not quickly pass away. Rather than directly attacking the Church, the state endeavored to co-opt it.[14] In exchange for being allowed to serve the Church, bishops and priests were asked to publicly declare their loyalty to the state and praise Soviet "peace initiatives." Some won the freedom to travel to ecumenical religious gatherings in the West, but only at the cost of remaining silent about state injustices and declaring instead that the Soviet Union protected religious freedom.[15]

"Unofficial" popular Orthodoxies remained active during these years and interacted in complex ways with the official, institutional Church, sometimes entering into its life and sometimes existing on its edge or even outside it. Scholars today, especially historians and anthropologists, shy away from the term "popular Orthodoxy," arguing that it has too often been used to discredit popular religious practice or to suggest that official, institutional religion is somehow better than, or different from, the people's lived piety.[16] But I believe that the term can still helpfully and neutrally refer to refer to forms of religiosity that manifest themselves apart from the official Church's public worship and organized institutional structures. One form of popular Orthodoxy in the Soviet era was characterized by devotion to religious rituals that had long established themselves as general cultural practices. Russian soldiers went into battle in World War II with icons of St. George to protect them from harm. Despite state disapproval, people continued to observe important holy days, make pilgrimage to holy sites, ask priests to bury deceased loved ones, and venerate icons and relics.[17] Where a parish no longer existed, people might gather in a cemetery chapel. Children were secretly baptized by priests or family members.[18]

Some scholars have argued that Communist rituals even helped sustain this popular religious sensibility. Russian historian Ol'ga Kaz'mina has written, "The religious cult transformed itself into a cult of great leaders. Elements of divinizing Lenin were apparent: whatever he said was regarded as indisputable truth, it was customary to venerate his body, and there was even a kind of sainthood accorded to his relatives and associates, of whom it was forbidden to speak negatively. Portraits of the great leaders were treated like icons, and the Ten Commandments were replaced by the Ten Principles of 'The Moral Codex of the Builder of Communism.' "[19] As an acquaintance in Moscow once told me, "The 1980s were a great time to be Orthodox in Russia. People were no longer being persecuted for their faith, and the general moral atmosphere reflected Christian values: sexual modesty, love of family and nation, honest work, and social solidarity."

A second stream of popular unofficial Orthodoxy was characterized less by adherence to traditional cultural rituals and more by efforts to preserve the core of Church belief and practice outside of a compromised official Church. One locus was the home. A Russian woman born in the mid-1970s related to me that her parents living in Moscow during the Khrushchev era had nothing to do with the Church, but whenever she went back to the family village, her grandmother told her Bible stories and taught her Orthodox prayers. No church was nearby, but the grandmother remembered the faith.[20] Another locus for this second strand of unofficial Orthodoxy was the catacomb or underground church. Representative is Gleb Kaleda, who made a brilliant public career for himself as a geologist while quietly studying theology. After his underground ordination in the 1970s, he secretly gathered a community in his home and celebrated the Divine Liturgy and the Eucharist. As Marxist-Leninist ideology lost credibility, such communities increasingly attracted members of Russia's intelligentsia, who found a free space there for intensive study of Scripture, church tradition, and Orthodox spirituality.[21]

Other members of this kind of "alternative" Orthodoxy found a niche in the official institutional Church. They gathered around "dissident" but Church-true priests such as Aleksandr Men' and Vsevolod Shpiller. Other Orthodox believers took a more critical stance. Figures such as Alexander Solzhenitsyn called on the Church to speak out against Communist oppression. Dissident priests such as Gleb Yakunin demanded that the official Church repent of its accommodations to state interests. Underground publications, *samizdat*, with religious and political themes proliferated.[22]

Still other "unofficial" ways of relating to Orthodoxy appeared. By the 1980s and 1990s, some Russians were rediscovering the nation's ancient historical traditions. Groups of enthusiasts worked to preserve or rebuild historic churches or monasteries. These people were not always motivated by religious faith. Many simply had a desire to recover a rich cultural heritage that had been obscured or even destroyed under Communism.[23]

Despite the vitality of these different ways of relating to Orthodoxy, the state's forced secularization of society could not but have consequences for both the Church and popular belief and practice. If baptism occurred at all, it was usually because a grandmother insisted on it, as President Putin has said of his own case. The child's parents no longer had a clear sense of Orthodox identity. And the Church itself experienced a deep crisis of identity during these years. Where to draw the line between faithless accommodation and faithful cooperation—or resistance—to the state was often unclear.

It now seems astonishing that at the end of the Soviet era, despite more than seven decades of Communist efforts to eradicate religion, 30 percent of the population could still identify as Orthodox.[24] It is equally astonishing that with the fall of Communism Russians turned en masse to the Church as a way of marking their break with the Soviet past. People of all ages and backgrounds asked to be baptized. Interest in monastic vocations surged. Travel companies began offering pilgrimage tours to Orthodox holy sites. Crowds gathered again at Christmas and Easter services. To be Orthodox was suddenly "fashionable," as one of my Russian friends told me.

As in the past, what people understood by "Orthodoxy" varied widely.[25] Few of the new Orthodox were regularly attending the Divine Liturgy or receiving the Eucharist, and even fewer had basic knowledge of Church teachings. Many associated "Orthodoxy" more with Russian cultural and ethnic identity than religious belief or practice.[26] And, as earlier in Russian history (one has only to think of Leo Tolstoy), some "Orthodox" were indifferent to, or even suspicious of, the official Church and its efforts to control and define faith. Those members of the intelligentsia who explored religion were as apt to dabble in yoga or Eastern spiritualities as to immerse themselves in Orthodoxy. Historical enthusiasts soon found themselves competing with Church authorities for control of religious sites.[27] Dissident priests such as Yakunin gravitated into politics.

Nevertheless, this new "Orthodoxy," whatever it meant, was the soil in which the institutional Church could again flourish. In the final years of Communism, the official Church increasingly came back into public view, as represented by the Gorbachev government's decision to allow the Church to celebrate the millennium of Christianity in Rus' in 1988. The Church was able to recover and renovate the ancient Danilov Monastery in Moscow; to canonize several historically significant Orthodox figures who had contributed to the nation's cultural, spiritual, and political greatness (including Andrei Rublev, the famous icon painter); and to speak publicly of Orthodoxy as an essential part of the nation's identity.

With the fall of Communism, the Church's efforts to shape Russian national identity accelerated. A reconstructed Christ the Savior Cathedral again dominated the view from the Kremlin; at Stalin's orders, the church had been razed in 1931 to make way for a massive Palace of the Soviets topped by a statue of Lenin 150–250 feet high; under Khrushchev, the project was abandoned, and a huge outdoor heated swimming pool took its place.[28] Another church destroyed under Stalin and even more historically significant, the Kazanskii Cathedral, was rebuilt on its original site on Red Square.

Orthodoxy again became part of public life. In December 1990, the government declared Christmas (January 7 in the Orthodox Old Style calendar) a national holiday. By then, the patriarch and other Church hierarchs had become honored guests at the Kremlin. After their presidential inaugurations, both Vladimir Putin (2000, 2012) and Dmitrii Medvedev (2008) walked across the Kremlin courtyard to the Cathedral of the

Assumption (Dormition) to receive a blessing and an icon from the patri-arch. The Easter Vigil began to be broadcast annually from Christ the Savior Cathedral on national television, with Putin, Medvedev, and other dignitaries in attendance.

By 2015, the Church had grown to more than thirty-five thousand parishes and eight hundred monasteries; slightly over half were in the Russian Federation, with the remainder in other countries of the former Soviet Union, especially Ukraine.[29] The Church was conducting a wide range of educational and social projects, and most Russians were identifying them-selves as Orthodox.[30] Could anyone really object to the Church calling these developments "miraculous," a veritable "rebirth" of Orthodox life after so many years of deep repression?

For many political commentators, the most striking feature of the new reli-gious situation has been the resurgence of traditional Orthodox notions of a symphonia between Church and state, a political arrangement in which they actively cooperate in promoting the good of the nation. Take note, the emphasis here is on the good of the *nation*. Whatever the Church's other-worldly ends, it also seeks people's moral, spiritual, and social well-being in a particular national-ethnic context. Moreover, according to the principle of symphonia, Church and state *cooperate*. While each has its proper sphere of activity in which the other does not interfere—the Church focuses on spiritual matters while the state seeks earthly peace and justice—Church and state complement each other. The state supports the Church's efforts to bring Orthodox moral values into society, and the Church respects the state's authority in worldly, political matters.[31]

The difference between notions of liberal democracy in the United States and Orthodox symphonia in Russia is embedded in the two nations' symbolic landscapes. Contrast the National Mall in Washington, D.C., with the Kremlin, an ancient fortress in the heart of Moscow. The Mall has "temples" to civil religion (the Lincoln Memorial, the Jefferson Memorial), but no church steeple is in sight. The Kremlin, however, has government buildings next to historic Orthodox churches. Even Stalin did not tear down every Kremlin church. Today, the visitor to the Kremlin enters the symbolic center of the Russian nation, and that center includes both Church and state. Symphonia is at the heart of Russian national identity.

The principle of symphonia finds idealized expression in traditional depictions of St. Sergius of Radonezh. Despite retreating into the thick woods north of Moscow to live by himself in a hermitage, he soon attracted many followers, and the hermitage eventually became a monastery. Artists such as Nesterov have represented Sergius as a humble monk to whom great princes such as Dmitrii Donskoi came for counsel about matters of state. The historical reality, however, has been different, at least in the eyes of many educated Russian Orthodox believers. They would say that the Russian state has regularly dominated the Church, and that Church leaders who resisted the state's abuse of power could expect exile or even execution. To this day, students of Russian Church history remember Philip, metropolitan of Moscow, who in 1568 confronted Ivan the Terrible during the Divine Liturgy and publicly rebuked him for instigating bloodshed and criminal acts that were destroying the nation. The tsar had him arrested and later killed.

Similar tensions arose when Patriarch Nikon, seeing Russia as the special protector of Orthodoxy, introduced liturgical reforms in the early seventeenth century that, he argued, would bring the Church into accord with Greek practice. A key point of contention was whether believers were to make the sign of the cross with three fingers (Russian tradition) or two (Greek). Tsar Mikhail Romanov promoted Nikon's program, resulting in a deep and enduring split in the Church. Those who resisted the reforms became known as Old Believers. Many of them, including most of the monks at Solovki, fled for their lives into other parts of Russia's remotely settled north. In the end, however, the tsar put Nikon in his place. The patriarch went into self-imposed exile in the Monastery of the New Jerusalem, which he had once hoped would be the new center of the Orthodox world over which he would rule.[32]

Today, many historians note that Church-state relations in eighteenth- and nineteenth-century Russia were complex and shifting. Although Peter the Great, Mikhail's grandson, replaced the Patriarchate in 1721 with a Holy Synod headed by a state-appointed procurator, Gregory Freeze, one of

America's most prominent historians of the Russian Church, has argued that the state's goal "was not to make the Church a 'department of state,' but an efficient organization capable of overseeing and regulating religious life."[33] Such figures as Metropolitan Filaret (Drozdov) advanced creative initiatives in education and parish life, seeking to promote "Christianization" of a society that seemed more Orthodox in name than in reality.[34]

Nevertheless, many of my educated Russian Orthodox acquaintances view the synodal period in largely negative terms. A recent biography of St. Serafim (Sobolev), a newly canonized twentieth-century bishop, succinctly expresses a sentiment shared more widely in the Russian Church today. According to Sobolev, Peter the Great "transformed the Church into a department of the state apparatus." Even worse, Peter broke the authority of the Church and gave free rein to "Voltairism, masonry, sectarianism, humanism, socialism, nihilism, and other erroneous movements." Catherine the Great further undermined the Church by closing four-fifths of the monasteries. As a consequence, the monarchy also lost authority in the eyes of the people, paving the way for the tragic events of the twentieth century.[35] I have also often heard the charge that Nicholas I and other conservative political leaders in nineteenth-century Russia viewed Orthodoxy primarily as a resource for securing state power, a view also shared by German historian Hans-Christian Diedrich: "The domestic politics—and therefore the religious policies—of the Russian Tsars from 1880 to 1905 were characterized by a Slavophile ideology of a three-fold resonance of Russian national consciousness and autocratic Tsardom bound together inseparably with Orthodoxy."[36] This program of "Autocracy, Orthodoxy, and Nation" ensured that the Church would enjoy social prominence, but only at the price of state control.

By the time of the October Revolution, deep fractures had appeared between a privileged Church hierarchy and an impoverished parish priesthood, and between the official Church and elements of unofficial popular Orthodoxy. Russians' outward allegiance to the Church hid their lack of knowledge and conviction about Christian faith. And while Orthodoxy still shaped the rhythms of village life, a growing proletariat and intelligentsia in the cities felt increasingly alienated from the Church. Even many candidates for the priesthood rejected Church authority; in several cases, seminarians assassinated rectors who tried to impose discipline.[37]

As one prominent priest told me, "If Russia had truly been an Orthodox nation in 1917, people would never have allowed the Bolsheviks to seize power. If Russians had truly been Orthodox, they never would have participated in closing churches and confiscating Church treasures." The principle of symphonia had broken down. The growing authoritarianism of the Russian state ultimately made the institutional Church dependent on the good graces of the tsars. A similar pattern eventually developed under Communism. After trying to eliminate the Church altogether, the Bolsheviks concluded that they could successfully use it, instead, for their own purposes: as a source of income, a pawn in Soviet foreign policy, and a means of monitoring political dissent.

Today I see a Church hierarchy that is ambivalent about symphonia. In a nuanced analysis of the Church's *Social Concept* of 2000, political scientist Irina Papkova concludes that the Church seeks both cooperation with and distance from the state. With the fall of the Communist regime, the Church, she writes, formulated "a vision of church-state relations that favors the symphonic model, calling for a high degree of church-state cooperation for the sake of society's greater good, while simultaneously explicitly rejecting state control over the church's internal affairs."[38] On the one hand, the *Social Concept* does not reject the possibility that Russia could someday restore an Orthodox monarchy and hence a Church-state symphonia. On the other, the *Social Concept* affirms the Church's ability to work within a secular political order that prohibits the establishment of religion and guarantees freedom of belief, as is the case with the current Constitution of the Russian Federation. Even advocates of symphonia acknowledge that the state today has a secular character.[39]

As Papkova and other political scientists have established, the Church, despite its hope for close cooperation with the state, has much less influence over federal legislation than is commonly assumed. The Church has not prevailed in restricting legal access to abortion or prohibiting sexual immorality in the popular media. And even where the state has appeared to support the Church, as in prosecuting members of the feminist activist group Pussy Riot after they staged a political protest event in Moscow's Christ the Savior Cathedral in 2012, the state has arguably acted primarily in its own interests, namely, to repress an incipient anti-Putin movement. The fact that Church and state interests sometimes coincide does not mean that the state is directed by the Church.[40] Church and state negotiate a variety of political outcomes according to their different interests.[41]

The Church has profoundly shaped Russian political life not so much in matters of formal governance, but rather by providing key narratives, symbols, and rituals that help Russians make sense of who they are as a nation.[42] The Communists tried to create the "new Soviet man" who would live by rational, scientific-atheistic assumptions about reality and commit himself to building an industrialized, technologically advanced society. The Church has declared, in contrast, that humans are created for harmonious, trusting relationship with God and each other. For Orthodox believers, the rebirth of the Church has meant, above all, the freedom of the Church to manage its internal affairs without state interference and to represent its moral values to Russian society.

From my perspective, however, this effort to restore Orthodox values to public life is a highly dubious proposition. As a theologian, I believe that the Church's raison d'être, whether in East or West, is to bring people into communion with the divine through active participation in Church life. Christianity is not primarily a matter of cultural or national identity, but rather of religious truth. And at times I see a Church in Russia that thankfully does go beyond just making Orthodoxy useful to the state for social and political stability. Despite its temptations toward worldly power, this Church continues to celebrate a liturgy and nurture a spirituality that offer people the possibility of salvation—victory over sin and death, and life eternal.

According to traditional Orthodox teaching, eternal life is not simply a state of being after physical death. The believer begins to experience eternal life even now, as he or she is mystically united with God.[43] The supreme expression of this union is the Eucharist, that Christian ritual in which believers receive bread and wine that have been transformed into the body and blood of the crucified and resurrected Christ, who in his very being unites divinity and humanity. Those who take Christ into themselves begin a process of *theosis*, a Greek word that can be translated as "deification" or "divinization." The idea of theosis goes back to early Church theologians such as Athanasius, who in the fourth century declared that God "assumed humanity that we might become God."[44] While an infinite distance between humanity and the divine "essence" always remains, those who commune with Christ nevertheless truly receive God's "energies."[45] Believers acquire the ability to pause in wonder at the divine presence in all creation and to live in harmony with the world. Just, loving community becomes possible.

Orthodoxy repatterns the life of the believer, so that he or she will become more attentive to the mystical power of the Eucharist and grow more fully into a holy life. The Church prescribes seasons of fasting and ascetic exercise in which people discipline physical and emotional impulses that easily enslave them to selfishness, pride, and destructive forms of sensuality. Each day of the Church year commemorates saints, who not only provide superb examples of faithful living but also promise to pray for those who venerate them.

The Orthodox tradition appoints hours of prayer that structure the course of each day for those who are attentive, as I once learned when I stayed in a hut in a remote Russian monastery. It was a late winter night, the snow lay deep on the ground, and all was still except for the low chanting of a couple in the room next to mine. They were reciting the Church's order for evening prayer. The Sunday Divine Liturgy calls the faithful even farther into the Church's vision of a new heaven and earth. The prayers and rituals aim at purifying each of the physical senses, so that they will no longer curve people selfishly into themselves but rather will open them to a transcendent spiritual world. Icons and frescoes of Christ, Mary, and the heavenly saints refocus people's sight from this world to the next. Music—sung by human voices, for Orthodox worship has no instrumentation—engages people's hearing with prayers, hymns, and Scripture readings about life in Christ. Clouds of incense delight people's sense of smell with heavenly perfume. People feel their bodies go to work as they stand (sometimes for two to three hours in a Russian church service), make the sign of the cross, bow, and especially during ascetic seasons perform prostrations on hard stone floors. And the eucharistic elements redirect worshippers' sense of taste. "O, taste and see how good the Lord is," they chant as they receive the spiritual food during special Lenten liturgies.

Legend recounts that Prince Vladimir of Rus' converted from paganism to Orthodoxy in 988 after he had sent emissaries to examine the religions of surrounding nations. Those who returned from the Cathedral of Hagia Sophia in Constantinople reported that the Orthodox liturgy so overwhelmed them with transcendent glory and beauty that "we no longer knew whether we were on earth or in heaven." Orthodox worship invites one momentarily to leave this world and join the angels and archangels, saints and martyrs who ceaselessly worship God on his throne in heaven.

Observing church rituals, however, is not enough to enter into this holy world. While attending the Divine Liturgy, keeping the Church's fasts, and receiving the Eucharist are essential, believers will also have to change their life orientation away from selfishness to love of God and neighbor. Deification is a long process of self-transformation in which humans cooperate with God to overcome sin and become like Christ.[46] Life in the Church, while transcending worldly matters, at the same time directs people to what is good for society as a whole: greater justice, mercy, and reverence for life. So again, we can conclude that the Russian Church's hope has been twofold: that the broader cultural phenomenon of "Orthodoxy resurgent" will help the Church draw more people into active participation in its life, and that people who seek eternal salvation will also help the nation secure those moral values that have historically made it great.

Both aspects of this religious vision of society are explicated with particular clarity in the Church's *Missionary Concept*, published in 2007 after nearly a decade of work under the leadership of Ioann (Popov), metropolitan of Belgorod and Starii Oskol and head of the Church's Department of Mission.[47] The document has served as the basis for a popular textbook, *Missiology* (second edition, 2010), and for the "special missionary emphasis" of the Belgorod Seminary, which prepares priests for ministry in a secularized, post-Communist Russia.

The *Missionary Concept* defines mission as "proclamation for awakening a person to faith."[48] This statement is striking in its focus on the individual and his or her personal relationship to God, a concern that to me is also decidedly Protestant. Many Russians take Orthodoxy to require formal allegiance to the institutional Church, faithful observance of religious rituals, adherence to Orthodox moral norms, and knowledge of Church doctrine. While affirming the importance of these activities, the *Missionary Concept* makes clear that the Church's goal is ultimately much more. The Church exists to invite people to experience salvation.

Despite these "Protestant" overtones, the document defines salvation in classic Orthodox terms. In contrast to a "born-again" experience (as emphasized by Protestant evangelicalism) or a trusting confidence in God's forgiveness of sins in Jesus Christ (as in classic Reformation teaching), Orthodoxy speaks of salvation in terms of a transfigured or deified self. Moreover, salvation or deification occurs only as one enters into the life of the Church. Especially by means of eucharistic fellowship, people receive the very life of God. According to the *Missionary Concept*, the Church strives to be a comprehensive presence in society because it seeks the transfiguration of every human being and, indeed, all of reality (3–4).

In contrast to traditional notions of Christian mission as conversion of non-Christian peoples, the *Missionary Concept* identifies the Russian people as the Church's first pastoral responsibility. The document asserts that the Bolsheviks tore Russians away from their traditional Orthodoxy. With the demise of Communism, Russians have become vulnerable to destructive cults, nontraditional worldviews, and the neo-pagan values of a secular society. Russia now needs nothing less than a "second Christianization" in which the Church brings its values back into Russian society. The goal, however, is not that people adopt Orthodoxy as a new social ideology to replace Communism, but rather that they experience communion with the divine (5–7).

The *Missionary Concept* assumes that the salvation of individuals and the transformation of their national culture go hand in hand. As Russians rediscover the ways in which Orthodoxy has traditionally shaped their national identity, they are more apt to participate in Church life. And as they enter more actively into Church life, they will commit themselves more fully to shaping a society that embodies Orthodox values (8). The

Church will give moral and spiritual foundations to the culture, and a culture embedded with Orthodox values will direct people to life in God.

The *Missionary Concept* recognizes that many Russians, even if they have been baptized and identify themselves as Orthodox, need basic catechetical instruction in order to participate responsibly in Church life. If people are to discover a transfigured life in God, they must learn to revere the Scriptures and Church tradition; to understand the structure and meaning of the liturgy; to participate in the Eucharist; and to shape their everyday lives according to the will of Christ (10).

The document emphasizes, however, that the spirit in which the Church offers this instruction is as important as its content. In approaching people, the Church should be a loving mother, not a strict judge. Quoting Patriarch Aleksii II, the document states that "spiritual direction is not a matter of manipulating people. It is the power of love, not spiritual violence" (15). The experience of authentic, intimate fellowship is perhaps the most important factor in drawing people into Church life. And this experience of Christian community often begins outside the church building as people participate in pilgrimages to holy sites or send their children to summer church camps (18).

Just as the Church should explore new strategies for reaching Russians today, it should find a new language for communicating its vision of life rather than relying on traditional catechetical resources, such as the nineteenth-century *Law of God* textbook, meant for people who were born and raised in an Orthodox culture and the Orthodox Church (6, 15). The *Missionary Concept* encourages greater use of contemporary art and musical forms in the Church's educational endeavors as well as exegetical preaching in the Divine Liturgy—emphases that, again, sound familiar to Western Protestants (19, 23).

A good deal of the *Missionary Concept* is devoted to practical methods of missionary outreach. Especially important, says the document, are missionary expeditions, in which groups of clergy, often with theological students, travel to areas of the country in which there is no established parish. Over the course of several weeks, the missionaries conduct baptisms, worship services, and catechetical classes.[49] The *Missionary Concept* has helped make such expeditions a key element of contemporary Russian

Orthodox theological education, not only at the Belgorod Seminary but also at other theological schools. Further, the *Missionary Concept* calls on the Church to reach into society by publishing popular religious literature, making effective use of the Internet and mass media, constructing chapels in airports and other public spaces, and organizing youth work.

The latter receives particular emphasis. The *Missionary Concept* recognizes that most young people in Russia are indifferent toward Orthodoxy and religion in general. They will be won to the Church not by forcing the outward forms of Orthodoxy upon them but rather by preparing them to make a conscious decision for active Church life. Every parish and monastery should develop educational and social initiatives that propagate Orthodox values in society and invite people into Church life. Every cleric, monastic, and layperson should think of him- or herself as a missionary (20–21).

The *Missionary Concept* is cautious about missionary outreach to members of other ethnic or religious groups in Russia. Unlike Moscow's Father Daniel Sysoev, who was murdered in his church in 2009—some speculate that radical Muslims targeted him—the *Missionary Concept* does not call for proselytization of members of Russia's other cultural-religious traditions. Rather, the document states that the Church is committed to dialogue and reconciliation with them, so long as they respect the Orthodox Church and its special place in Russian culture. The *Missionary Concept* argues that these traditions affirm the same basic moral values as the Church's and are equally concerned to counter the corrosive influences of a globalized secular culture. From this point of view, not every Russian must become Orthodox, but every Russian should be able to support the Church's social agenda. The *Missionary Concept* adds that members of other religion groups should not take advantage of Russians, many of whom are still weak in their Orthodox faith because of Communism's secularizing influence. The document is especially critical of "sects," arguing that they manipulate people rather than respecting their cultural identity and freedom to choose for themselves (13–14).

The Russian Orthodox Church, as I see it today, holds forth a vision of perfect unity and harmony in relation both to the nation and to the life of the Church. The nation and the Church can be one within themselves and in relation to each other. While this unity is always subject to tension and even misuse by one "interest group" over and against another, the Church foresees a world in which genuine progress toward unity is possible. This vision of Holy Rus' does not emphasize the tragic compromises that inevitably accompany social-political life, but rather those remarkable moments in which people truly experience the earthly realization of a transcendent order of perfect community, even if just momentarily.

The longing for a world in which people live in transcendent peace with God, each other, and indeed the whole of creation is not exclusive to Orthodoxy. I think of the nineteenth-century American Quaker artist Edward Hicks, whose famous paintings titled *The Peaceable Kingdom* depict the wild beasts of the forest gathering with domesticated animals, while in the background white-skinned Quakers and red-skinned Indians offer each other gestures of peace. Here, the prophecy of Isaiah 11 seems to come to fulfillment:

> The wolf shall dwell with the lamb,
> and the leopard shall lie down with the young goat,
> and the calf and the lion and the fattened calf together;
> and a little child shall lead them.
> The cow and the bear shall graze;
> their young shall lie down together;
> and the lion shall eat straw like the ox.
> The nursing child shall play over the hole of the cobra,
> and the weaned child shall put his hand on the adder's den.
> They shall not hurt or destroy
> in all my holy mountain;
> for the earth shall be full of the knowledge of the Lord
> as the waters cover the sea. (English Standard Version)

Nesterov's *Holy Rus'* and *The Way to Christ* offer a Russian interpretation of the same vision, although with greater emphasis on the Christ who heals all human pain and sorrow.

For Russian Orthodoxy, perhaps the most important visual depiction of this image of harmony and peace is Andrei Rublev's Trinity icon. A monk in the early fifteenth century at the Holy Trinity–St. Sergius Monastery, Rublev painted the icon for the iconostasis of the Trinity Cathedral, in which the relics of St. Sergius repose. Rublev took a traditional iconographic theme, the visit of three angels to Abraham and Sarah (Gen. 18), and transformed it into a spiritual commentary on the nature of the divine.[50]

The association of the three visitors with the three persons of the Trinity derived from early Christian teaching, but earlier Russian iconography had interpreted the events as a divine visitation to humanity. Typically, the three angels sit at a long table. Abraham and Sarah, to the sides, kneel and venerate the angels as God's presence with them. Behind the table stand a house and a cluster of trees in the wilderness.

Rublev removes Abraham and Sarah from the scene, and the house, a tree, and a rock cliff become mere outlines that nearly dissolve into the background. The focus now is clearly the three angels, who are no longer at a banquet table but rather around an altar table. The angels nod toward each other and make signs of blessing; their almost identical youthful faces seem to transcend maleness or femaleness. The one behind the altar table and the one to the right look toward the one to the left.

Rublev does not identity the three persons of the Trinity, but some commentators have suggested that the colors of their robes are significant. The angel to the left is mostly in brown (perhaps symbolic of the hiddenness of God the Father), the one behind the altar table is in purple and crimson (perhaps representing the passion of the Son), and the one to the right is mostly in green (perhaps associated with the life-giving power of the Holy Spirit). Or it may be that Rublev simply wishes to suggest such perfect unity and intimacy among the three that any one of them could be Father, Son, or Holy Spirit.

On the altar table stands a chalice in which we see a scarlet liquid or object representing Christ's sacrificial death and the eucharistic Communion that are at the very center of the Orthodox liturgy. The perfect communion that constitutes the inner life of God is now offered to humanity through the Eucharist. The angels sit at three sides of the altar table; the side toward the viewer is open for humanity, as though to say that those who receive the Eucharist sit at the fourth side of the table and enter into the inner life of God.

A contemporary version of Rublev's Trinity icon (author's photograph)

In 1929, Soviet authorities confiscated the Trinity icon and moved it into the national art museum in Moscow, the Tret'iakov Gallery, where it now hangs under protective glass. When I first viewed the icon, I was surprised by its dimensions. The angels are as large as the viewer. And I was overwhelmed by the glistening white background, to which no reproduction can do justice. A pure light flows from the icon to the viewer. Some visitors cross themselves as they approach the icon; others kiss the protective glass.

For me, the ideal harmony and community of Rublev's Trinity underlies the Church's social vision today. Humans can enter into a world that shines with divine light. They can live at peace with God and each other. Church and state can cooperate with each other to support social harmony. This kind of symphonia is not merely a political principle; it is nothing less than a religious assertion about ultimate reality.

THREE

Religious Education

In the sixteenth century, the Sretenskii Monastery lay on Moscow's outskirts. Today it is near the city center, only a few blocks away from the infamous "Lubianka," the headquarters of the KGB and now its successor organization, the FSB (Federal Security Service). The Bolsheviks closed the monastery in the 1920s, and part of the complex was used for imprisonment, torture, and execution. When the monastery was returned to the Church in the 1990s, Patriarch Aleksii II dedicated a large stone and cross to those who had died here for their faith. Every Friday evening I would pause by this memorial before hurrying on to the Bible study class in the nearby building that houses the monastery's seminary.

Inside the front door, a student would be stationed at a table to keep guard. On my first visit, I wondered what the young man would make of the fact that I was clearly a foreigner, but he politely led me to the room in which the group met. Plaster was falling from the walls, the window frames were brittle and cracked.[1] Thirty old school desks were crowded together, such that latecomers had to shove their way through those of us seated at the front to get to the free seats at the back.

I soon observed that there was a core group of fifteen to twenty participants, with another ten to fifteen occasional visitors. The regulars consisted largely of women aged fifty to sixty-five. Before class began, they would share gossip, remind each other of the previous week's lesson, and prepare tea for the class. It did not take long for them to inquire who I was and what had brought me to Moscow and their Bible study. One of the women, Irina, a grandmotherly figure close to retiring from a job in a local government office, soon adopted me. I got to know her friends Tat'iana and Liudmila, too.

The class typically began ten to fifteen minutes late. Then Father Julian, a middle-aged monk with a straggly ponytail, would arrive and lead the group in prayers to Mary, whose icon hung at the front of the room. When he had seated himself at an old, wobbly table, he would begin grilling his students: "What did we talk about last time? Who can remember?" His belligerent style shocked me at first. He seemed determined to put the students—and especially the women—in their place. Some evenings he would glare at a class member and demand, "Why didn't you bring a Bible?" or "Why do you bother to come if you can't remember what I talk about?" He nearly brought one young woman to tears when she asked him to repeat a point. To American sensibilities, Father Julian was rude and sexist.

But equally astonishing to me was that the women were totally unfazed. Irina and her friends would push back, respectfully but insistently: "Well, we're just trying to understand you better" or "You know that we need more help." Sometimes they even grinned and chuckled as they spoke. Father Julian would declare how much they frustrated him, and in response they would insist that they really liked the class and him personally. He would finally throw up his arms in despair and launch into his lecture, working verse by verse through the Gospel of John. An hour later, the class would end with another chanted prayer, and as the class dispersed, Father Julian would offer a personal blessing to anyone who wished. Even the young woman whom he had viciously scolded asked and received.

What is religious education all about? Themes of deification, transfiguration, and glimpsing heaven are prominent in formal explications of Orthodox belief and practice, but these topics hardly appeared in the Sretenskii Bible study class. Was the real point to demonstrate the power and supposed intelligence of a male clerical hierarchy over and against laywomen, who still constitute the majority of active Church participants and helpers? Alternatively, were the women successfully creating a support group over and against an indifferent teacher? Or was the banter between instructor and students good natured? And with so few people in attendance

at the Church's educational programs—whether at Sretenskii or elsewhere—could Church ambitions to in-church Russian society stand a
chance? As a seminary teacher myself, I understood why the Church would
want people to know what it believes and practices. Orthodoxy should be
more than merely a synonym for "ethnic Russian." But religious education
is clearly not a simple proposition.

Since the fall of Communism, the Russian Orthodox Church has established an impressive infrastructure of schools, universities, seminaries,
publishing houses, and mass media. These educational initiatives have
helped the Church promulgate its values in Russian society. People now
have the opportunity to learn openly about all aspects of Church doctrine,
history, morality, and worship. Basic information for laypeople is as available as scholarly literature for experts.[2] To be sure, the quality and purpose
of these educational offerings vary widely, and Russians avail themselves of
them to varying degrees. And two perhaps not entirely compatible impulses
seem to be at work: to make Russians better Christians, and to help Russians
know what makes their nation great.

Religious education as an exercise in civic education struck me on my
first visit to a Sunday school in Moscow. The parish of St. Seraphim of
Sarov, closed under Communism and now reopened, is located in an attractive residential neighborhood on the west side of the city.[3] Many of its
members are middle-class, professional Russians with children. When I
visited, a small wooden barrack was serving temporarily as the parish church;
government officials had not yet approved the parish's proposal to construct
a tall stone edifice on the site, where a monastery and church had stood
until the Bolsheviks demolished them. Father Aleksandr Narushev, one of
the three priests on staff, has primary responsibility for religious education.

Father Aleksandr is a bright, energetic man who has wasted no time in
organizing a popular children's summer camp and a weekly Sunday school
program. I attended a class for children aged ten to twelve that took place
after the Divine Liturgy. In typical Russian pedagogical style, the children
sat quietly and politely at wooden school desks. When Father Aleksandr
launched into a half-hour talk about the importance of Orthodoxy to

Russian culture, their eyes seemed to glaze over, and when he asked, "What is culture?" they were silent. But Father Aleksandr was not perturbed. He quickly answered, "Orthodoxy and Russian culture belong together." And to reinforce the point, he asked each child to go home and write a paragraph on the theme "What I Love about Russia."

As a North American Protestant, I bristled at first at Father Aleksandr's pedagogical strategy. What, I asked myself, did educating children about their Orthodox cultural identity have to do with helping them grow in Christian faith? As we lunched together after class, Father Aleksandr helped me see that I was making an artificial distinction. For him, as for so many Orthodox leaders whom I met, Russian culture itself makes a witness to the gospel because that culture and its literature, music, architecture, and art were decisively shaped by Orthodoxy. From this perspective, when Russians learn how Orthodoxy has shaped their national heritage, they also learn something about what it means to be a Christian. I think that Father Aleksandr would say that religious faith is more than cultural or national identity, but he nevertheless wants Russians to see divine glory in the noblest accomplishments of their nation.

As I understand it, an Orthodox education involves more than transmitting cultural or national identity, because Orthodoxy has traditionally regarded humans as capable of deification and transfiguration. An official Russian Orthodox Church document notes, "Church education is in principle wider and deeper than an intellectual process of transmitting and mastering knowledge and information. The center and meaning of Church education is to be found in the gracious transfiguration of man's entire nature in communion with God and his Church."[4]

Elena Ivanova, a Russian Orthodox pedagogue, roots this understanding of education in the monastic wisdom of St. Siluan of Mt. Athos, an early twentieth-century Russian monk whose spiritual writings have become influential in Russian Orthodox circles today.[5] Ivanova notes that Siluan sees divinization as God's gracious gift to humans. Christ and Christ's saving work make divine-human fellowship possible, and humans should offer their praise and thanksgiving in response. But, according to Ivanova, Siluan adds that this transformation of the self also depends on human efforts to follow Christ and his commandments. Only as a person freely submits to God can he or she enter into God's life.

For Ivanova, an Orthodox pedagogics will attend to both dimensions of divine-human fellowship. Because God uses people whose lives are filled with divine grace to offer divinization to others, an Orthodox education depends first of all on the teacher and the quality of his or her life. What a good teacher is communicating is not primarily information about God or Church tradition but rather God's loving, transforming presence as manifest in the teacher. A good teacher also opens up space for the student to decide for him- or herself to serve God and become like Christ. In Ivanova's thinking, this transformative space is to be found above all in the Church and its way of life. There a person learns to overcome his or her selfish will, to pray, to trust that God is guiding his or her life, and to love others, especially one's enemies.

I have sometimes seen how Church authorities use doctrine and ritual to keep people under their thumb. But I can also interpret the Church's educational work more sympathetically. I can understand that a good priest would want to protect people from errors of thought and behavior that are destructive of self or relationships with others.[6] Perhaps right understanding and worship of God ("Orthodoxy" can be translated as "right glorification") really can help people discover a divine dimension to their existence and right relationship with their fellow human beings.

My young, vivacious Russian friend Anna and I often debate these matters. She reminds me that intellectual knowledge of doctrinal propositions does not guarantee salvation. She notes that Jesus' first disciples were illiterate fishermen. She insists that today, too, a simple believer may live more faithfully than an educated theologian: "If a person wants to learn more about the Church's beliefs, that's fine. But we should not expect that of everyone. Those who live according to Orthodoxy are filled with love and reverence, and that's what really matters." And I, the North American theologian and professor with a Ph.D., reply that religious education is nevertheless not just for intellectuals. Learning Church belief and practice can help every believer see more clearly the contours of true life in God. A person does not love God with the mind alone, but love of God includes the mind.

While the formulation "faith seeking understanding" has been more typical of Western than Eastern theology, the Orthodox tradition has also valued intellectual inquiry, especially when it deepens people's ability to pray and offer loving service to others.[7] I would like to believe that the Russian Church's educational initiatives will teach Russians today not only that they have a cultural Orthodox identity but also that they can pursue and experience holiness.

The Russians whom I have gotten to know have decisively shaped my way of framing these issues historically. Anna would say that "faith seeking understanding" actually plays a much larger role in the Russian Church today than traditionally. For centuries, Orthodoxy was embedded in folk practices. To be Orthodox was not primarily a matter of learning the meaning of Church doctrines or rituals; rather, it was a way of life shaped by the rhythms of village life. A general sense of wonder and awe before the powers of nature was reinforced by the experience of the holy in the Divine Liturgy. Efforts in formal education emerged only as the Church began to see faith less as a vague "mystical" experience and more as a matter of right doctrine and practice.

In folk Orthodoxy, the Church year was coordinated with the cycles of agricultural life. Russian peasants traditionally associated the veneration of the Prophet Elijah (July 20/August 2) with prayers for a good harvest.[8] On the anniversary of the Birth of the Mother of God (September 8/21), one of the most important holy days of the year, peasant women in some parts of Russia greeted autumn by processing to nearby rivers and lakes, eating blessed jellies and breads, singing folk songs, performing dances, and playing games.[9] A blend of mutually reinforcing beliefs and practices from Christianity and local nature religions provided the "sacred canopy" that bore village life from one generation to the next.[10]

Attending church, especially on great holy days, was a vital part of these traditions. Education occurred implicitly as people attended the Church's prayers and worship. Orthodox theology is, above all, "liturgical theology."[11] The Church teaches through its symbols, narratives, and rituals. As a Russian priest once said to me, "John, if you want to learn Orthodox theology, go to the liturgy, not the library." From this perspective, icons—the pictures that the Church paints of holy persons—are not only objects that command believers' veneration but also vehicles for teaching them theological truths. Similarly, the Church's prayers and hymns set forth biblical language and central Church doctrines, just as the Church's fasts and holy days direct believers to key events in the life of Christ, Mary, and the saints.

However, as general educational levels rose in Russia in the eighteenth and nineteenth centuries, religious education became more formalized. Church authorities were increasingly concerned to combat the "superstitious" dimensions of popular folk Orthodoxy. The Church's worship and prayer no longer seemed to do the job; few people understood the Church Slavonic, last revised in the early seventeenth century, in which the liturgy was celebrated, or comprehended the meaning of basic Christian rituals, such as baptism and the Eucharist. The Church charged priests to intensify their preaching and catechetical work in order to familiarize their parishioners with Scripture and Church teaching.[12]

About the same time, the tradition's key texts became more accessible to laypeople. For centuries, the language of the Russian Bible, like that of the liturgy, had been Church Slavonic. Like the Roman Catholic Church, the Orthodox Church had long worried that vernacular translations would undermine Church teaching and authority, a charge that Orthodox leaders regularly leveled against Protestants with their seemingly arbitrary, subjective interpretations of the Bible.[13] But in the early nineteenth century, a Church-sponsored Russian Bible Society began work, and in 1876 the Church enthusiastically promoted an authoritative translation of the Bible, the so-called Synodal Bible (because it was approved by the Church's Holy Synod).[14]

Traditionally, Orthodoxy has attended not only to Scripture but also to the writings of the Church Fathers. Especially important has been the *Philokalia*, a collection of ancient and medieval spiritual writings originally used for guiding monastic life. As was the case with the Bible, Russian translations first appeared in the nineteenth century. And while few laypeople would read deeply in the *Philokalia*—its enigmatic sayings are not always easy to unravel—it inspired a genre of popular spiritual literature that did reach many people.

Especially important were the spiritual writings of such figures as St. Dmitrii of Rostov in the late sixteenth and early seventeenth centuries and Bishop Ignatii (Brianchaninov), who translated parts of the *Philokalia* and helped renew monastic life in the nineteenth century.[15] Equally popular was *The Way of a Pilgrim*, the spiritual diary of a peasant who wanders across the Russian countryside with a copy of the *Philokalia*, searching for a holy elder who can teach him how to "pray without ceasing" (1 Thess. 5:17). He eventually learns about the Jesus Prayer—"Lord Jesus Christ, have mercy on me"—which he repeats like a mantra, in search of mystical communion with the divine.[16]

A third kind of Orthodox educational literature that emerged in the nineteenth century was catechetical in character. One of the first and most famous catechisms was prepared by Metropolitan Filaret (Drozdov), who had also played a key role in promoting the Synodal translation of the Bible.[17] Closely related to catechisms were textbooks for formal instruction of religion (law of God) in parishes or Russian primary schools, many of which were operated by the Church.

Other kinds of educational literature proliferated. Church newspapers and journals promulgated statements of hierarchs, decisions by councils, and reflections by theologians.[18] Journals for laypeople exploded in popularity. And in the late nineteenth and early twentieth centuries, a group of remarkable and sometimes controversial theologians and philosophers— such as Sergei Bulgakov, Nicholas Berdyaev, and Vladimir Soloviev— profoundly shaped Orthodox intellectual circles.[19]

These new efforts at educating people in Orthodox values and ways of thinking had only a brief life. Soon after the October Revolution, the Bolsheviks shut down the Church's educational work. Government decrees separating Church and state removed the Church from public school education. Sunday schools and Church publications were prohibited, and theological seminaries were closed. Many of the Church's great intellectuals went into exile. As the Bolsheviks embarked on programs of industrialization and urbanization, the indirect education in Orthodoxy that folk traditions once provided was severely weakened, though never completely lost. The formative power of the liturgy also declined as the Bolsheviks closed parishes and monasteries and discouraged people from attending services at those that remained open. Even when state religious policies relaxed after 1941, the state tightly controlled Church seminaries, kept priests under close surveillance, limited the number of parishes, restricted Church publication work, and undertook popular campaigns of antireligious, atheistic education. Most religious education went underground, largely hidden from both the state and the Church hierarchy.

In these hidden spaces, some believers read and studied their tradition's holy texts on their own. But two other forms of education also became important: instruction by a wise leader and group study. One activity could include the other, but they could also take place independently. The wise leader might lead a group study, but individuals might also come separately to the wise leader for instruction.

Russian men's and women's monasteries had long paired their younger members with an older, wiser monastic who would hear confessions and provide spiritual guidance. This practice also came to influence parish life. Believers needed a spiritual counselor before whom they could make confession and receive spiritual instruction. Normally this person was their priest, but they might also seek out another counselor—a monk, a nun, or a priest in a different parish who had won a reputation for spiritual wisdom.[20]

By the nineteenth century, the phenomenon of holy elders further shaped people's perceptions of spiritual counsel. Especially associated with the monastery at Optina Pustyn', these holy elders attracted uneducated peasants as well as some of Russia's most famous public intellectuals, such as Leo Tolstoy. The holy elders seemed to have extraordinary spiritual insight. Usually (though not always) male, they could look into a person's heart, see into his or her future, and provide practical counsel for how to live the Christian life and resolve personal problems. While the holy elders did not provide formal Christian education in Scripture or the teachings of the Church Fathers, they distilled and transmitted the spiritual wisdom they had gleaned through many years of immersion in Church prayer, worship, and tradition.

In the Soviet period, holy elders assumed a new importance, often attracting visitors from afar and establishing informal networks of spiritual children. In turn, these spiritual children sometimes met on their own, especially if their spiritual father was exiled or executed. Such underground "cell groups" represented a new development in Russian Orthodoxy. A "lay church" emerged outside the formal structures of the official, state-approved Church.[21]

This lay church, with its deep commitment to understanding Church teaching and practice, was distinct from traditional folk Orthodoxy. Further, the democratic character of this lay church contrasted with the implicit authoritarianism of the holy elders. A spiritual child did not question his or her holy elder but rather accepted his counsel, whereas members of the underground church took the initiative for educating themselves in the Scriptures and the Church's great texts.

To be sure, the line between the two phenomena should not be drawn too strictly. A lay church could remain attached to a charismatic priest or monk, and a holy elder could encourage his spiritual children to sustain the faith even in his absence. But the circumstances of Soviet Russia taught some believers that the "Church" resided less in hierarchical structures than in believers' conscious commitment to understand and guard Church doctrine and practice.

In the early twentieth century, this lay church was powerfully represented by such movements as the World Student Christian Federation, which drew thousands of young intellectual Russians into small ecumenical circles that studied the Bible and nurtured spiritual fellowship. Although many Orthodox Church leaders were suspicious of the movement, others sympathized with it, and still others had risen to leadership because of their participation in it. Some of these study groups survived even into the 1920s, before the state completely disbanded them.[22]

As Communist persecution accelerated, some parishes, sometimes with the encouragement of their priest, organized themselves into small circles that, like the student movement, offered a protected space for spiritual growth and support. In some cases, these groups also helped preserve liturgical life. They hid icons and liturgical books, implements, and garments—and sometimes their spiritual father. If he was arrested, they might travel thousands of miles to visit him in his place of exile.[23]

The Church of St. Nicholas in Klennikakh, a historic neighborhood near the center of Moscow, offers one outstanding example of the importance of both venerated leaders and lay initiative for Orthodox education during the Communist era.[24] When the Bolsheviks came to power, Aleksei Mechev, the parish's beloved priest, foresaw that the Church's traditional way of life was threatened. He prepared his parishioners to live a monastic kind of existence in this world. They would have to learn to meet in secret and devote themselves intensely to defending the Church's traditions.[25]

When Aleksei died in 1923, his son Sergei succeeded him and continued to build circles of intense spiritual fellowship that could survive in case of his arrest and imprisonment.[26] Even after the state sent him into exile in 1929, he guided the community by way of letters. In one, he writes: "Do not grieve about yourselves, because you still have what is most important but has been denied to many others, including me: worship. Guard it. Indeed, this is my commandment to you, not only to my spiritual children but also to my friends. Guard worship, guard the clergy. . . . Instruct one another, strengthen one another, comfort one another. 'Bear one another's burdens and in this way obey the law of Christ' (Gal. 6:2)."[27]

When the Communists closed the church in 1932, parishioners valiantly preserved the spiritual inheritance they had received from both Mechevs. They regularly visited Aleksei's grave in a Moscow cemetery and prayed for his help. Groups of ten to twelve believers would gather in a parishioner's apartment. A trusted lay spiritual leader, male or female, would guide the group. On Saturday evenings, the group chanted vespers, matins, the hours, and *akathists* (special hymns to a saint). On Sundays, a priest would secretly celebrate the liturgy; he and the members of the groups were risking years of exile or even execution if the secret police learned of their activities.

Eventually, political repression scattered the parishioners, but several survived to celebrate the reopening of the parish in 1991. One noteworthy spiritual daughter of Aleksei and Sergei was Maria Sokolova, who helped preserve ancient traditions of icon painting. In the 1920s and 1930s, she carefully made copies of major icons that she feared might be destroyed by the

Communists. In 1934, she painted the first version of an icon to honor "all the saints who shone forth in the Russian land," saints to whom the Local Council of 1917–18 had assigned a day of commemoration, although the Church was not able to celebrate it publicly until 1946.[28]

Since the fall of Communism, both Aleksei and Sergei have been canonized, and Aleksei's remains have been transferred to the reopened Church of St. Nicholas in Klennikakh, where I have stood in line to venerate them. Some of my Russian Orthodox friends honor the Mechev community as an example of what the Church should be today: a space in which laypeople take an active role in educating themselves about Christian faith and sustaining Church practice.

Toward the end of the Soviet period, several other powerful Church personalities promoted religious education. Father Aleksandr Men' became especially well known. Spiritually nourished as a child and young man by key figures of the underground church, Father Aleksandr devoted himself to advanced theological studies and in 1960 was ordained to the priesthood. Because a secret government directive at that time forbade highly educated priests from serving in Moscow, he was assigned to small parishes on the city's outskirts.

Father Aleksandr thought deeply and wrote prolifically about the Christian faith, relating it to the sciences and other world religions and encouraging critical study of the Bible and Church tradition. His curiosity and enthusiasm not only touched his parishioners but also won him a wider following. By the late 1980s, his lectures and books had helped spark a religious renaissance among Russian intellectuals seeking an alternative to the ideology of the collapsing Soviet state. In 1990, he founded an academy for lay theological education.[29]

Father Aleksandr was brutally murdered later that year under circumstances that remain unclear and troubling; some speculate that the KGB was involved. Although the Church hierarchy had honored Father Aleksandr for his missionary zeal, certain circles in Church and society were threatened by his open-mindedness and popular influence. Some priests even labeled him a heretic and prohibited their parishioners from reading his books. Today his followers regard him as a martyr, and Moscow's Church of Cosmas and Damian has taken a leading role in preserving his legacy by publishing his works and promoting lay participation in parish life.[30]

The range of approaches to education and spiritual leadership within Russian Orthodoxy is further illustrated by two other famous spiritual fathers who, like Men', began influencing wide circles of the Church in the 1950s and 1960s: Ioann (Krest'iankin) and Nikolai (Gur'ianov). Neither would be martyred, but both suffered imprisonment. Like Men', they were priests, but one belonged to a monastic community, while the other lived a monastic-like existence. Both Ioann and Nikolai came to be popularly regarded as holy elders, but Ioann remained firmly within the bounds of the official Church, while Nikolai was sometimes claimed by groups more on its conservative, nationalistic fringe.[31]

Ioann lived for forty years in the Pskov-Pecherskii Monastery, the only Russian Orthodox monastery never to have been closed by the Soviets; the area belonged to Estonia until Soviet annexation in 1940, was occupied in 1941 by the Nazis, and came under Soviet control again only after the war. The monastery's remote location and the spirited leadership of one of its abbots, Alipii (Voronov), helped it survive the Khrushchev era. Ioann, like Aleksandr Men', became famous for his infectiously joyful faith, had hundreds of spiritual children, and welcomed a steady flow of visitors up to his death in 2006.[32] Nikolai served as a priest on the island of Zalit, not far from Pskov, until his death in 2002 and was especially well known for his devotion to the royal family and his predictions of the imminent end of history, at which time a tsar would be restored to Russia.[33]

With the fall of Communism, the institutional Church quickly reestablished education as a priority. To the Church's thinking, Soviet scientific atheism had once tried to rob Russians of their historic cultural identity.[34] Now there were new threats. Yoga, Buddhism, and other Eastern spiritual movements had become popular in some intellectual circles. Western religious groups, especially North American evangelical Protestants, were sending thousands of missionaries to "convert" Russians to the gospel. The Church was not content with the fact that more and more Russians were calling themselves Orthodox. It wanted them to *know* and understand what the Church believed.

Some Church leaders now believe that renewed attention to traditional Russian culture—such as the classics of Russian literature or music—will transmit Orthodox values and ways of thinking to people. Other priests, such as Father Vladimir Klimzo in the village of Davydovo in the Iaroslav Region, are reintroducing folk songs and celebrations to their parishes as a way of disseminating Orthodox moral values. From the perspective of still others, remnants of popular Orthodoxy that went underground during the Soviet period—such as pilgrimages to sacred springs or displays of icons at home—can now be ways for the Church to educate people about Orthodox faith. And perhaps the liturgy itself, now widely accessible, will draw people into a vision of Holy Rus'. But it seems to me that while historic Russian culture, folk traditions, popular piety, and the liturgy all have their place, none is sufficient. They may simply encourage people "to do Orthodoxy" on their own, not with the Church's guidance. I agree with those Church leaders who, as in the nineteenth century, say that more formal means of education are also necessary.

In a post-Communist, urbanized world, publication initiatives and media programming are playing an especially important role in the Church's efforts to educate the wider populace in Orthodox teachings. Today, a vast array of religious newspapers, journals, books, CDs, DVDs, and radio and television programs target a "nonchurched" but Church-friendly audience. The Sretenskii Monastery in Moscow operates one of the Church's largest publishing programs, a veritable Barnes & Noble of the Orthodox world. The monastery publishes more than one hundred new titles each year, covering all aspects of Church life for all age groups: Christian spirituality, Church history, Scripture, Church music and arts, Orthodox ascetical practices, monasticism, liturgy and prayer, and the lives of the saints. The monastery also maintains one of the Orthodox Church's best Internet sites (www.pravoslavie.ru), which offers detailed explanation of saints, icons, and historical events associated with each day of the Church year.

Orthodox Internet sites and radio and television outlets provide additional education in Christian faith. Radio Grad Petrov in St. Petersburg and

Radio Radonezh in Moscow are especially noteworthy, with the former providing not only popular educational programming but also scholarly presentations on Russian Church history, doctrine, and liturgics. Orthodox television stations such as Spas and Soiuz also have a growing audience, although the technical quality of their programming still lags far behind that of the nation's major channels.

Until he became patriarch in 2009, Kirill had a weekly half-hour program each Saturday morning on one of Russia's major television stations. He became widely known for interpreting pastoral-theological questions in a compelling way to a popular audience. Metropolitan Hilarion (Alfeev), Kirill's successor as head of the Church's Department of External Church Relations, now hosts a weekly television program in which guests interview him about Church life, as did I in 2013.[35] Like Kirill, Hilarion is renowned for his capacity to communicate the Church's theological legacy to a popular audience. His books on Orthodox theology reach beyond scholarly circles to educated, interested laypeople.[36]

In Soviet times, the Scriptures and the great spiritual writings of the tradition were available, if at all, only in highly limited quantities. Today they are being republished in inexpensive popular editions. Representative are recent publications of the Gospel of Mark, the shortest and perhaps most readable of the four New Testament biographies of Christ. One of these popular publications presents the Gospel along with the classic commentary of an eleventh- to twelfth-century Byzantine theologian, Feofilakt of Bolgar. The introduction argues that a person cannot understand European and Russian literature, art, and philosophy without a familiarity with the teachings of Christ.[37] A second book offers a commentary by Bishop Vasilii (Preobrazhenskii) of Kineshma, who died in internal exile in 1945.[38] In 2012, the Patriarchate's department for information, in cooperation with its department for missions, distributed for free a third commentary, prepared by Aleksei Uminskii, a popular Orthodox priest, publicist, and television personality in Moscow. Uminskii's commentary aims at attracting new readers to the Bible. Through simple journalistic language he invites people to discover how Christ speaks to them today.[39] And a fourth publication, from the Sretenskii Monastery, simply presents the text of the Gospel of

Mark along with lavish photographs of its Middle Eastern setting and Orthodox icons that illustrate key scenes from the life of Christ.[40]

Church publishing houses have also made the great spiritual writings of the Orthodox tradition accessible to a popular audience. The publication program of the Sretenskii Monastery is again noteworthy: a new five-volume edition of the Russian version of the *Philokalia* and works of classic Russian spiritual authors, such as the eighteenth-century St. Tikhon of Zadonsk.[41]

While Sretenskii operates firmly within the Church's institutional structure, many Orthodox publishers have no official Church status. In the past, their publications often included a commendation from the patriarch or a metropolitan, although the hierarch had never given explicit permission. In recent years, the Church has taken a more active role in exercising "quality control" to ensure that people get the "right" answers. The Church's Publications Committee now seeks to evaluate all religious publications. Those it regards as theologically reliable may carry the imprimatur "Recommended for publication by the Publications Committee of the Russian Orthodox Church" on the copyright page. While this oversight is exercised primarily over Orthodox publishers, the committee also invites secular publishing houses to secure the Church's imprimatur for any of their publications that address religious matters.[42]

Today Russians have more access to religious educational resources than ever before. Nevertheless, in my observation, few Orthodox believers read the Scriptures on their own and even fewer delve into the Church's spiritual classics. Moreover, they rarely ask their parish priest for help. Men are perhaps reluctant to display their ignorance, be perceived as a bother, or take the time. Women, from what I can see, are more apt to consult their priests, but usually about personal problems, not Church teachings.[43] Instead, people turn to Orthodox publications, radio programs, and Internet sites in search of "right answers."

The Sretenskii Monastery in Moscow again provides an impressive example. For many years, the monastery website invited people to submit their "questions to a priest." By 2010, three monks were responding full-time to the more than fifteen hundred requests that arrived each month. As questions and answers became increasingly repetitive, the monastery ceased accepting questions and established an online search function that allowed people to access answers from the archives. The man with principal responsibilities for this project, Archmonk Iov (Gumerov), is a small, wiry man, now in his seventies, who converted to Orthodoxy during the Soviet period, was ordained as a priest, and then took monastic vows and entered Sretenskii after the death of his wife. In 2009, he compiled *One Thousand Questions to a Priest*. The first quarter of Father Iov's nine-hundred-page book provides basic information about the Church's liturgical and ritual life: the symbolic arrangement of a church building; icons and relics; holy days; the structure of the Divine Liturgy; veneration of the saints; miracles; remembering the dead; sacraments; and basic ascetical practices such as fasting and prayer. The book's next five hundred pages are devoted to the Church's central beliefs: the Trinity; Christ as God and Savior; Mary, the Mother of God; the human as soul, spirit, and body; temptation and sin; the character of the spiritual life; and the authority of the Scriptures. The last section of the book discusses the position of the Orthodox Church in relation to other churches and religions; sects and occultism; philosophy, literature, and culture; and secular society.[44]

While Father Iov's book is intelligent and sophisticated, it reflects Orthodoxy's—and especially Russian Orthodoxy's—attention to right ritual practice. The great schism of the seventeenth century ("Old Believers") resulted in part from Church efforts to reform the way in which people made the sign of the cross.[45] Today, much popular religious literature in Russia also emphasizes right ritual behavior. People want to know how to pray or fast or use holy things in order to be truly Orthodox.

A pamphlet that Iov has coauthored with his son, Father Pavel Gumerov, further typifies this concern. Entitled *The Christian Household: Traditions and Holy Things*, the work offers simple instructions for making one's home a holy place: how to arrange an icon corner, consume holy water and blessed bread (*prosphora*), or recite the Church's morning and evening prayers.[46] Their booklet is representative of hundreds that have appeared for a popular Church audience, focusing on how right ritual behavior trains a person to perceive divinity in the midst of everyday life.

Another dimension of "getting things right" is women's attire. Some monasteries, such as the Danilov Monastery for men in Moscow, keep a barrel containing wraparound skirts at their entrances so that women arriving in slacks can be properly dressed on the grounds. At the Martha and Mary Monastery for women, a sign with a big X through a pair of bright-red lips warns women wearing lipstick not to kiss the icons. Monasteries and parishes often provide headscarves for women who have neglected to bring their own. From the Church's perspective, such matters are not just an oddity of the Russian tradition or merely a result of people's insecurity about what they have to do to be religious. Rather, ritual behavior shapes a person's inner self. Religion is as much about what one does with one's body as about what one believes. Even Western Protestants, despite their historic suspicion of ritualistic practice, have begun to acknowledge the importance of such practices as fasting, pilgrimage, and setting aside times and places for prayer.[47]

To be sure, some Russian priests and parishioners are obsessed with ritual because they want to demonstrate their power to regulate others' behavior. It is not unusual for a newcomer to an Orthodox church in Russia to be scolded for doing something wrong. I once had a monk demand that I bow more deeply when the priest came through the church to swing his censer over the icons and worshippers.[48] Another time, a church helper asked me to leave because I was simply observing the space rather than buying and lighting candles, and so was obviously a "tourist" rather than a believer.

My friend Pavel, who works with an Orthodox youth organization, worries that the Church too often turns off young people by imposing external forms of religiosity on them.[49] "Young people too often hear from the Church that they are wearing the wrong clothes or crossing themselves in the wrong way," he says. For those who believe that the ultimate goal of an Orthodox education is communion with the divine, ritual practice is not an end in itself. Rather, ritual practices makes sense only if they help a person become more aware of the world as divinely transfigured.

While a sensitivity to divine beauty is not missing from Iov's writings, it is more prominent in another book published by the Sretenskii Monastery. *The Unknown World of Faith* opens readers to a world that may be "unknown" to them because they have never encountered the Church and its teachings about an "unknown" world beyond their everyday world. Every human being nevertheless poses questions of ultimate meaning and seeks God, says Archimandrite (now Bishop) Tikhon (Shevkunov), head of the monastery, in an introduction.[50]

Beautifully illustrated, *The Unknown World of Faith* has enjoyed numerous printings and is widely used in Orthodox schools.[51] The book opens with a discussion of the authenticity of the Shroud of Turin, which is especially venerated by the monastery—a full-size photographic copy of the shroud is displayed in an underground chapel in the monastery church. The book then explores Orthodoxy's remarkable world of miracles, saints, and beauty; Orthodox worship, doctrine, and prayer as entry points into that transfigured world; and Russia's special responsibility for safeguarding Orthodoxy. The book concludes with personal testimonies to Orthodoxy's truth from a variety of historical and contemporary figures, including well-known Russian writers, artists, musicians, and scholars.[52]

In 2011, yet another book from the Sretenskii Monastery invited Russians to glimpse this transfigured reality. Written by Bishop Tikhon, *Everyday Saints* (or, more literally, *Unholy Holy Ones*) is a collection of stories about contemporary monastic life in Russia.[53] In contrast to Orthodox "getting things right" books, *Everyday Saints* depicts Orthodoxy's human face, a Church that is composed of people with warts and flaws, through whom God nevertheless works for good. Even though it is six hundred pages long, the book had sold more than 1.5 million hard copies and tens of thousands of electronic copies within three years and today is ranked among the best-selling books in Russia since the collapse of Communism. In contrast to most of Sretenskii's books, *Everyday Saints* has been marketed not only in Church bookstores but also in supermarkets and other mass outlets.

Bishop Tikhon is a skillful storyteller. He traces his journey out of Soviet atheism into Orthodoxy and then into monasticism. In his opening pages, he extols "this beautiful world [of the monastery] that lives by entirely different rules from those of ordinary life—a world of endless light, filled with love and joyful discoveries, hope and happiness, struggle, victory and insight into the meaning of defeat—and most importantly about the mighty revelation of God's power and help" (7). Significantly, what Tikhon emphasizes about Orthodoxy is not doctrine or even the beauty of the liturgy (although he does not deny their importance) but rather the experience of the holy in everyday events and people. For Tikhon, miracles and wonders are never far away. A person can never predict when they will occur, but life in a disciplined Christian community prepares a person to recognize them.

Tikhon's book draws out that strand of traditional Russian Orthodox thinking that looks for the wise elder who will guide his spiritual children into truth. Tikhon refers specifically to Ioann (Krest'iankin), although Tikhon notes that Ioann never made any such claims about himself. For Tikhon, Ioann was more than just a wise, experienced counselor; he had the uncanny ability to discern God's will for a person when that person could not see it for him- or herself. Ioann's extraordinary spiritual insight had direct implications for Tikhon's life. As a young man, Tikhon despaired about his future until Ioann directed him to take steps that eventually resulted in Tikhon's assignment to the Sretenskii Monastery. Today Tikhon and the Sretenskii monks regard Ioann as their intercessor, spiritual instructor, and benefactor. As Tikhon declares in *Everyday Saints*, "His sermons, letters, and instruction are [our] basic textbooks" (56).

While honoring Ioann's special authority, Tikhon also democratizes elderhood. The greater part of Tikhon's book is about ordinary monks, nuns, priests, and believers who nevertheless turn out to be more than ordinary. Tikhon introduces the reader to a set of unforgettable, sometimes outrageously humorous characters, such as Father Antipa, Father Gavriil, and Father Rafail. Each has personal peculiarities and foibles, even neuroses; none has a claim to holiness. For Tikhon, all of them nevertheless reveal something of God's holy presence in everyday life.

Tikhon began his monastic career in the Pskov-Pecherskii Monastery, where his friend Father Rafail also served for six years before being assigned to a small parish in an isolated rural area. Tikhon describes Rafail as an energetic and ebullient but also willful personality who gave as much as he could to God and others but never overcame a tendency to take unwarranted risks, especially when driving cars. Rafail often seemed lazy and ineffective as a priest. His preaching was disorganized and confused. Some of his parishioners could not stand his rough-edged personality, but others found him mesmerizing. What Father Rafail liked best was inviting people to join him for tea, then regaling them with stories that often turned out to be tall tales.

Tikhon was once hosting several distinguished female relatives of the patriarch, and on the train back to Moscow they ran into none other than Father Rafail, about whom Tikhon had already made them so curious. Rafail was going to the city to buy auto parts. As he sat with his new acquaintances, he captivated them with stories of his encounters with wild animals near his village. He asked the women if they would know what to do if confronted in the forest by a bear or a wild boar. His descriptions of the dangers both frightened and fascinated them. Finally, he asserted that the best strategy for escaping from a pursuing bear would be to climb a tree and throw a sweater at the bear if it too came up the tree. Father Rafail claimed that the beast would mistake the sweater for a human, grab at it, come crashing to the ground, and break its vertebrae. The women knew that he was pulling their leg but roared with laughter.

Tikhon further reports that Father Rafail had long dreamed of buying a really fast automobile, but one thing after another had frustrated his plans. Here Tikhon draws out a spiritual lesson: God may try for a long time to save us from ourselves, but if we are unrepentant and stubborn he will finally allow us to bear the consequences of our actions. We then learn that Rafail eventually succeeded in acquiring a used but powerful Mercedes and soon afterward crashed and died.

Rafail was no saint in the ordinary sense of the word, but Tikhon argues that all who participate in the Eucharist receive Christ's holiness, despite their sins and flaws. Nineteen years later people still remember Father Rafail's remarkable spirit. In his presence, they sensed a world filled with God's glorious presence and boundless love. An ordinary sinner became an extraordinary instrument of divine grace (547–60).

Perhaps Bishop Tikhon is also an unholy holy one. For months I tried in vain to set up an interview with him. One day he phoned me out of the blue and said that he had time for me, but only if I could get there right that very moment. I dropped what I was doing and rushed forty-five minutes across town, worried he would be gone to his next appointment by the time I arrived. At the monastery, a secretary escorted me to an exquisite reception hall, where I nervously waited alone. When Tikhon finally entered, he had three telephones in his hands, and an assistant kept handing him papers to sign. But Bishop Tikhon—reputed at the time to be President Putin's personal counselor—was generous with his answers to me and, at the end of our talk, made a point of saying how much he appreciated Protestants.

An Orthodox education has many dimensions, but imparting to people a sensitivity to transcendent beauty and glory in the everyday is especially important and helps explain why the line between cultural identity and religious faith is so difficult to draw in Russia. Orthodoxy, as I understand it, ultimately aims to move people beyond "right" answers to a vision of the perfect harmony and unity that have shaped the nation in the past and should shape their lives and society in the present. Books such as *The Unknown World of Faith* and *Everyday Saints* invite ordinary Russians to glimpse this possibility. Moreover, the Church suggests they will see more and more of Holy Rus' if they enter into the Church's life, where they will learn how and why to pray, participate in the Divine Liturgy and the sacraments, live moral lives, care for the weak and needy, and pursue a transfigured life.

Of the Church's many educational initiatives, five deserve particular attention—religious education in the public schools, prebaptismal catechization, parish-based religious education, Orthodox university education, and the development of academic disciplines of "comparative theology" and "sectology."

Religious education in the public schools. Until the Bolshevik Revolution, half of Russian elementary school education was in the hands of the Church.[54] Today the nation has a well-established system of state-run public schools. But with the collapse of Communism the Church has again been able to operate its own educational system. The number of Church-sponsored kindergartens, elementary schools, and *gymnasia* has grown rapidly, although it represents only a tiny percentage of the nation's educational institutions.

Russians send their children to Orthodox schools for the same reasons some Americans and Europeans are attracted to parochial education. Active Orthodox believers often desire a school that will reinforce religious beliefs, practices, and moral values that they cultivate in their family or parish. For people more distant from the Church, Orthodox schools appear to devote greater attention to the individual needs of children or to protect children from corrupting moral influences in the state public schools.

The Church has aimed, however, not only at acquiring a niche for Orthodox schools within the nation's larger educational infrastructure but also at including religious education in the state school curriculum. Such proposals are highly controversial. While some regional governments have implemented extensive programs of Orthodox religious education, others have resisted.[55] In the Belgorod Region, children receive religious education at every grade level, and local Church and government authorities are planning to make religious education a standard part of the curriculum at the city's state university. Elementary school classes go on field trips to parishes, where priests explain the different parts of a church building or how believers venerate icons. But in more secularized, urbanized parts of the country—such as Moscow or St. Petersburg—religious education has not been part of the regional curriculum, and Orthodox priests have sometimes complained about not even being permitted to accept invitations to speak in classes.

Given these complexities, federal authorities long resisted Church proposals that religious education be part of the nationally mandated curriculum. Vigorous debate inside the Church further complicated the question. Some Church leaders argued that religious education should be framed in terms of the foundations of Orthodox culture. The goal would be to describe the Church's contributions to Russian history and culture rather than to promulgate Orthodox doctrine and practice. Others parts of the Church wanted religious education to be more like catechization, along the lines of the "law of God" curriculum of the prerevolutionary period.[56]

A breakthrough in Church-state negotiations occurred soon after Patriarch Kirill's enthronement in 2009. In a sudden turnabout, the federal government agreed to explore offering religious education in the public schools. In 2009–12, federal officials conducted a pilot program in nineteen regions of the country. In February 2012, Prime Minister Putin announced that the program would be introduced nationally in the fall. Nevertheless, Church leaders could claim no great victory. The government insisted that parents be able to choose for their children from six course options: the foundations of Orthodox, Jewish, Islamic, or Buddhist culture; the foundations of world religious cultures; or secular ethics. The course would be limited to one hour a week over thirty weeks in the fourth and fifth grades, and the state, not the Church, would determine the qualifications for teachers of the new subjects.

The state's decision was met with controversy. Most schools did not have the personnel to offer all six tracks. Instruction in Judaism, Islam, and Buddhism would occur only where the local population included large numbers of these adherents. Moreover, most schools, not having the financial resources to hire additional teachers, would have to recruit teachers from other subject areas to pick up instruction in religious education. Additional questions arose about the content of the instruction. How well would young children understand abstract religious concepts? Would thirty hours of instruction be so limited as only to confuse children about religion? Would teachers fairly represent religion? In some schools, the new teachers of religion were former Communists, once indoctrinated in atheistic Marxism-Leninism. And would teachers sympathetic to the Church be able to invite priests into their classrooms or organize field trip to religious sites? Some Orthodox priests and parents further feared that placing religious education in the public schools would make it just one more academic requirement and therefore turn children off from religion.

While few Church hierarchs saw the situation as ideal, Orthodox universities with state accreditation began training teachers for the new course, and the Patriarchate recruited Andrei Kuraev, a leading Church publicist and an ardent promoter of Church outreach to Russian society, to write the textbook. Because the patriarch believes that Russian culture implicitly preaches the gospel, he perhaps hoped that the foundations of Orthodox culture would not only be informational but also invite children to become aware of their innate Orthodox spiritual identity.

Kuraev's textbook reveals both the possibilities and the limitations of this approach. Kuraev goes far beyond describing Orthodoxy's historical influence. He skillfully presents Orthodoxy in a way that assumes no prior knowledge on the part of the children. At the outset, he defines religion in a distinctively Christian (and Orthodox) way: as a conviction that humans are not alone in the world—that next to and above them exists "a rational and spiritual world of God, angel, spirits."[57] This conviction, he notes, has historically shaped entire cultures, such as Russia's. Further, the textbook guides pupils specifically into the world of Russian Orthodoxy. Kuraev explicates major Church teachings about God (creation; Christ's incarnation, crucifixion, and resurrection; and the Last Judgment), morality (the Ten Commandments and the Beatitudes), religious practice (prayer, worship, and fasting), sacraments (penance, baptism, and Eucharist), great exemplars of Christian faith (monks and saints), and the emergence and role of Orthodoxy in Russian history.

Perhaps because he is speaking to children, Kuraev does not introduce the term *deification*, emphasizing instead the moral dimensions of Orthodoxy. He says that the Church teaches love, honesty, faithfulness, diligence, and patriotism. God rewards good and punishes evil (36–41, 68–69, 84–93). In contrast to Bishop Tikhon's *Everyday Saints*, Kuraev downplays Orthodoxy's interest in the miraculous. Rather than discussing miracle-working icons or relics, he speaks of the "miracle" that occurs when one person chooses to help another in a time of need (71). Similarly, Kuraev emphasizes the moral dimensions of Lent rather than the ascetic practices that Orthodox believers have traditionally exercised to discipline their physical desires. While mentioning that adherents of Orthodoxy refrain from certain foods, he sees Lent primarily as about devoting more time than usual to prayer and good works. Says Kuraev, "If a person decides to act according to Christ's commandments . . . then that person belongs to the Kingdom of Christ, and the Kingdom of Heaven is already here" (65).

Kuraev argues that this moral ideal is what Russians have always meant by Holy Rus'. From Prince Vladimir in the tenth century to the present day, Orthodoxy has inspired the Slavic peoples to seek holiness, and even though they have often fallen short, this striving for holiness has made them one

(60). Nevertheless, for Kuraev, as for Bishop Tikhon, an Orthodox way of life also draws one into a vision of a transfigured world of divine beauty, peace, and joy. Kuraev includes Alexander Solzhenitsyn's famous words: "The key to the sense of peace that the Russian landscape generates is in its churches. . . . Wherever you are in the fields or wandering in the meadows, far from any habitation, you are never alone . . . the cupola of a bell tower always beckons. And people have always been selfish and even bad. But the bells for evening prayer have rung . . . reminding them to set aside trivial earthly matters and offer the moment to eternity" (60–61).

Despite this acknowledgment of transcendent beauty as a key element of Orthodoxy, Kuraev's textbook ultimately does not escape the danger of reducing Christianity to a moral code that supports the social and political status quo. Rather than showing how God seeks the transformation of society, Kuraev portrays Christians as good citizens of this world. He argues for the possibility of Christian participation in "just war" while avoiding discussion of circumstances under which Christians should resist the state (88–91). He calls on Christians to be diligent and honest in their work but does not note social and political factors that contribute to poverty or social inequality (92–93).

The textbook's presentation of Orthodoxy is further constrained by the first and last chapters, which frame the textbook as a whole and also appear in the textbooks for the other five tracks of religious-ethical education. Written not by Kuraev but rather by pedagogue Aleksandr Daniliuk, they emphasize love of nation and respect for all of Russia's cultural and religious traditions. Religion is viewed as a political instrument for promoting social unity and harmony.

Perhaps it is inevitable that a textbook for public school use will honor religion for its contributions to securing established political arrangements rather than its impulses for social reform and therefore its potential to destabilize those arrangements. Despite these limitations, Kuraev's vision of a morally transformed Russia is more attractive than many of the regional curricula and their focus on historical facts and traditional teachings.[58] While less than a catechism, Kuraev's textbook offers more than cultural studies. It aims at inculcating an Orthodox vision of reality.

Some Church leaders undoubtedly hope that high-quality religious education in the public schools will draw children into parish life, where they can receive further religious education. Nevertheless, the new curriculum still lacks widespread support, especially in Russia's larger cities. In Moscow, less than a quarter of schoolchildren have enrolled in the foundations of Orthodox culture; in St. Petersburg, only 9.5 percent. The vast majority has chosen secular ethics instead.[59] Many Russians, even those who call themselves Orthodox, remain suspicious of any school program that suggests ideological indoctrination, such as occurred under Communism.

Prebaptismal catechization. Receiving Orthodox baptism helped Russians mark the new era that dawned with the fall of Communism. Most Russians, however, did not know what baptism meant in Orthodox teaching—that it represented the beginning of a process of self-transformation toward holiness and deification. They did not regard baptism as necessarily leading to regular attendance at the Divine Liturgy, reception of the Eucharist, submission to Church authority, or personal repentance and reformation.

In 2011, the Church's Holy Synod asked all parishes to institute a broad set of new educational initiatives, including premarital counseling, adult Sunday school education, educational work in conjunction with Church holy days and pilgrimages to holy sites, and prebaptismal catechization.[60] Priests were to conduct at least two preparatory conversations with people seeking baptism for themselves or their children, especially in cases where people were not active church members. The first conversation was to focus on the meaning of baptism, the second on basic Church doctrine (as set forth in the Nicene Creed) and moral practice (as set forth in the biblical commandments). Adults seeking baptism would attend a third meeting, at which they would be asked to confess their sins. All of the conversations were to make clear that baptism entailed a commitment to reforming one's life in accord with the Church's understanding of God's purposes for humanity and the world.

The question of prebaptismal catechization had been actively debated in Church circles.[61] Initially, discussion focused on catechization of adults seeking baptism. The Church's *Missionary Concept* proposed recovering the ancient practice of a "catechumenate." Adults would enroll in a program that would prepare them for baptism over several months or even years.[62] Some parishes, such as Prince Vladimir's Cathedral in St. Petersburg, developed innovative catechetical programs both for people preparing for baptism and for people wanting to understand the baptism that they had already received.

Some priests, however, opposed making catechization a formal requirement for baptism. At issue was how exactly to understand the Church's conviction that Russians, by virtue of being Russian, were already implicitly Orthodox or connected to the Church. In 2010, Bishop Antonii (Cheremisov) of Krasnoiar and Enisei delivered an address in which he strongly affirmed every Christian's lifelong need for catechization but opposed making baptism conditional on knowledge of Church doctrine or practice. Antonii argued that the Church has always had only one condition for baptism, namely, a person's desire to receive it. In the early church, said Antonii, people needed catechization prior to baptism because they had been pagans. Today the situation is different: "Those who come to us . . . are people with a genetic composition from the thousand years of Christianity in Russia. . . . They are not pagans but rather our brothers. They come to us from the very heart of our common Russian Orthodox life. How can we possibly refuse [to baptize them] . . . when they consciously accept everything that has determined the spiritual life of their pious forebears?"[63] Antonii argued that the Church should therefore rejoice, rather than put up obstacles, when people after decades of atheistic propaganda still had "a little flame of the faith of their ancient forebears."[64]

The debate within the Church became even sharper in relation to prebaptismal conversations with parents and godparents. Many priests feared that people would perceive the Church to be legalistic rather than welcoming. The Church could best encourage people to grow in their understanding of the faith after they had been received as infants into the Church.

According to traditional Orthodox teaching, baptism as a sacrament has an inherent power to draw people into the mystical presence of Christ, regardless of their level of knowledge. But as a theologian, I could understand the case for prebaptismal conversations. Since the ancient catechumenate could last as long as three years, a requirement of two to three short meetings prior to baptism hardly seems burdensome.[65] Prebaptismal counseling, it seems to me, encourages parents and godparents to be aware of their spiritual responsibilities to their children. And prebaptismal catechization of adults invites them to understand baptism as entry into the life of the Church rather than just a matter of personal salvation or social custom. The Church's move to mandate even minimal prebaptismal catechization suggests that at least some of its leaders would agree with me that a person who becomes more aware of his or her cultural Orthodox identity will not necessarily find the way to Orthodoxy to be a matter of deification. To our thinking, formal education about Church doctrine and practice should accompany baptism.

Parish-based religious education. While religious education in the public schools may help some people overcome their anxieties or indifference about stepping into a church, only a longer, more comprehensive program of religious education can help them become secure about basic Church teaching and practice. Similarly, prebaptismal catechization will be successful only if it helps people see the need for continuing religious education. In response, parishes are establishing Sunday school programs, especially for children and young people. Many parishes are also offering adult education, including Bible study, instruction in Church doctrine, and even the opportunity to learn Church Slavonic, the language of the liturgy.[66] In addition to parishes, monasteries have become important centers of lay religious education. Russian monasteries have always welcomed pilgrims for prayer and service, and some monasteries have a tradition of social ministries to the needy. New, however, is the intense commitment in some monasteries, especially in urban areas, to nurturing parish life, beginning with baptism, although the Russian Orthodox tradition has normally restricted baptism to parish churches.

Moscow's Sretenskii Monastery has one of the largest worshipping congregations in Moscow. Its priest-monks hear hundreds of confessions in the course of a week and take turns celebrating the liturgy and preaching. Bishop Tikhon is especially renowned for his sermons—many of the stories in *Everyday Saints* were originally sermon illustrations—and the Sretenskii choirs are among Russia's best. The monastery sponsors a Sunday school for children as well as the Friday evening Bible study class for adults that I attended.

The class illustrates key challenges to the Church's educational work. As in the West, parish-based religious education in Russia attracts only a small proportion of active believers. Seven hundred or more people were regularly attending the Divine Liturgy at Sretenskii, but the Bible study class was the only adult educational offering. And participants seemed to value the class as much for the caring fellowship that they had developed as for its rich educational content.

Father Julian was usually frustrated that his pupils had so few questions about his lectures. People would sit glumly and silently until someone risked a comment, knowing that Father Julian might well dismiss it as "stupid." But one evening the class came alive when Irina and her friends managed to change the conversation. Tat'iana boldly asked, "Father Julian, what do people most often ask you about being a monk?" Father Julian was normally not amused by such diversions, but this time he could not resist answering: "They wonder what a monk wears beneath his robe!" The class began to titter, and Irina jumped in, "Well, and what do you say?" Without skipping a beat, he replied, "That I wear a normal shirt and trousers, of course." And for the next half hour the class peppered him with questions about a monk's daily schedule and tasks. Afterward Irina whispered to me, "That was one of the best classes that we've ever had."

Orthodox university education. For the first time in Russian history, the Church has established Orthodox universities. Especially prominent is St. Tikhon's Orthodox Humanitarian University in Moscow, whose board of directors is chaired by the patriarch. The university receives no Church funding and only limited state financial support but has successfully attracted private sponsors—Arkadii Rotenberg, one of Russia's wealthiest businessmen and a close associate of President Putin, supported renovation of the historic Moscow Diocesan Building as the university's new administrative home. Named in honor of Patriarch Tikhon, the university seeks to follow the progressive legacy of the 1917–18 Local Council, which met in the Diocesan Building and restored the Patriarchate.

The founder of the university, Father Vladimir Vorob'ev, was trained as a physicist. In the Soviet period, he was deeply influenced by Father Vsevolod Shpiller in Moscow's parish of St. Nicholas in Kuznetsakh, on whose grounds the university was founded. A powerful, creative thinker who was not afraid to relate Christian faith to science and society, Shpiller attracted a remarkable group of Soviet intellectuals, several of whom became priests, including Vorob'ev, who after Shpiller's death eventually became head of the St. Nicholas parish.[67]

In the 1990s, Father Vladimir began organizing a wide range of educational activities in the parish, including a theological institute for laypeople. With the fall of Communism, the institute developed into a full-fledged university, with Father Vladimir as its rector. Today the university boasts three thousand students and ten faculties: theology, missions, history, philology, religious education, church arts, sacred music, sociology, information technology and applied mathematics, and continuing education. The university has state accreditation and is ranked as Russia's best nonstate institution of higher education.[68]

While St. Tikhon's does train men for the priesthood, its broader aim is to educate a new Orthodox intelligentsia to bring the Church's values into Russian society. Recent promotional materials describe the university as "an important missionary project aimed at overcoming the devastating effects of Soviet atheism. The university seeks to restore the Orthodox faith and its principles of morality, to shape a spiritually healthy culture for a new generation, and to promote understanding of national history and devotion to the Motherland."[69]

The university is an Orthodox oasis in the midst of a huge bustling city. Instructors are active believers, both male and female; many of the male teachers are also priests. All students, women as well as men, take classes in theology. Many students also participate in missionary trips that help the Church establish a presence in remote areas of the country that do not yet have a parish or a priest. On major holy days, students and faculty gather together in the Church of St. Nicholas, where Father Vladimir and other professors celebrate the liturgy.

Despite its compelling vision of educating students to help re-Christianize Russia, I learned that St. Tikhon's has had limited success in placing its graduates in jobs. Bishops often prefer to ordain graduates of traditional Church seminaries, which are usually located in monasteries and characterized by a monastic rather than university ethos. Graduates of other departments have even fewer prospects for Church-related work; those who complete degrees in sociology or philology often find that nonchurch institutions prefer to hire graduates of state institutions.

Another challenge to the university has been the changing character of the student body. Because of state accreditation rules, the university no longer requires applicants to submit a letter of recommendation from a priest. Even though most students continue to identify themselves as Orthodox, many have limited grounding in Church doctrine and practice. In 2012, the university appointed, for the first time, a priest to provide for the spiritual development of its students. If St. Tikhon's graduates were to "Christianize" others, they themselves would first have to be "Christianized."

The development of "comparative theology" and "sectology." Post-Communist Russian legislation on religion affirmed separation of church and state and protected freedom of conscience, but by the late 1990s disappointment with economic and social liberalization led many Russians to question further Westernization of their society. One indication of the new attitude was the 1997 Law on Freedom of Conscience and Religious Associations, which noted Orthodoxy's special place in Russian culture, privileged religious organizations that had been legally established in Russia for at least fifteen years, and restricted the activities of newer religious movements—not only Western Protestant evangelical groups but also Mormons, Scientologists, Jehovah's Witnesses, and Muslim missionaries from Turkey and the Middle East.[70]

The Russian Orthodox Church strongly supported the new legislation, arguing that many foreign religious groups were failing to respect Orthodoxy's deep roots in Russia, using coercive methods of proselytization, and taking unfair advantage of the ideological confusion that the collapse of Communism had triggered. At the same time, the Church intensified its efforts to educate Russians about the difference between Orthodoxy and other religious groups.

Seminary education of priests now includes required coursework in "comparative theology," which aims not only to describe but also to evaluate the history and basic religious principles of the Roman Catholic Church and major Protestant denominations. In my observation, however, comparisons are weighted toward establishing the superiority of Orthodoxy and the errors and shortcomings of other Christian groups. Father Maksim Kozlov, professor at the prominent Moscow Theological Seminary and Academy and author of a standard work on the different Christian churches, critiques Catholicism in terms of its deviations from Christianity's core teachings about salvation, Mary, the sacraments, and ecclesiastical organization.[71] Father Valentin Vasechko, head of the comparative theology program at St. Tikhon's University, describes Lutheranism as a renewal effort that went awry from the beginning, and Calvinism as taking the Reformation to logically consistent yet absurd ends.[72]

Oversimplification sometimes tends toward caricature. I learned that students of comparative theology in Russian Orthodox seminaries typically regard the Protestant Reformation as a justified reaction against distortions of doctrine and practice in the medieval Catholic Church. But they largely ignore Luther's principle of justification by grace through faith and instead accuse his followers of being obsessed with "works" and moral purity. When it comes to John Calvin, students focus almost exclusively on the doctrine of predestination, even though it has a secondary place in his writings and plays almost no role among contemporary Calvinist theologians in churches such as my own.

Besides comparative theology, the Church has promoted the academic study of "sectology" to track the activities of religious sects and cults, and to evaluate and publicize their religious errors. The Church's leading sectologist is Aleksandr Dvorkin, who was born in Russia but grew up in the United States and returned to Russia after the collapse of the Soviet Union. Dvorkin now heads the Russian Association of Centers for Study of Religions and Sects, regularly lectures at St. Tikhon's University and other Orthodox educational institutions, and advises Church and state officials about new religious groups in Russia. While less concerned about historic Catholic and Protestant churches than what he calls "totalitarian sects," such as the Unification Church and Hare Krishna, Dvorkin strongly defends Russia's historic Orthodox identity. In a 2013 memoir that received considerable attention, he described his confused spiritual searchings during his time in America and his journey back to Orthodoxy and, ultimately, Russia.[73]

Another important figure is Vladimir Martinovich, who heads up the sectology work of the Belorussian Orthodox Church (Moscow Patriarchate). Martinovich maintains an extensive database of new religious movements in Belarus, lectures widely, and works closely with the state office for religion and nationalities. While noting that sects are a normal phenomenon in every society and typically conduct themselves quietly and peacefully outside of public view, Martinovich argues that some pose a danger to society.[74] As I sat in his office in Minsk, he turned to his computer and pulled up photographs of every Seventh-day Adventist leader in Belarus, showed me his biography and address, and recounted the number of members in each group.

While destructive sects and cults have at times drawn attention to themselves in Western societies—Martinovich has worked closely with sectologists in Germany—the development of sectology in the Russian Orthodox Church reflects a concern that Russians not lose their historic identity in Orthodoxy. In his book *Nontraditional Religiosity in Belarus*, Martinovich appends relevant sections of the Church's *Social Concept*: "The Church constantly reminds society of what Christianity has deposited into the treasury of world and national culture. . . . We must not ignore the danger that secular schools will be penetrated by occult and neo-pagan influences and destructive sects, under whose activity a child may lose himself, his family, and society."[75]

I wonder, however. The Orthodox Church's very efforts to re-Christianize society may provoke the emergence of "sects." In resistance to the Church's efforts to reshape society, dissident religious groups emerge. Their teachings about personal commitment and religious community as an alternative to dominant social norms suggest deficits in the Church's working assumption that Russians are somehow Orthodox by nature. The absence of a self-critical moment in the Church's work in comparative theology and sectology again raises the question of whether the Church's educational efforts tend toward "right answers" and indoctrination rather than entry into a religious vision of divinity in and around the everyday.

These representative initiatives—religious education in the public schools, prebaptismal catechization, parish-based religious education, Orthodox university education, and the development of academic disciplines of comparative theology and sectology—reveal the breadth of the Church's efforts to re-Christianize Russian society. We could also name other important projects. Every November the Church sponsors a major historical exhibit in Moscow's Manezh, near Red Square. In recent years, the focus has been on cooperation between Church and state in different historical periods, including the years of Communism. Also noteworthy are the annual "Christmas Educational Lectures," which have taken place in Moscow since 1993 and are sponsored by the Patriarchate's Department for Religious Education and Catechization. For five days in late January, thousands of people attend plenary addresses by major Church, social, and political figures, as well as hundreds of presentations in fifteen sections covering all aspects of the Church's work.[76] In all of these ways, the Church endeavors to ensure that no Russian will grow up without basic familiarity with the nation's Orthodox heritage, the Church's teachings and practices, and the differences between Orthodoxy and other Christian and religious communities.

Nevertheless, the success of education in any field ultimately depends on persuasive, thoughtful teachers, and the case is no different here. In recent years, the Church has greatly improved theological education of its most important teachers: ordinary parish priests. As the Church quickly reestablished itself in the 1990s, bishops often ordained priests without first educating them. Today the Holy Synod requires a seminary education for new priests and continuing education for priests who were ordained without a seminary degree. The Church has also established doctoral programs to train a new generation of theologians and religious scholars. These programs include sustained dialogue with new theological and philosophical movements in the West. The Holy Synod has recently established "faith and science" as a major theological priority.[77]

The legacy of the holy elders and great charismatic teachers of the nineteenth and twentieth centuries continues to shape religious education as well. Father Vladimir Volgin, head of Moscow's Church of St. Sophia, the Wisdom of God, knew some of these figures at the end of the Soviet period. As a young priest, he briefly served with Aleksandr Men', and for many years Ioann (Krest'iankin) was Father Volgin's spiritual father. Father Volgin believes that the days of the holy elders are now over, but he wants the Church to explicate the wisdom that they left behind.[78]

Although a handful of monasteries are known today for having a holy elder, none of them enjoys the stature of Ioann (Krest'iankin) or Nikolai (Gur'ianov). A new kind of spiritual leader has emerged instead: the educated, eloquent priest who wins a reputation for his ability to explicate the faith persuasively. These priests often head large urban parishes, appear regularly in both Church and secular mass-media outlets, and have extensive social and political connections. Their model is not so much the holy elder but rather St. John of Kronstadt (d. 1908), who was renowned for his spiritual wisdom as a priest, preacher, teacher, and organizer of parish life.[79]

The phenomenon of the "wise, eloquent priest" is especially apparent today in Moscow, whose major churches are concentrated in the city center, while the city limits extend fifteen to twenty miles outward. The parish principle no longer functions. Many "parishioners" are not from the "parish" in which they live but rather travel into the city from far away. They select a congregation based on their attraction to a particular priest and his preaching and leadership. Among these outstanding personalities are several priests already mentioned—Vladimir Volgin, Bishop Tikhon (Shevkunov), Vladimir Vorob'ev, and Aleksei Uminskii (Church of the Holy Trinity in Khokhlakh)—as well as Dmitrii Smirnov (Church of St. Mitrofan of Voronezh on Khutorskii Street).

Each of these priests is highly intelligent and well educated (often, originally, in a secular discipline—Vorob'ev the physicist, or Shevkunov and Volgin, who were cinematographers). They are regarded as authoritative interpreters of Orthodoxy. All regularly offer public commentary on the Church's position in relation to current events or issues, although not always in concert: Smirnov is more associated with conservative political groups, whereas Uminskii has sympathized with those seeking democratic reform. All five men are gifted speakers and regularly appear on television; Vorob'ev is more soft spoken and better known from articles and interviews. All are passionate about the Church's ministry, and their personal exemplification of Orthodox moral and spiritual values may be as important to their followers as the content of their words.

Volgin is especially known for the emotional intensity that he brings to his preaching.[80] People crowd to the front of the church to hear him; some use cell phones to record his message. The sermon often lasts twenty minutes or longer, even though it comes at the end of the liturgy. Volgin speaks without notes and has a charisma that enables him quickly to establish a personal bond with his listeners. He does not hesitate to confront them directly with what he understands to be the demands of the gospel in a world of perpetual temptation and distraction, nor is he reluctant to use his sermons to call on the government to support the Church and Christian values.

Father Volgin also connects with many parishioners as a confessor and is reputed to be a spiritual father to more than two hundred people. The line of people who want him to hear their confessions on a Sunday morning is often so long that he offers a general absolution to those who are still waiting at the time of the Eucharist—in the Russian Church, confession before a priest in required prior to communing. Volgin regularly invites people to his home; meals with him are constantly interrupted by phone calls or visitors dropping by for counsel. Some of Moscow's leading businesspeople and political leaders look to him for spiritual guidance, but many "ordinary" believers also feel close to him.

As in the Soviet period, the spiritual children of a particular priest or spiritual father will sometimes gather to offer each other encouragement and assistance. During summer vacations, they may live close to each other in a village or a dacha settlement. On Church holidays, they may share meals in each other's homes. Rarely will they organize a formal study of Scripture or a classic spiritual text, but neither will they meet simply to shoot the breeze. In informal but significant ways, they share insights about the faith and support each other in knowing and practicing their faith.

Nevertheless, matters of religious belief and practice in Russia, as elsewhere in the Western world, have become highly individualized. A few people will gather in Sunday schools or small groups, but many more will learn about Orthodoxy in fragmentary, unsystematic ways: as they step into a church to light candles, make pilgrimage to icons or relics reputed to work miracles, observe folk traditions handed down in their families, or consult religious and secular Internet and media sources. Their formal education in belief and practice will be fragmentary.

The challenges to "Orthodox education" are also evident in the efforts of a new generation of priests to reach Russia's intelligentsia. Metropolitan Hilarion (Alfeev)—an accomplished composer, theologian, and public intellectual—has acknowledged the deep alienation that many Russian intellectuals feel from the Church. He believes that the Westernizing reforms of Peter the Great pitted the Church and the intelligentsia against each other; today the Church must try to overcome this rupture. Russian culture, such as during the "Silver Age" of Russian philosophy and art in the early twentieth century, achieved its greatest results when intellectuals worked creatively within the nation's Orthodox spiritual traditions.[81]

Metropolitan Hilarion recognizes that the Church needs its intellectuals if it is to articulate an intelligent Orthodoxy to a Russia that increasingly strives for, and is shaped by, Western standards of science, education, and lifestyle. Influential priests such as Volgin and Vorob'ev reach some of these Russians, but more politically liberal and democratically minded intellectuals often view them and other Church leaders as providing overly simplistic "right answers" to complex questions. Some critics, such as famed novelist Liudmila Ulitskaia, have accused the resurgent Orthodox Church of being more interested in indoctrination than education, more concerned to teach people to submit to Church and state authority than to wrestle with difficult questions of faith, morality, and politics. Her writings have been condemned by some Church figures.[82]

To be sure, the Church's educational work is still in its infancy. In contrast to Western Protestantism and Catholicism, the Russian Orthodox Church is still developing age-appropriate Sunday school materials and learning how to train Sunday school teachers and instructors of the foundations of Orthodox culture. So far, only 1 percent of self-identified Orthodox believers know Church Slavonic. Only 3–5 percent regularly read the Bible; indeed, fewer than one out of six believers owns a complete copy of the Bible. Only a third confidently believe in life after death. Only 9 percent report being familiar with the doctrine of the Trinity, a foundational teaching in

Christianity and of particular importance to Orthodox theology and worship. The gap between city and village raises further concerns: 15 percent of self-identified Orthodox believers in cities such as Moscow are able to identify Church teaching about the Trinity, while the percentage in the countryside is close to zero.[83] Seventy-three percent of Russians report never attending the Church's educational offerings, while a third of Russians — including 16 percent of Orthodox believers — state that they believe in astrology and magic.[84]

Under these circumstances, I can understand the temptation in some Church circles to settle for forms of religious education that simply instill pride in Russia's distinctive "Orthodox" national identity. But then, as I see it, Holy Rus' would no longer mean a vision of the transformation of this world into a fellowship of love and mutual care, but rather the blessing of the existing social-political order with its guarantees of institutional Church stability. If the Orthodox Church is to be true to the vision that I have been sketching out, it will ask itself: how can religious education draw people into the freedom of the gospel rather than simply encourage unthinking submission to Church authorities or reduction of religion to social custom or national identity? And how can the call for Russians to know Orthodoxy not obscure the essential contribution of minority religious communities — including Catholics, Lutherans, Baptists, Muslims, Jews, and Buddhists — to Russia's national heritage?

Even as I see deficits and problems in the Church's work, I remain deeply impressed. Russians are learning more about Orthodox belief and practice than ever before. As the Church establishes new parishes (approximately three hundred every year), new Sunday schools, youth groups, and adult educational activities also appear. To be sure, some Russians will learn only to submit to Church authority, but others will catch a glimpse of that holy world to which Church leaders as different as Bishop Tikhon (Shevkunov) and Deacon Andrei Kuraev point.

Even a rudimentary education in "right answers" is not all bad. As people learn about Orthodoxy's central place in Russian history and culture, they may also see the importance of right social relationships. A recent sociological study suggests that the Church's educational efforts have succeeded in making the current generation of university students more aware of basic Church teachings. When given a list of moral values, a large majority of students, even at state universities, correctly identified Orthodox versus secular ones.[85] Of course, factual knowledge, as we have noted, does not automatically translate into a commitment to self-transformation. Nevertheless, as a theologian, I believe that religious symbols, narratives, and rituals ultimately defy simple political instrumentalization. They open up a space for interpretation that allows people to imagine possibilities beyond the present.[86]

Two years after regularly attending the Sretenskii Bible study, I returned to Moscow. One afternoon, I traveled across town to browse in the monastery bookstore. As I prepared to leave, two women entered: of all people, Tat'iana and Liudmila. We paused and looked at each other curiously, and then began to smile. "Good day," I said, "I recognize you. I used to attend the Bible study class." "Oh, we remember you, too" they replied. "We have missed seeing you. Where have you been?" "Unfortunately, I don't live in Moscow anymore. I'm back for just a few days. Will you be meeting on Friday?" "No," they said, "we're on summer break now." "And Irina," I added, "does she still attend?" "Yes, of course. We'll be sure to tell her that we saw you. And we'll let Father Julian know, too. He'll be very pleased to hear that you asked about the class." Not quite sure how to say good-bye, I stumbled about and finally said, "It really is wonderful to see you." But Tat'iana and Liudmila had just the right words: "Please pray for us, and come join us again. You are part of our class." In that moment, I glimpsed what I call Holy Rus', that wondrous space in which people not only know something about the divine but also experience mysterious bonds of friendship that transcend time and space.

FOUR

Social Ministry

Let us again pause for a moment before Nesterov's striking mural of Holy Rus' in Moscow's Martha and Mary Monastery. Russia's poor and sick, maimed and elderly walk across a landscape of gently rolling hills. It is a cool summer day; the unspoiled beauty of the Russian countryside enfolds human suffering in its embrace. Orthodox Sisters of Mercy accompany and guide the pilgrims, keeping them from stumbling and falling. Jesus waits with his arms outstretched. His body is radiant with light. He promises that time will be transfigured by eternity, human longing transformed by divine presence.

The Orthodox Church brings its values into society not only as it educates Russians about their religious heritage but also as it reaches out to individuals who have material, physical, or emotional needs. Since the collapse of Communism, the Church has developed an impressive number and range of social ministries. Orthodox hospitals, hospices, orphanages, feeding and housing programs, and drug and alcohol rehabilitation centers—in these and many other initiatives, the Church has taken a leading role in caring for Russia's poor and needy.[1] The Church's work has been all the more important in view of the fact that government-sponsored social work has lagged even as Russia has experienced new and pressing social problems. In some areas of social service, such as drug rehabilitation work, the Church has pioneered models of effective treatment and stimulated government efforts to respond more adequately.

From many years of observation and conversation, I have come to the conclusion that the Church's social programs aim first of all at helping people in need, not making them churchgoers. The Church believes that its social work should be an expression of Christian love that expects nothing in return. At the same time, the Church hopes that these initiatives will open up space for people to enter into its life. As people experience the Church's love, they will perhaps be moved to know more about the Orthodox faith. Physical and emotional healing will be a prelude to spiritual healing, which from an Orthodox perspective can be found only within the Church's worship and sacraments. While faithfully attending to people's this-worldly needs, the Church prays that people will ultimately concern themselves with eternal questions—how to turn away from temptation and sin and find a trusting relationship with the divine source of life that Christians call God. Perhaps more than any of its other initiatives, the Church's social work has helped make the Church and its life more widely known and accessible to Russians.

Drug addiction began to emerge as a major problem in Russian society in the late 1980s as national borders became more porous and as social, economic, and political instability increased. By the mid-1990s, drug abuse had become epidemic. According to 2010 U.N. statistics, 1.64 percent of Russians between the ages of fifteen and sixty-four were addicted to narcotics, double the rate of the rest of eastern Europe. Of these 2.5 million addicts, 90 percent were using heroin, 90 percent were suffering from hepatitis, and 60 percent had HIV/AIDS. Drug addiction shaves as much as 2–3 percent off the nation's GNP.[2]

A small, rural Orthodox parish has pioneered Russia's new drug rehabilitation work. St. George's Parish is located three hundred miles to the northeast of Moscow, along the banks of Russia's mother river, the Volga. One January I rode a local train through the night from Moscow to the town of Kineshma, where one of the monks, Father Amvrosii (Mikhailov), met me and several other pilgrims. It was a cold winter day; the sky was steel gray, the ground piled high with snow. Father Amvrosii loaded us into a Gazelle (the Russian name for a small passenger van) and drove out of town to the banks of the Volga, where he announced, "We will walk from here."

It is possible to take a road from Kineshma over a bridge to St. George's, but the way is long and indirect and sometimes impassable in winter. As we stepped onto the frozen river, a small sign with carefully stenciled black letters warned, "Danger: Do Not Cross." Father Amvrosii nevertheless led the way. With each step we sank into a foot of snow. Beneath the snow we encountered a thin layer of water over the ice. That made us nervous. Was the river really frozen hard? It was. Two hours and one and a half miles later, we arrived safely on the other side, where a second monk, Father Pavel (Shvets), met us in an old work truck and drove us down a snow-packed dirt road to the parish.

St. George's consists of a small compound of wooden houses surrounded by a low stone wall. Just outside the wall stands the parish church with its bell tower and glistening silver steeple, and next to the church lies the parish cemetery. Nearby is the village of George, a collection of ramshackle, tilting wooden huts. On the other side of the parish, an even smaller cluster of houses, comprising the village of Zarinov, hugs the bank above the mighty river.

St. George's was one of the few churches in Russia that remained open throughout the Soviet era, although a priest was not always available to serve.[3] In the late 1980s, the local bishop appointed Father Mefodii (Kondrat'ev) to head the parish. Father Mefodii soon established a small community of monks who maintained a monastic discipline while renewing parish life. The challenges were formidable. The agricultural economy of the area had collapsed after the fall of Communism. Young people were moving to the cities; only the poor and elderly remained.

In 1991, several people from St. Petersburg who were involved in drug rehabilitation work bought abandoned houses nearby and renovated them as dachas. Father Mefodii soon drew them into the parish's life, and they told him about their work with drug addicts. In 1993, another event further impelled the monks to think about drug rehabilitation. A young addict came to the parish desperately seeking help with recovery, and the monks allowed him to live with them for several months. As they got to know him, they were horrified to learn about the terrible crimes to which addiction had once driven him. But they also saw a person who otherwise was not much different from other young unchurched Russians. And the encounter with Church life seemed to be healing to him.[4]

Group therapy session, St. George's Parish, Ivanovo Region (with permission of St. George's Parish)

The monks eventually came to believe that God was asking them to establish a special ministry to drug addicts. In coordination with Father Mefodii's spiritual children from St. Petersburg, the brothers began accepting up to eight young men at one time to live in the parish for a year or more. All of the addicts have completed a first stage of rehabilitation; many see St. George's as a last opportunity to change their lives. The recovery program includes physical exercise and religious observance as well as both individual treatment and group therapy based on widely known secular models, such as the twelve-step program. The young men also receive "film therapy," which consists of watching and discussing popular movies in which they become more aware of the emotional dynamics that motivate good or destructive behavior—and thereby get in touch with their own emotional life, which, according to Father Mefodii, has often been stunted. "The young men will seem normal to you," he told me, "but in fact they are very ill."

The natural landscape around St. George's is remarkably beautiful and tranquil. City life with its endless overstimulation of people's senses and desires seems far away. In summer one can walk alone for hours through abandoned fields and forests. In winter the landscape becomes a vast frozen expanse, and the silence is deafening. This wondrous setting has given Father Mefodii time and space to reflect deeply on questions of religion and culture. He believes that drug addiction is more than a matter of personal weakness; it has profound social dimensions. Post-Communist Russian society lost its moral and spiritual foundations in Orthodox Christianity. Secular Western values, especially evident in contemporary youth culture, are shaping people's lives instead. The consequences have been disastrous.[5] People have become egotistical and deeply alienated from one another. They no longer ask fundamental questions about the meaning of life but rather succumb to consumerism, materialism, and a cult of pleasure.[6]

According to Father Mefodii, these new social forces have seriously undermined family life. Many addicts come from broken homes in which parents have placed pursuit of personal interest and pleasure above care for their children. The pain of emotional neglect and sometimes physical abuse leads these children to drugs, which seem to promise ecstasy, creativity, and an escape from personal problems. Narcotics use, however, inevitably harms a person's health, ensnares him in criminal activity, and impedes his ability to establish healthy relationships with others.

Father Mefodii also draws on Orthodox notions of sin and salvation to understand drug addiction. While agreeing that addiction has characteristics of a physical or emotional illness, Father Mefodii insists that it implicates, above all, the individual's sinful will. Social and familial factors may contribute to drug abuse, but the individual remains responsible for his behavior. He has chosen to use drugs, and "with God's help he can choose at any stage of his addiction to quit. And if he refuses, he is just further implicating himself in sin."[7] In contrast to those Protestant traditions that emphasize "by [God's] grace alone," Father Mefodii follows Orthodox teaching that humans must work at overcoming sin. But if salvation is not in the hands of God alone, neither is it a divine reward for extraordinary human efforts, a position that Orthodoxy typically ascribes to Roman Catholicism. Rather, humans must cooperate with God to achieve salvation. The key factor in drug rehabilitation is a person's desire to change—and therefore only individuals with strong motivation are admitted into St. George's program.

Because addiction is at its heart a spiritual problem, humans need spiritual resources to combat it. While Father Mefodii recognizes a social dimension to addiction, he does not focus on measures that the state should take to restore Russia's moral and spiritual foundations but rather emphasizes the Church's care for individuals. The process of personal spiritual reformation has two major dimensions.[8] First, St. George's introduces the young men to the great achievements of human culture, especially Russian culture. Because, in the Church's view, Russian culture necessarily transmits Orthodox values, a person who becomes "cultured" is also reshaped spiritually. Cultured people have an appreciation of beauty and transcendent values. Culture, therefore, opens them to the divine.

Acquiring "culture" has several aspects. At St. George's, it begins with practicing simple, everyday good manners. The young men are expected to speak "normal Russian" and to forswear the slang and profanity that typically characterize their speech. They are also expected to practice basic etiquette, such as waiting to eat until the priest has blessed the meal. Appreciating great music is another component of being cultured. Father Mefodii argues that "it is necessary strictly to prohibit listening to hard rock, rap, psychedelic music, and other styles . . . that exercise a destructive influence on the psyche." Those in recovery should listen rather to Church music and classical music, or should even learn to enjoy silence—although Father Mefodii acknowledges that changing a person's musical tastes is not easy and that compromise with people in recovery will often be necessary. Father Mefodii further recommends introducing recovering addicts to Orthodoxy's great spiritual writings and to classic works of world and Russian literature. Exposure to the natural world is equally important. Father Mefodii notes that "some [of the young men] notice sunrises and sunsets for the first time since childhood." Recovery from addiction depends on renewing a person's ability to find joy in everyday existence.

The second dimension of personal spiritual reformation revolves around the experience of genuine loving community. People in recovery need to live and work with emotionally and spiritually healthy people. In studying secular rehabilitation programs Father Mefodii has become especially interested in the notion of a "therapeutic community" in which counselors and patients relate to each other with love and respect. He believes that this kind of approach is deeply Christian in its affirmation of the value of every human person. Father Mefodii, however, asks the Church to go even further in its understanding and formation of community. In his experience, individuals have the best shot of overcoming addiction if they become fully integrated into the life of the Church. Father Mefodii argues that parishes and monasteries, rather than freestanding rehabilitation centers, are therefore the best places for drug rehabilitation. What recovering addicts need, above all, is incorporation into the life of the Church.

In-churching has several facets. As the young men participate in community worship and receive the sacraments, they experience a transcendent dimension of existence that they perhaps never knew before. Further, the monks encourage the young men to work with a skilled spiritual father who can help them recognize, confess, and battle their destructive impulses. For many of the young men, the time at St. George's will offer them the first opportunity in their lives to establish a trusting relationship with a person who is morally grounded and spiritually wise.

For Father Mefodii, the Church's ascetical traditions play an especially important role in spiritual reformation of the self. They help people overcome the tyranny of selfish desires so that they are able to give themselves in service to others. The program at St. George's asks the young men to discipline themselves in prayer, fasting (including a six-week Advent fast and an eight-week Lenten fast, both of which ask Orthodox believers to remove all animal products from their diet), and "obediences"—menial and sometimes unpleasant tasks that the monks ask the young men to do for the sake of the community's well-being, such as cleaning out the chicken coops, tending the vegetable gardens, catching fish, chopping wood, helping with meal preparation and cleanup, or undertaking maintenance and construction projects.

In recent years, Father Mefodii has also given more attention to the role of religious education in assisting spiritual reformation. In the hope that the young men will participate with greater understanding in the parish's worship and service, the monks provide basic instruction in Scripture, liturgics, and "the law of God." Those members of the community who learn Church Slavonic join the monks in chanting prayers and hymns in the times of worship.

Separation from the world in order to be able eventually to live in but not of the world—such is the goal of the program at St. George's. For the few months they live at St. George's, the young men immerse themselves in a world that offers an alternative to the chaos that afflicted them as addicts. Everyday life at St. George's is marked by beauty, harmony, and peace, although here, too, conflicts can arise and on occasion a young man must be asked to leave. Most of the young men, however, catch at least a glimpse of what all faithful Orthodox believers strive to see: heaven on earth.

The challenge then becomes how to keep the young men morally upright and spiritually focused when they leave St. George's. St. George's works closely with its partners in St. Petersburg to integrate the young men into parish life when they return. Participation in the liturgy, sacraments, and life in Christian community should sustain them as much back home as it did at St. George's. Some of the young men, however, fear falling back into their old habits. I remember a young man with tattooed arms who baked the community's daily bread. His time at St. George's would soon end, but he told me that he longed to remain in its enchanted world.

St. George's claims a success rate of approximately 60 percent; the general remission rate for drug addiction programs in Russia is only 3–5 percent.[9] Because of the expertise he has developed, Father Mefodii now heads up a new patriarchal department for drug rehabilitation work and in 2014 was appointed bishop of Kamen' and Alapaev. He travels throughout the country to introduce his model of rehabilitation to parishes and monasteries that are considering such work.

Weekday mornings at St. George's begin with the hours of prayer. The young men, the monks, and any pilgrims gather at 6 a.m. in a church that for much of the year is still dark and illuminated only by a few candles. I have stood with them in a circle as each person went forward to venerate the icon of the Mother of God and then embraced the other members of the community one by one. It seemed to me for a passing moment that the promise of healing, forgiveness, and reconciliation—and the hope that mortal life will be transfigured by eternity—took away any difference between therapist and patient, healthy personality and addicted psyche, or monk and layperson. In the words of the Apostle Paul, "All are one in Christ Jesus" (Gal. 3:28).

As important as in-churching is to the program at St. George's, Father Mefodii is careful to acknowledge that rehabilitation, in the narrower sense of quitting drugs, can happen without incorporation into Church life. Not all recovery programs have to be based in a parish or monastery, and the Church can support rehabilitation centers that use secular methods alone. As Father Mefodii notes, the young men who come to St. George's are motivated, first of all, not by what the Church considers central—to know God and the meaning of life before God—but rather a personal desire to resolve a practical problem that has made their everyday lives unbearable.[10] A person does not have to become a Christian in order to quit drugs, and the drug rehabilitation program at St. George's seeks first and foremost to make the young men productive members of society.

There is a second reason to distinguish in-churching from addiction recovery. According to Orthodoxy teaching, a person can pursue salvation only freely and not under compulsion. As in matters of religious education in the public schools, Church social ministry will have integrity only as it respects a line between making people aware of Orthodoxy, on the one hand, and integrating them into Church life, on the other. Father Mefodii argues that those who enter a Church rehabilitation program must be willing to receive instruction in the Orthodox faith and attend Orthodox worship services. But they remain free to decide for themselves whether or not to pray, receive the sacraments, or make confession of sin before a priest.[11] Most, but not all, of the young men at St. George's do participate.

It is not easy, however, to know just where to draw the line between familiarizing people with the Church and integrating them into Church life. The program at St. George's operates with the same assumptions as Andrei Kuraev's textbook *The Foundations of Orthodox Culture*, namely, that people can be drawn into a new way of life just by becoming aware of the great achievements of Russian culture as shaped by Orthodoxy. Father Mefodii observes that "not all of those going through rehabilitation in a Church setting will become active Church participants, but the majority of them will change their moral orientation."[12] And if the young men do enter more fully into the Church's life, they will be more likely, the monks believe, to overcome the inner emptiness that drove them to drugs in the first place. Dealing with drug addiction can become the occasion for discovering, as Orthodoxy calls it, "life in God." The monks cannot choose salvation for the young men, but the monks will never stop reminding them not only that they can be healed physically but also that they can be transfigured spiritually.

The question of what it means to become "Orthodox" is complicated, and "entering into the Church's life" has various gradations. To belong to the Church in the fullest sense is to participate regularly in its liturgical and sacramental life and to live according to its moral dictates — and not out of sheer habit or social pressure but rather with the desire for salvation. But to the way of thinking that I have been sketching out, even those persons, such as the young men at St. George's, who are still developing a sensitivity to transcendent beauty and just beginning to become "cultured" are somehow already within the Orthodox world, whether they know it or not. As they become aware of what is great in their Russian heritage, they implicitly "hear" Orthodoxy's call to self-transformation, and to the extent that they embrace their nation's "traditional values," they are given an impulse to reorient their lives toward God. At St. George's, as elsewhere, the Church hopes that its social outreach will touch people with a divine love that will draw them into a vision of heaven on earth. Deification is a long and gradual process, but it sometimes begins when a person in need experiences, for the first time in his or her life, the love, awe, and wonder that the Church cultivates.

St. George's sees itself as a model for other parishes, especially in rural areas. The fact that it is staffed by four monks, however, is significant.

Monasteries are playing a leading role in renewing the Church's social ministries today, in part because monasteries often command resources that parishes do not have. Monasteries can assign social work to their members, while parishes depend on volunteers. And monasteries often have more space and funding for social ministries.

In the Orthodox tradition, the monastic emphasis on personal salvation has never justified neglecting people in need, whether in or beyond the monastic community. Monasteries have long been concerned to care for people who have come to their doors, whether as pilgrims or people in search of material assistance. And while the monastic life has always required separation from the world for the sake of prayer and ascetic discipline, some monasteries have long traditions of social ministry.[13] A key figure in Russian Orthodox history is St. Joseph of Volokolamsk, who in the early sixteenth century argued that monasteries needed to accumulate wealth in order to provide social services. His own monastery developed a home for the elderly, a hospital, and programs for children.[14]

Nevertheless, the degree to which almost all monasteries today are involved in social outreach is striking. Service to the needy is a spiritual discipline that is as important as prayer or fasting. And as in the past, women's monasteries, such as the Martha and Mary Monastery, are in the movement's forefront.[15] Prior to the October Revolution, Elizabeth and her Sisters of Mercy regularly visited Moscow's poorest neighborhoods; offered medical care, financial assistance, and spiritual counsel; established a home with rooms for young village women who had moved to the city to work in factories; and founded another home, for women with tuberculosis.[16] When I visited almost a century later, the reestablished community consisted of fifteen sisters, sixty professional employees (all of whom were active Orthodox believers), and a large sisterhood of lay volunteers. In contrast to the practice in Elizabeth's community, five of the fifteen sisters, including the abbess, Mother Elisaveta (Pozdniakova), had been tonsured. These "black sisters" observed a stricter monastic regime than the others, thereby helping to keep prayer and worship at the center of the community's life. The "white sisters" had special medical training and took the lead in the monastery's social work.[17]

Today the community sponsors concerts and lectures, maintains Elizabeth's living quarters as a museum, operates a dormitory and school for young orphaned girls, runs a summer camp for invalid children, and offers cutting-edge social service programs, such as classes for parents with autistic children or for people caring for aging and ailing relatives. The monastery also sponsors a parish that has a regular cycle of worship services open to the public and a small Sunday school.[18]

Mother Elisaveta's youthful energy is infectious. For her and the sisters, the basic spiritual disciplines of monastic life help them meet the demands of social service. The day begins at 5:30 a.m. with prayer and the Divine Liturgy. On Mondays the sisters set aside time for spiritual conversation. In the weeks prior to the Great Lent, they discuss controlling the passions; during Lent, the meaning of the liturgy. On Thursdays a professor, often from St. Tikhon's University, presents a lecture on a theological topic. Each of the sisters has a spiritual father before whom she regularly makes confession of sin, and Bishop Panteleimon, head of the patriarchal department for social ministry, provides spiritual oversight of the community as a whole.[19]

As at St. George's, the social ministries at the Martha and Mary Monastery draw people out of an everyday world of suffering and pain into an extraordinary world of divine beauty and harmony. Here the Church's commitment to helping people in physical and emotional need extends to recognizing their need for spiritual rest and healing. Not all who come to the Martha and Mary Monastery will depart with a new sense of the meaning of life. Not all will choose to participate more actively in Church life. But few will fail to sense the extraordinary love and care that the monastery offers to people in need and how the sisters seek to renew Russian culture and tradition.

I have gotten to know another St. Elizabeth's Monastery, this one in Minsk, Belarus. While not formally affiliated with the Martha and Mary Monastery in Moscow, St. Elizabeth's in Minsk has the same commitments to prayer and social service. It reaches out to people in desperate need and invites them into new life in the Church. The story of its founding is no less extraordinary than that of the Martha and Mary community.[20]

In 1996, the metropolitan of the Moscow Patriarchate churches in Belarus, Filaret (Vakhromeev), gave his blessing for the organization of a sisterhood in Minsk dedicated to the memory of St. Elizabeth. At that time, the sisters' principal service was to men in a psychiatric hospital, one of Europe's largest, on the edge of town. The sisters dreamed of establishing a monastery nearby to anchor their ministry spiritually, and as men were released from the hospital, they offered, as a gesture of thanks, to help the women construct a church.

The sisters and their spiritual father, Andrei Lemeshonok, are quick to mention Nikolai Gur'ianov, the famous holy elder and Father Andrei's own spiritual father. In late 1997, when public opposition and lack of funding threatened completion of the church, Father Andrei traveled to Nikolai on his remote island. As they spoke, Nikolai pulled out a 5-ruble note, handed it to Father Andrei, and assured him that donors would soon step forward. Moreover, declared Nikolai, the sisters would become "white nuns." In 1999, his predictions came true. Metropolitan Filaret approved establishment of a women's monastery dedicated to St. Elizabeth, and soon afterward the lower part of the church, in honor of St. Nicholas, was completed.

As other men were released from the hospital or simply came looking for work, the sisters trained them in various church arts and crafts. Workshops for iconography, church furniture and implements, ironwork, and liturgical garments soon opened. To provide additional work, the monastery established a skete about 20 miles away on 300 acres of land near the village of Lysaia Gora. Here, men in especially desperate straits—homeless, unemployed— could help raise animals, till crops, and construct buildings.

Today the monastery has ninety sisters (both "black" and "white") assisted by a small brotherhood, two hundred members of a lay sisterhood, and several hundred craftsmen and farm workers.[21] The monastery complex includes two major churches and three smaller ones. A four-story building houses forty workshops. A bakery and a cheese factory are in operation. New construction includes a hostel for pilgrims and a cultural-educational center with a meeting room for five thousand people. The monastery has become a large economic enterprise; its sisters regularly travel to Orthodox exhibitions hundreds of miles away—Moscow, Kiev, even New York City and Pittsburgh—to sell their products.

As at the Martha and Mary Monastery, the sisters believe that spiritual disciplines ground social ministry. Prayer, worship, and spiritual reflection lie at the heart of their communal life. Even the iconostasis in the monastery Church of St. Elizabeth communicates the close relationship between prayer and service. The first row includes the icons of Elizabeth and Barbara. In the third row are icons of Patriarch Tikhon (who, as we have seen, faithfully led the Church through the first years of Bolshevik persecution), John of Kronstadt (who as a parish priest developed an impressive array of social ministries in the late nineteenth and early twentieth centuries), Aleksei Mechev (the parish priest in Moscow who promoted an active laity), and Veniamin of Petrograd (who in the early 1920s headed Church efforts to gather money for Russians suffering from famine even as he resisted Bolshevik confiscation of Church treasures, for which he was martyred in 1922).

Father Andrei has given especially eloquent expression to the relationship of prayer and service. Nikolai Gur'ianov taught him that a monastery should provide everything: "work, prayer, and relaxation—and bread and sugar." St. Elizabeth's turns no one away. It even has an arrangement with the police to deliver newly released prisoners to its farm, where they can live and work until they transition back into society. Some of these men have a history of drug abuse, crime, and even murder. Often they have no legal documents or money. Many see the monastery as their last chance to make good.

The experience of Christian community is as important here as at St. George's. The men at the monastery farm are in constant contact with each other, Father Andrei, and the sisters. According to Father Andrei, "We have constructed everything for dialogue . . . so that people will talk, not isolate themselves, but rather speak out and build trust. If this will happen, there will be a kind of unity . . . like a family. . . . Conversation is an essential element of our life here, as well as confession and, thus, revealing one's thoughts. When we speak aloud the things that are bothering us, it helps everyone. . . . So, as far as I am concerned, there is only confession and conversation. And the liturgy."[22]

Father Andrei wants each man to have the opportunity to come to God. Each must see himself as he really is: a sinner who is nevertheless loved by God and others. Father Andrei tries to keep even the troublemakers in this circle of love. Some, of course, will choose to leave rather than to live in a community shaped by the seasons of the Church year, daily prayer and worship, and Orthodox moral and spiritual values. But others will discover the ability to love, even as they have been loved. Father Andrei speaks proudly of the six rehabilitated men who recently became monks.

The social ministries at St. George's, the Martha and Mary Monastery, and St. Elizabeth's in Minsk all draw a close connection between healing human brokenness and educating people in religious faith. The Church believes that as people come to know and practice the Orthodox faith, they will experience spiritual well-being and deal more effectively with physical and emotional problems. Where their own sinfulness has contributed to their problems, they learn to purify themselves. Where they suffer at the hands of forces of evil that they cannot control, they find new strength to endure patiently.

The relationship between healing and education is especially evident in the social ministries of the Iosif-Volokolamsk Monastery, an hour outside Moscow. The monastery's great sixteenth-century leader, St. Joseph, not only founded a school for children but also fed children who were suffering hunger at a time of famine.[23] The monastery's special connection to children in need continued during the Soviet era. Although the Communists closed the monastery in 1922, they housed a public school and later an orphanage in the monks' living quarters. Today the monastery again sponsors social and educational work with children and teenagers, including an innovative Scouting program.

Of special interest is the work of Father Moisei (Semiannikov), the monastery's business manager. Father Moisei is an energetic young monk with a thick black beard and twinkling brown eyes. He regularly visits two nearby villages that have government-sponsored social rehabilitation centers for delinquent children and teaches a class, the foundations of secular ethics, in an elementary school in a third village. In each place, he combines deep compassion for children with basic instruction in Orthodox values.

Father Moisei has learned that establishing a trusting relationship with the children is the most important factor in promoting their spiritual reformation. Only when solid human relationships are in place can the children begin to imagine a trusting relationship with a divine power. When Father Moisei visits the social rehabilitation centers, he does not discuss faith in a theoretical way but rather introduces the children to basic spiritual practices that, he believes, will strengthen them. Today when he stands before an icon and asks the children who among them wants to pray with him, he hears, "I do, I do, I do . . ."

Father Moisei tells of one boy who decided to leave home because his parents were deeply troubled and even abusive. Because the boy knew and trusted Father Moisei, he chose not to look for a secular job or turn to petty crime but rather to live and work at the monastery. Today the boy continues to attend school while participating in the monastery's life of prayer.

Father Moisei has also won over most of the pupils in his class on secular ethics. While the director of the school has forbidden him to talk directly about God or faith, the children respond positively to Father Moisei's confidence that they can resist using alcohol and drugs or deceiving and lying to others. Many class sessions end with lively debates about moral integrity.[24] Even the few children who are openly hostile to his ideas are touched by his patience and joy.

In my observation, religious education and social ministry support each other. Religious education never remains abstract knowledge; rather, it aims at spiritual reformation. And social ministry does not limit itself to helping people with their immediate worldly needs; rather, it invites people to learn and practice a living faith in God. Religious education and social ministry work together to strengthen both historic Russian culture and Orthodox faith. The Church, it seems to me, wants people who will benefit society even while they attend to their eternal destiny. Religious education and social ministry are further interconnected by virtue of the fact that both sets of initiatives depend on teachers and caregivers who establish a deep level of trust with those whom they serve. Whether we speak of St. George's, the Martha and Mary Monastery, St. Elizabeth's in Minsk, or Father Moisei in Volokolamsk— the Church strives to shape communities of mutual care and accountability.

However, one dimension of the Church's initiatives in religious education and social ministry is noticeably missing, at least from a Western perspective. The Russian Orthodox Church still gives little attention to unjust social structures that contribute to poverty, broken families, social delinquency, drug and alcohol abuse, and other social crises. The Church's criticism of Western ideologies of success and consumption has not yet yielded to closer analysis of state and social policies and arrangements in Russia that undermine the moral and spiritual foundations of Russian society.[25]

The religious vision of culture that shapes the Church's social work today is deeply rooted in the Church's past. Like Christians of other traditions, Orthodox believers have long believed that they must fulfill Christ's command to care for the poor and the stranger, the hungry and the suffering. In the nineteenth century, problems related to growing industrialization and urbanization demanded a more systematically organized response. John of Kronstadt founded a settlement house in St. Petersburg in which migrants from the countryside to the city could learn practical work skills.[26] Wealthy businessmen—among whom Old Believers played an important role—endowed hospitals, orphanages, and other charitable institutions. Lay sisterhoods helped care for soldiers wounded in war.[27]

The Church's Holy Synod called for establishment of new monasteries that would coordinate "monastic life with charitable or educational work." By the late nineteenth century, at least forty-seven such monasteries had appeared. Social ministry also became a priority for parishes, which by 1889 were operating 660 homes for the elderly and 480 hospitals. Some parishes became especially well known for their work with alcoholics or prisoners. And not only did the Church operate its own institutions, it also supported various municipal and private initiatives. But after 1917, the Bolsheviks closed or nationalized the Church's organized charitable work. Lay brotherhoods or sisterhoods involved in social ministries were abolished. The state alone was to provide social services. While Orthodox believers never ceased to help each other in their times of need, officially organized Church social work could not resume until the end of the Soviet era.[28]

Lay sisterhoods, such as at Moscow's Martha and Mary Monastery or Minsk's St. Elizabeth's, have played a prominent role in renewing the Church's social ministries. Among the first and most important of these groups in Russia is the Sisterhood of St. Dmitrii in Moscow. Dynamics that we have observed at St. Elizabeth's are also evident here: the leadership of a strong spiritual father, the blessing of a holy elder, a reestablished connection to prerevolutionary traditions of Church social work, efforts to ground service in prayer, and a desire to combine social outreach to the needy with an invitation to them to enter into the Church's liturgical and sacramental life.

The Sisterhood of St. Dmitrii is associated with what has traditionally been one of Moscow's largest hospital complexes, now known as the First City Hospital.[29] At the beginning of the nineteenth century, Dmitrii Golitsyn, a wealthy Orthodox businessman, endowed the first part of this complex, including not only a hospital that would treat patients free of charge but also magnificent grounds with ponds, an orangery, and an art gallery. In the very center of the hospital building was a church into which patients could directly walk or be wheeled from their rooms. The church was dedicated to the donor's namesake, the Tsarevich Dmitrii, who had died under suspicious circumstances in 1591 in the midst of a political power struggle after the death of Dmitrii's father, Ivan the Terrible. Dmitrii was canonized in 1606 as a "passion bearer," one who faced suffering and death with Christian equanimity and faith.

The church was closed in 1922 and during the Soviet period served as a canteen and smoking area. In 1990, a reclusive holy elder, Pavel (Troitskii), who had become a spiritual father to several of Moscow's leading Orthodox priests, blessed efforts to recover the church from the state. In May of that year, for the first time since the Communists had closed the church, Father Arkadii (Shatov), one of Pavel's spiritual children, was allowed to offer ministerial services in the hospital. The number of patients wishing to receive Communion exceeded all expectations. At about the same time, volunteer Orthodox Sisters of Mercy were allowed to assist with basic tasks in the hospital, such as mopping floors, changing sheets, and washing patients.

In July 1990, Father Arkadii's wife died after a prolonged illness. She had predicted that the hospital church would be returned to the Church after her death. About the same time, the holy elder Pavel made a similar prediction: Father Arkadii would soon be appointed priest of the hospital church. A few months later, hospital administrators indeed transferred the hospital church into the hands of the Church. Patriarch Aleksii II reconsecrated it, and Father Arkadii became its priest.

Father Arkadii and some of his spiritual children from other churches soon organized a parish in the hospital church. Parishioners regularly joined the Sisters of Mercy in visiting patients after worship services. Among those in attendance was Agrippina Istniuk, who earlier in the century had been trained at Moscow's Martha and Mary Monastery and had personally known St. Elizabeth. Agrippina later served as an assistant to the holy elder Pavel and to Father Vladimir Vorob'ev, himself one of Pavel's spiritual children and head of the Church of St. Nicholas in Novokuznetsakh.

In 1991, the Sisterhood of St. Dmitrii was formally organized under the spiritual leadership of Father Vorob'ev. The work of the sisterhood has steadily expanded ever since. Besides its work in the hospital, the Sisterhood of St. Dmitrii gives special attention to homebound patients and assists in many of the parish's social projects, which now include several orphanages, a home for juvenile delinquents, an assisted living center for elderly people, an Orthodox elementary school, a Sunday school, and summer camps for children and young people. In 1992, the hospital agreed to give the Church space for a school, now licensed by the state, to train Sisters of Mercy. The school, the only one of its kind in Russia, offers high-quality medical education as well as classes in theology, liturgics, and Church Slavonic. Graduates serve not only at the First City Hospital but also in hospitals and charitable institutions in other parts of Russia.

Members of the sisterhood recall that in the early 1990s, hospital doctors and administrators were deeply ambivalent about the sisterhood.[30] On the one hand, the hospital staff welcomed the sisters' practical assistance at a time when the hospital was greatly underfunded and understaffed. On the other, few of the doctors and administrators were Orthodox believers, and they did not want the sisters speaking about religious faith with the patients.

Today the place of the sisterhood in the hospital is secure. While most of the hospital staff remains uninvolved in Church life, some doctors and administrators do identify themselves as Orthodox and regularly attend prayer services and liturgies in the hospital church. And the sisters have learned to discuss religious questions only at a patient's request. The position that the Church has taken in other areas of social work applies here: the Church should be free to touch people with its love in the hope that they will want to enter into Church life, but no one should feel coercion.

The Church's comprehensive presence in post-Communist Russian society is represented by the unhindered access that the Church has to patients in the First City Hospital. In early January, on the Orthodox holy day of Kreshchenie (Theophany, associated with the baptism of Christ and the revelation of the Trinity), Father Arkadii (now Bishop Panteleimon) or another priest processes through the hospital halls and rooms and sprinkles them and the patients with holy water. Similarly, the sisters are permitted to work in every ward. While all of them are ready to answer basic spiritual questions, several with advanced theological training have been designated to assist patients who express interest in being baptized, making confession, or receiving the Eucharist.

Leaders of the parish and the sisterhood emphasize that most patients value the Church's presence and therefore the Church's implicit invitation to enter into its life. Especially important has been the sisters' service in the hospital's center for cardiovascular surgery, which brings patients and their families to Moscow from all parts of Russia, including many areas without an Orthodox church. Every week several baptisms take place, and twenty to sixty people receive Communion.[31]

Public response to the Church and its ministry has also been positive in the Hospital of St. Aleksii, just a few minutes away from the First City Hospital.[32] Like the First City Hospital, the Hospital of St. Aleksii was founded and endowed prior to the revolution by wealthy Orthodox businessmen. Like the First City Hospital, St. Aleksii's claims a connection to great Church figures of the past: St. Elizabeth (Romanova) and her husband, Sergei, were present for its opening in 1903. And both hospitals treat patients from all religious backgrounds free of charge.

St. Aleksii's is different, however, insofar as it is operated today by the Church, not the state. Not only patients but also hospital personnel attend services in the hospital church. Icon corners have been set up in each ward. During seasons of fasting, the hospital cafeteria prepares special food for those whom the doctors permit to observe the fast. A brochure about the hospital notes that "many people entering the hospital, even at age sixty to seventy, participate for the first time in their lives in the sacrament of confession, many others are baptized—approximately sixty adults every year."[33]

At both the First City Hospital and St. Aleksii's, the Church points with pride to its success in in-churching Russians. The loving service of the Sisterhood of St. Dmitrii has introduced many patients to Church life. Or, stated alternatively, many Russians who in times of personal crisis have been touched by the Church's ministry have reclaimed Orthodoxy as part of their personal identity. They have found spiritual and emotional strength in returning to what they understand to be their nation's ancient religious traditions.

It is important, however, not to exaggerate the Church's place in Russian society. While St. George's (four monks), the Martha and Mary Monastery (fifteen nuns), St. Elizabeth's in Minsk (ninety nuns and two hundred members of a sisterhood), and the Sisterhood of St. Dmitrii (seventy members, fifty of whom focus on help to homebound patients) are accomplishing impressive work, they hardly make a dent in Russia's vast social problems. Only thirteen sisterhoods exist in Moscow, a city of at least 12 million; approximately seventy sisterhoods exist in Russia as a whole.[34] Volunteerism is still a new concept in Russian society and the Church. While the patriarchal department for social work is rapidly expanding its initiatives, department representatives told me in 2012 that they had a network of approximately one thousand volunteers for all of Moscow. While the Church is rapidly expanding its drug rehabilitation programs, they are still counted by the dozens rather than the hundreds, and they face competition from programs run by the government and private organizations; conservative Protestant groups, such as Seventh-day Adventists, have been especially active in this work. Orthodox parish-based social ministries in

Russia are still in their infancy. Nevertheless, there is every reason to believe that Church social work will continue to grow and touch more Russians.

As we have seen, a religious vision of society guides these efforts. Many Church leaders believe that when people in physical or emotional need encounter the Church's love and care, they become aware of their need for spiritual healing as well. People discover how the Church's moral and spiritual orientation can strengthen both their personal lives and Russian society as a whole. As they come closer to the Church, they learn to overcome selfish, sinful desires in order to give their lives in love to others. They begin the way of deification.

Although key ideas about Church and society, body and spirit, and illness and healing implicitly guide the Church's social ministries in post-Communist Russia, few Church thinkers have given these ideas explicit attention. Theological reflection on the Church's outreach will perhaps develop more fully as Church social work expands. Some Orthodox believers doubt, however, that the Church needs grand theological theories about social service. The people who serve in these ministries typically speak of simply trying to obey Christ's command to love your neighbor as yourself.

Perhaps for this reason, the Patriarchate's official document "The Principles of Organization of Social Work in the Russian Orthodox Church" focuses not on a theoretical justification for social ministry but rather on the kinds of social services that the Church should be developing. The document also emphasizes that the responsibility for social work lies with all the Church's constituent parts—individual believers, parishes, dioceses, and monasteries alike. The opening section of the work consists largely of references to Old and New Testament passages about love of neighbor: first of all, love of those in one's religious community, and then of those on the outside as well.[35]

Some Church leaders are now calling for thinking through more carefully the purpose and motivation for social ministry, as at a roundtable discussion in January 2012 sponsored by the synodal department for charitable work. Chairing the event was Father Arkadii (Shatov), who in 2010 was elevated to the rank of bishop and assumed the name Panteleimon, in honor of the fourth-century saint-martyr who had served as a physician to the suffering and needy in Asia Minor. Deacon Oleg Vyshinskii, a lecturer in social work at Moscow's St. Tikhon's University, noted that Russian Orthodoxy has a less well-developed understanding of social ministry than Catholic and Protestant churches in the West.[36] In the Catholicism that emerged after the Council of Trent in the sixteenth century, social ministry was impelled by the idea that good works contribute to a person's salvation. Calvinist Protestantism, of course, rejected this idea. God's mercy in Christ alone, not good works, brings about salvation. Nevertheless, Calvinist Protestantism emphasized that those who trust in God do good works as a divine calling that confirms their salvation. Orthodoxy, in contrast, has been more cautious than either Catholicism or Reformation Protestantism about social ministry. According to Vyshinskii, good works have been regarded as only one dimension of life before God, and believers should be careful not to see people in need as a means for selfishly working out their own salvation.

Vyshinskii also noted historical factors specific to Russia that have hindered development of social ministries. Social activism has often been associated with Protestants sects or the Renovationists, those Orthodox priests and believers who at the time of the October Revolution supported radical social change, allied themselves with the Bolsheviks, and attempted to remove Patriarch Tikhon from office. Other observers have argued that state suppression of the Church and its social ministries under Communism caused Russian Orthodoxy to focus almost exclusively on individual salvation.[37] The Church survived by turning inward and leaving social work to the state. Even today it is not unusual to meet priests and monks in Russia who oppose the Church's new post-Communist emphasis on social ministry. To them, the Church should focus on people's eternal salvation while demanding that the state fulfill its obligations to society, including care of the poor and needy.[38]

In his presentation, Vyshinskii concluded that the Orthodox Church will be able to justify its social ministries only if it demonstrates how they contribute to people's salvation and deification. Bishop Panteleimon did not respond directly to Vyshinskii's challenge, but in other venues he has argued that people are indeed spiritually transformed as they engage in social ministry. While the Church calls on the state to fulfill its responsibilities to society, a commitment to social ministry is also essential to Church life. To be sure, the Church's document "Principles of Social Work" warns monks and nuns that social ministry should not undermine their principal calling to prayer and ascetic practice.[39] Correspondingly, social work should not divert any member of the Church from pursuing deification. But overall the post-Communist Church has taken Bishop Panteleimon's position that the spiritual life goes together with social service.

Symphonia, especially during the synodal and Communist periods, often restricted the Church to a spiritual sphere of influence. Bishop Panteleimon has compared the Church of that era to a man who has a heavy rock on his chest and nearly suffocates. After Communism, the Church can again breathe deeply and devote itself to the two tasks that should always lie at the heart of its life: love of God and love of neighbor. Panteleimon notes that the Church often delivers higher-quality social services than does the state. Even though social work places providers in situations of extreme human need that can easily overwhelm them, their spiritual resources will sustain them. And although most Church social workers receive a lower salary than state providers or even serve as volunteers, many Russians, noticing their good-hearted motivations and the high quality of their work, prefer the Church's social services to the state's. Panteleimon therefore has called on the state to support the Church's social initiatives, and he welcomes new laws that have made the Church eligible to receive government funding for social ministry.[40]

In the preceding analysis, I have emphasized how Church social work is an important means for inviting people into the Church's liturgical and sacramental life. Social ministry is closely related to in-churching. The Church, however, often stresses a different but no less significant dimension to its social work: service to people in physical need also draws providers more deeply into the Church and the Christian life. To answer Vyshinskii's question from this angle, social ministry is essentially related to salvation because through service to others, one grows in deification.

Bishop Panteleimon notes that many Christians have difficulty with an intellectual approach to the faith, such as studying the gospel or thinking about the meaning of life. It may be, rather, the act of participating in social ministry that first opens them to a deeper relationship with God. Panteleimon speaks of his own life experience. After the premature death of his wife threw him into deep grief, he came to understand that the only way ahead was to help others who were suffering. The opportunity to minister in the First City Hospital saved his life.[41]

This theme often repeated itself in my visits to Church social service projects. In St. Petersburg, a member of the Sisterhood of the Great Martyr Anastasia Uzoreshitelnitsa, the city's most prominent sisterhood, told me that many sisters had been drawn more deeply into Church life through social service.[42] Work in a hospital inevitably confronts one with desperate situations of human suffering and death that can easily trigger a personal spiritual crisis. A sister who for the first time is asked to change a patient's Pampers may be so repulsed by the experience that she resolves to leave the sisterhood. But with the loving support of the other sisters, she may find that such an experience actually becomes a profound moment of personal spiritual growth.

Father Andrei Lemeshonok at Minsk's St. Elizabeth Monastery makes a similar point about social service and the spiritual life. The spiritual solitude that, according to Orthodox teaching, should characterize a monk's life is a matter not of withdrawing from society but rather of living prayerfully. Care for people in need draws the monk into deeper prayer, and prayer brings peace with God. The true monastic does not allow him- or herself to become obsessively despondent about his or her sinfulness. Rather, one learns that in giving one's life to others one is spiritually transformed and filled with light. Father Andrei points to the examples of the holy elders Ioann (Krest'iankin) and Nikolai (Gur'ianov), who despite their deep suffering under Communism became renowned for their deep peacefulness and joy.[43] The document "Principles of Social Work" further notes that service to others can help a believer grow in Christian virtues of love, self-denial, humility, patience, and wisdom.[44] Another Church paper speaks similarly of how serving the ill can teach the server greater compassion toward others and greater faith in God's provision.[45]

Because service to people in need is a spiritual exercise, it requires personal discipline and communal support. Members of Moscow's Sisterhood of St. Dmitrii meet once a week for the Divine Liturgy, often celebrated by Bishop Panteleimon. Once a year, the sisters make pilgrimage to the famous women's monastery at Diveevo, where the relics of one of Russia's greatest saints, Seraphim of Sarov, repose.[46] Members of the sisterhood in St. Petersburg speak of the extraordinary Christian fellowship that they forge among themselves.[47] Both the Sisterhood of St. Dmitrii and the Sisterhood of the Great Martyr Anastasia Uzoreshitelnitsa regularly meet with a spiritual father for prayer and counsel.

A recent Church document on combating drug addiction offers a helpful summation of the Church's understanding of social ministry. According to the authors, Russian Orthodoxy teaches that illness is an opportunity for a person to grow spiritually. Regardless of one's level of faith, illness (and presumably other hardships) invites one to seek "that fullness of being, which is possible only in unity and communion with God as Creator of the world and Savior. . . . Illness frequently becomes a moment of divine visitation."[48] The experience of sickness or disability may help a person find new strength to repent of sin—and especially any sins that have contributed to the person's difficult situation. At the same time, the Church calls on its children to show love and solidarity with those who suffer, and especially with other members of the Church. In reaching out to those who are ill, Christians grow in compassion and faith.

The document applies these insights specifically to people with HIV/AIDS. In an introductory essay, Metropolitan Hilarion (Alfeev), head of the Church's Department of External Church Relations, argues that HIV/AIDS offers the sufferer an opportunity to reexamine his life and free himself from sinful passions (5). The Church, however, refuses to condemn people with HIV/AIDS; on the contrary, it lovingly accepts all who turn to it out of their neediness. Illness not only challenges the sufferer to repent but also spurs members of the Church to learn greater compassion. Just as Father Mefodii regards drug addiction as ultimately indicting all of society, Metropolitan Hilarion sees HIV/AIDS as a result of social disorder, not merely personal failure: "Neglect of moral norms and principles, growth of spiritual emptiness, [and] loss of the sense and purpose of life" are the fundamental causes of the HIV/AIDS crisis (5). Like Father Mefodii, Metropolitan Hilarion repeats the accusation that the West and liberal democracy have infected Russia with the moral relativism and spiritual decay that contribute to drug use. Not only those individuals who suffer but also the nation as a whole should repent of sin and recover the moral values that Russia's traditional religious communities — and especially the Orthodox Church — have taught and guarded. Of central importance for renewing society, Orthodox believers typically say, are social measures for strengthening families, which have historically preserved and transmitted the nation's foundational values. And the Church further believes that if people enter into its life, their moral orientation will be firmer and therefore the nation will be stronger.

Not all Russians will ultimately choose to participate in Church life, but the Church hopes that all of them will be educated in Orthodox values and encouraged to live by them. From the Church's perspective, the nation will be stronger if the state promotes such initiatives as religious education in the public schools and Church social work. And, more generally, the Church believes that the state will benefit Russian society by securing and honoring the place of Orthodoxy, because it helps secure the moral foundations of the nation.

At conferences and in publications, Church leaders affirm Church-state cooperation in social outreach. But behind the scenes, I have often heard Church leaders complain that the state is more concerned to secure its own power than serve society or help the Church. Some point to practical difficulties that the Church has faced in carving out legal space for its work. Often the state imposes conditions, such as licensing of Church-related social programs and certification of Church social workers, that the Church finds overly restrictive. A Soviet mentality still persists among too many Russian bureaucrats. Because they believe that the state should control every area of society, they are reluctant to give the Church more space for its social work, despite the high rates of public approval that the Church enjoys in this area.

Liberal critics of the Church wish that it would speak out publicly against the Putin government's authoritarian features. But in a highly centralized state such as Russia, the Church knows that it will be able to develop its social ministries only if it maintains a good working relationship with government officials. A policy of quiet but persistent negotiation with the state seems more fruitful than open confrontation, even if such a policy comes at the cost of making the Church seem dependent on and even subservient to the state.

The Church's social work is complicated not only by Church-state relations but also by deficiencies in the Church's understanding of culture and society. Russia does not exist today as a nation hermetically sealed off from the rest of the world. Political leaders' commitment to strong economic development has brought values of the global marketplace into Russian society. The Church cannot simply dismiss consumerism, construction of multiple lifestyle niches, or the drive to enhance personal freedom of choice as alien values imposed by the West. Rather, many Russians themselves freely embrace these values in their aspirations to achieve a Western standard and style of living.

The Church's understanding of culture and society is deficient from another angle as well. Its "anti-Western secularism" rhetoric fails to offer a nuanced analysis of the strengths of liberal democracies. As I suggested earlier, the Church's social work would benefit by greater attention to social structures that contribute to such problems as drug addiction and poverty. Thus far, the Church has spoken out about certain broad ideological dimensions to Russia's social problems and how to minister to individuals who suffer from them, but has done little to examine how state economic policies, population movement from country to city, or a culture of corruption undermine the nation's life.

The Church's understanding of human freedom raises additional questions about the Church's social work. According to traditional Orthodox teaching, humans never lose their freedom to choose God. Even illness and personal hardship need not diminish human freedom; on the contrary, they can activate it. Both the one who is suffering and the one who lovingly reaches out in mercy to the sufferer have the opportunity to grow in religious faith. Human freedom, however, is a complicated matter both theologically and personally. Take the young men at St. George's. Why have they been able to choose recovery while so many other drug addicts do not? Why do illness and hardship sometimes become the opportunity for a "divine visitation" that positively reorients some people while others lose the moral-spiritual compass that once guided them? And, at St. George's, how much of the daily regime do the young men really choose for themselves? Do they attend the liturgy because they freely seek God or because everyone else in the community goes? Does in-churching strengthen their freedom to resist drugs, or is the enchanted, holy world of St. George's only a temporary escape from Russia's everyday reality? St. George's claims a high success rate, but in their more reflective moments the monks wonder why some of its young men will nevertheless return to drugs.

The dynamics of human freedom are no less complex for those who serve in Church social ministries. As Vyshinskii noted, social service can be selfishly motivated. Providers can become proud of their good deeds. Has the Orthodox Church developed its social ministries simply out of Christian love for people in need, or has it been motivated by desire to counteract the influence of its religious and secular competitors? And has the Church become so proud of developing its social ministries that it has been willing to compromise itself with an authoritarian state? Do state policies that privilege the Orthodox Church in education and social work—all in the name of promoting "traditional moral values"—respect Russians' freedom to choose faith for themselves, or do these policies inevitably compromise freedom of conscience? Sorting out true from false freedom may be more difficult than Church statements about social ministry acknowledge.

None of these questions should cast doubt on the genuine good that the Church is doing. Its social ministries make an extraordinarily positive contribution to a Russia that is still finding its way after the collapse of Communism. While the Church's work is still limited in scope, it touches thousands of lives and offers creative models of treatment and outreach that help orient government and private social service agency efforts. Russia desperately needs the Church's vision of a Holy Rus' in which the needy and those who care for them lead all members of society toward the life-giving solidarity represented by Nesterov's Christ. Even the most cynical critics of Church-state relations can give thanks for the Church's remarkable social achievements.

The Church's vision of a better society, however, must not obscure its attention to the profound mystery and sometimes painful tragedy of human freedom. The monks at St. George's know this lesson well, and that is why they ultimately pray for courage yet humility in the face of disappointment. The lesson came home to me when my family and I traveled to St. George's for Christmas. Heavy snows were falling around Kineshma, but the Volga was not yet frozen, and the monks had to drive us the long way around to reach the parish. The roads were barely passable, and at one point the Gazelle got stuck by the side of the road. All our efforts to push it back onto the road failed. A car went by but did not stop when Father Pavel, our driver, tried to flag it down. He shrugged his shoulders and said, "Some people hate priests and monks." We waited another forty-five minutes until a truck driver appeared, took mercy on us, and pulled the Gazelle out of the ditch. When we finally arrived at St. George's, night was already falling.

Although we were exhausted, the parish seemed more beautiful than ever. Just before midnight, we and other pilgrims gathered in the parish church. The recovering addicts were already there, stoking the old cast-iron furnace with logs until the metal glowed orange and red. Others tended the candles before the icons or chanted the Church's ancient prayers. When the Divine Liturgy finally ended in the wee hours of Christmas morning, all of us walked over to the parish kitchen and broke the Advent fast with a feast of grilled fish, potato and noodle salads, and chocolate candies. That afternoon, after a few hours of sleep, we gathered again, and the young men put on costumes and presented a humorous skit complete with Ded Moroz and Snegorochka (Russia's rough equivalent of Santa Claus and his helper).

Among the pilgrims were two very kind and pleasant women from St. Petersburg. A friend later quietly related to us that each of these women had had a son who went through the rehabilitation program at St. George's. The young men's days along the Volga had been the best of their lives, but when they returned to St. Petersburg, neither was able to stay clean. Both had later died of an overdose. The mothers had brought their sons back here to be buried in the church cemetery. And every Christmas these two women, now friends in grief, returned to the parish. The monks could no longer do anything for their sons, but the two women wanted very much to do something for the parish. They cooked and washed, decorated and cleaned, attended worship, received the Eucharist, and contributed to the loving, supportive community that makes St. George's a special place.

Now, as Christmas Day drew to a close and night again fell, each woman would walk to the church cemetery, stand by her son, and do the only thing left to Orthodox believers to do for the dead: kiss the simple metal cross on the grave, look up into the starry heavens, and pray for the Lord to have mercy.

FIVE

The New Martyrs

On Friday, November 4, 2011, Russians celebrated one of their nation's new holidays, Unity Day. Few Russians were aware that Unity Day formally marked the anniversary of the expulsion of Polish occupiers from the Kremlin in 1612. Most, however, would have understood that Unity Day had been established in 2005 to replace the Soviet commemoration of the Bolshevik Revolution on November 7. On Unity Day 2011, ten thousand young rightist nationalists marched on the outskirts of the city, accusing Putin and his party, United Russia, of tolerating Jews and Muslims.

Pious Orthodox believers observed November 4 in a different way. For them, it was the feast day of the icon of the Mother of God of Kazan, and most parishes celebrated the Divine Liturgy. A priest in our parish gave a sermon in which he criticized the government for neglecting to make the nation aware that Russian warriors had prayed before the Kazan icon prior to driving out the Poles. In the afternoon, thousands of Orthodox faithful gathered outside the Manezh, the city's huge exhibition halls just north of the Kremlin walls. Although they would wait up to two hours in the bitter cold to gain admittance, the mood was festive; some sang traditional hymns to the Mother of God as they tried to stay warm. I joined these pilgrims to venerate the fourteenth-century icon of the Theotokos of Tikhvin and visit a Church-sponsored exhibition entitled *Rebirth*, which reviewed the revival of Orthodox Christianity since the fall of Communism.

On Monday, November 7, state-sponsored activities drew another large crowd. Thousands gathered in Red Square to commemorate the seventieth anniversary of the formation of a famous battalion of volunteers that had pledged to defend Moscow as German troops laid siege. A few hours later, I tried to visit the Orthodox exhibition *Rebirth* a second time. It was the closing day, and the line was still long. Frustrated by how slowly it was moving, I finally abandoned it and went to find the source of the impassioned voices blasting from loudspeakers nearby. I soon discovered that in the square in front of the Bolshoi Theatre several thousand members of the Communist Party had gathered to commemorate the October Revolution.

They, too, were singing—not Orthodox prayers to the saints, of course—but rather old socialist songs with refrains such as "Lenin, Party, Komsomol!" Elderly party veterans were selling Soviet-era souvenirs and Party literature, red flags, and posters with images of Lenin and Stalin. From the platform, speakers lashed out at Putin and United Russia for trying to steal the parliamentary elections that would take place on December 4.

I returned to the Manezh. Night had fallen, the line was gone, and the police had closed off the area. Every two minutes, a lonely voice from a loudspeaker solemnly declared, "The Orthodox exhibition is closed. The Orthodox exhibition is over." Nevertheless, about twenty-five women in traditional Orthodox dress—long skirts and headscarves—waited by a metal barrier and pleaded insistently with the policeman to admit them. I stood nearby, waiting to see what would happen. The policeman finally relented. I followed the women in, becoming the exhibition's very last visitor.

These rival events at the center of Moscow reflect the competing narratives that define Russian nationhood today.[1] President Putin has appealed especially to the symbols and stories of the Great Patriotic War. Russia is a great nation because of its extraordinary sacrifices in World War II and victory over Hitler's Germany. In 2015, Russia observed the seventieth anniversary of the victory over Germany with a massive military parade and a procession of more than five hundred thousand people holding photographs of relatives who fought and/or died in the war.[2] For the Communist Party and its supporters, the collapse of "real existing socialism" has not diminished the compelling power of the Marxist vision of a just society in which the working class holds political and economic power. They celebrate the Lenin and Stalin who transformed Russia from a backward nation of peasants into an industrialized superpower. New rightist nationalist groups, in contrast, call for an authoritarian government that will guarantee Russia's Slavic purity. They sometimes call for a new tsar and idealize Russian society prior to the revolution.

While the Church itself advances several different narratives, I wish to explore one in particular. By this account, Orthodoxy is an essential part of Russian national identity; Orthodox rituals, such as veneration of great icons and prayers for national protection, have shaped Russians' way of life from one generation to the next; and Orthodoxy helped save the nation from its enemies at critical historical moments, as in the seventeenth century against the Catholic Poles. Bolshevik persecution of religion has added to this narrative: Russians suffered under Communism because the nation had rebelled against God, but the twentieth-century Russian martyrs opened the way to national repentance, the collapse of Communism, and social renewal.

Nationalist, state, and Church narratives sometimes overlap. Putin promotes revival of the Church and the nation's Orthodox heritage, as when he visits famous monasteries or endorses religious education in the public schools.[3] Nationalist groups carry the prerevolutionary flag of St. Andrew and call for an Orthodox political order. The Church emphasizes its contributions to the war effort against the Nazis or allies itself with the Putin government's rhetoric against Western efforts to dominate Russia. But these narratives also have key points of tension. Just how should Russians evaluate Stalin, who led them to victory in World War II but also was responsible for horrendous crimes against his own people? Does the Church share some of the social ideals of Communism, even though the Bolsheviks tried to eradicate religion? If Russia was truly an Orthodox society prior to the revolution, why did Russians allow the Bolsheviks to come to power? When can Church and state cooperate, and when will they find themselves in opposition? Just what happened to Russia under Communism, and what would it mean for Russians to come to terms with this part of their past?

Since the collapse of Communism, Russians have struggled to understand their nation's place in the world. What was once a great empire broke into different countries: Russia, Belarus, Ukraine, the Baltic nations, and the Central Asian republics. The great achievements of the Soviet Union in science, technology, and industrialization could no longer hide how far the country had really fallen behind the West. The transition to democratic government and a market economy resulted in massive social insecurity.

Life expectancy, especially among men, fell dramatically. Corruption was rampant. A small group of "oligarchs," business entrepreneurs with close connections to government officials, bought up state-owned resources and enterprises at rock-bottom prices and made extraordinary profits, even as millions of ordinary Russians struggled to make ends meet. Elderly women on miniscule state pensions gathered outside metro stations to sell old magazines, knick-knacks, or scarves that they had knit. Basic public infrastructure—roads, bridges, the public health system, and housing stock—crumbled. In 2000, Russia's gross domestic product was not even double that of tiny Denmark.[4] While the end of Communism brought new freedoms of travel, press, and political organization, many Russians felt that they had little to be proud of.

The relegation of Russia to the status of a second-class European nation—no longer a commanding superpower, even if it still had a huge nuclear arsenal—produced a crisis of national identity. Russians' resentment at their new situation was exacerbated by their perception that the West, especially the United States, was glad to use Russia's misfortunes to dominate and humiliate it. NATO expanded to the borders of Russia. A nationalist, anti-Russian movement arose in Ukraine, a nation that Russians had typically regarded as eternally united in friendship with (and dependent on) their own. Russians confronted, for the first time, social phenomena—such as drug addiction, pornography, and international criminal organizations—that seemed to be malicious invaders from a secularist, consumerist West.

In their search for a new national identity, Russians reached back into their history to retrieve ancient motifs and symbols of Russia's unique greatness. Although the Soviet Union had collapsed, many Russians believed that their nation was more than a junior partner to the West or a minor

European power. Russia continued to have a national identity that made it distinct from and in some sense perhaps even superior to the West. And some people turned to Russia's Orthodox legacy to articulate their nation's unique identity.[5] As in past centuries, Russia, they believed, had an errand to the world to defend the highest moral and cultural values of Christian civilization.

From this perspective, efforts to retrieve Orthodoxy as part of the Russian past cannot jump over the seven decades in which the Bolsheviks sought to eradicate religion. When Church leaders today cite the famous words of the ancient Christian theologian Tertullian, "The blood of the martyrs is the seed of the Church," the implications are twofold. Those whom the Communists killed for their faith sowed the renewal of Russia today, and Russia will find its way into the twenty-first century only by honoring these martyrs.[6]

Attention to the victims of the Bolsheviks had already begun in the Soviet era. Especially important was Alexander Solzhenitsyn's *Gulag Archipelago*—written between 1958 and 1968, published in the West in 1973, and distributed in samizdat in the Soviet Union. It spurred other efforts to document the crimes of the Soviet regime. As the Soviet Union collapsed, leading dissident intellectuals founded the human rights organization Memorial, which maintains a huge database of victims and sponsors conferences, historical research, and publications.[7] Other organizations founded museums at sites of Communist political repression, such as Solovki and near Perm.[8]

While federal legislation provides for political rehabilitation of victims of Soviet repression, the state has been cautious about making a public reckoning with the Communist past. State authorities perhaps worry that documenting the human rights abuses of the Soviet era will encourage criticism of the present political order. In any event, government officials in recent years have tightened access to police and KGB archives, Memorial has experienced tremendous pressure to curtail its activities, and school textbooks have emphasized Stalin's positive achievements while downplaying his atrocities.[9]

The Church, too, has a checkered history of coming to terms with the Soviet past. No official process of lustration has taken place to identify Church hierarchs and members who collaborated with the secret police.[10] The Church has not publicly acknowledged its complicity with the government in such matters as silencing dissident priests. Nor has the Church spoken openly and candidly about the horrible compromises that, to the hierarchy, seemed necessary to save the Church from complete destruction. When speaking of the Communist past, the Church prefers to present itself as a victim of oppression rather than a tragic collaborator.

Despite the hierarchy's failure to examine these matters with complete honesty, some in the Church have taken a leading role in reminding contemporary Russian society of the dark side of the Soviet era. Through memorial sites, historical research, educational endeavors, and veneration of the new martyrs and confessors of Russia, these Church leaders pose key questions: Is there any way to make sense of the nation's suffering under the Bolsheviks? Are there lessons for today? How can the Russian people ensure that such things never happen again? For these Church leaders, the Church interprets the Communist past in order to bring Orthodox values into society today.

The long line into the *Rebirth* exhibition continued into the first hall, where people, now at last able to warm up, walked up one by one to the Tikhvin icon of the Theotokos and offered their veneration. In 1941, the Nazis confiscated the icon and transferred it to Orthodox believers in Riga, Latvia, a German-occupied area. At the end of the war, Bishop John (Garklavs) brought the icon in safety to the Holy Trinity Cathedral (Orthodox Church in America) in Chicago. In 2004, leaders of the Orthodox Church in America returned the icon with great fanfare to the Russian Orthodox Church and its home in the Tikhvin Monastery several hours by car east of St. Petersburg.[11] Today people from all parts of Russia make pilgrimage to it, and the opportunity to venerate it in Moscow was a major event.

I, too, went forward, offered my veneration, and followed others into a long narrow hall whose displays traced the Bolshevik persecution of the Church from 1917 on. A huge photograph captured the implosion of Christ the Savior

Cathedral at Stalin's order in 1931. An accompanying label noted that the state later used marble from the church for walls and benches in several Moscow metro stations. A large poster presented a table of grim statistics.

	1914	1939	1952	1965
Church members	120,000,000	55,000,000	—	—
Monasteries	953	0	62	18
Churches/chapels	75,000	100	13,786	7,873
Seminaries	246	0	10	5
Hierarchs	139	4	65	77
Clergy	68,928	200	12,254	7,347
Monastics	94,629	0	4,639	1,500

Melancholy orchestral music played as we continued into a darkened tunnel on whose walls were projected historical film footage of scenes of persecution, secret police mug shots of people arrested for their faith, and inspiring words that the martyrs spoke prior to their execution.

The next hall moved us from the sacrifice of the martyrs to the rebirth of the Church—and from dark shadows to brilliant light and color. The 191 dioceses of today's Russian Orthodox Church introduced their social initiatives, mission work, and parish life. Priests answered visitors' questions. An adjoining hall was dedicated to the renewal of Orthodox arts: icons, liturgical garments and implements, Church choral music and bell ringing, and Church architecture. Many of the items on display had been produced by students at St. Tikhon's Orthodox University in Moscow.[12]

In the last exhibition hall, Church-related organizations introduced themselves: the Church's synodal departments, Orthodox charity funds for education and social work, Orthodox seminaries and academies, Miloserdiia (the largest Orthodox organization for social ministries), and St. Tikhon's University. Even the Moscow mayor's office had a booth, explaining how the city was supporting the Church's initiative to build two hundred new churches in areas of the city currently without a parish.

On my second visit, a crowd had gathered before the Tikhvin icon as the exhibit came to a close. A group of priests was performing a *moleben* (prayer).

Accompanied by the joyful singing of the assembled believers, the priests carefully hoisted the icon on their shoulders and processed out of the exhibition hall. As the rest of us left, a few pious women gathered scraps of paper and bits of dirt that had accumulated on the platform where the icon had stood. They would take them home and venerate them, confident that even these "leftovers" had been sanctified by their proximity to the icon and would bring blessing.

The *Rebirth* exhibition was more than a series of informational displays. It powerfully communicated a religious understanding of the events of the twentieth century: Bolshevik persecution of the Church has nevertheless led to religious renewal; the deaths of the martyrs under Communism have made possible the resurrection of Orthodox faith and life after Communism; God has used Soviet desecration of the Church to bring about a consecration of new churches, monasteries, and Church-related institutions; Russia is again being filled with the holiness of ancient Rus'; and Russia's future depends on a society and state that protect and promote the Church.

The displays made religious persecution the central story line of the Soviet era. They did not explain why Communism had arisen or directed its ire against the Church, nor did they place the Church's suffering within a larger context of national devastation and loss. Rather, the magnitude of the Church's suffering was emphasized. From having been present in every area of society in 1917, it had been nearly obliterated twenty-four years later. Even after Stalin's change of course during World War II, the Church remained a pale shadow of its former self.

The exhibition personalized the Church's suffering. The Soviets had not simply attacked the Church as an institution; they had put flesh-and-blood believers to death. Here again the exhibition focused on those who had died for their faith, not on the fact that the Bolsheviks had aimed at eliminating every trace of the old social order: the monarchy, the nobility, and privileged peasant landholders (the so-called *kulaks*).

Drawing on traditional Christian motifs, the exhibition portrayed how those who were faithful unto death ultimately gave life to others. Just as Christ died for the sins of the world, the Russian Orthodox martyrs sacrificed themselves for the sins of their nation. And just as God vindicated Jesus by raising him from the dead, God vindicated the new martyrs by bringing the Church that they loved back to life. The exhibition presented this rebirth as institutional, liturgical, and social in scope. The Church again has a comprehensive network of dioceses and parishes throughout and beyond Russia; Orthodox worship can be celebrated in all its glory; and the Church is able to shape society through initiatives in education, social work, and parish life. For pious Orthodox believers, this renewal of Church life after years of intense persecution is nothing less than miraculous. Equally miraculous to them is the transformation of the Russian state, which once tried to destroy the Church but now regards it as an essential part of Russian society.

When I left the exhibition, I walked over to the metro station at Biblioteka Imeni Lenina (Lenin Library) and rode the escalator deep underground. I noticed an ad on the wall go by me. Against a clear bright blue sky stood an ancient, domed Orthodox church, gleaming white. Printed below were the words: "Strengthening spirituality. Russia is reborn. Master Bank."[13] That commercial moment captured everything that the *Rebirth* exhibition was trying to say.

Recent work by leading Church historians adds depth and detail to this way of interpreting the events of the twentieth century. A center of historical research has been St. Tikhon's Orthodox University, whose rector, Father Vladimir Vorob'ev, has promoted scholarly and popular attention to the new martyrs. The university has established a database with information on more than thirty-five thousand individuals who suffered for their faith and has organized major historical exhibitions such as *Rebirth*.

Father Aleksandr Mazyrin, a professor at St. Tikhon's and a priest at St. Nicholas in Kuznetsakh, which Vorob'ev heads and on whose grounds university buildings are located, argues that the attack on religion was not an afterthought but rather at the very heart of the Bolshevik program.[14] What made the Church so threatening to the new state was not merely its traditional alliance with the monarchy or that, according to Marxist thinking, the Church offered the oppressed masses spiritual opium rather than social justice. Rather, the Church had an understanding of human dignity and freedom that directly clashed with a Marxist worldview. The Church insisted that humans were defined first of all not by material economic conditions but rather by the freedom to love God and others.

Mazyrin and other church historians have established that the arrest, imprisonment, and execution of Church leaders began immediately after the October Revolution. Less than a week after the storming of the Winter Palace, Father Ioann Kochurov was assassinated by Bolshevik soldiers in Tsarskoe Selo, the home of Catherine the Great's famous palace. Three months later, Metropolitan Vladimir (Bogoiavlenskii) of Kiev became the first bishop martyr. By the summer of 1918, Church officials had documented 121 martyrdoms and were investigating reports of others. By 1920, the number of martyrs exceeded twelve thousand, including twenty-eight bishops.[15]

A government decree that established legal separation of Church and state in February 1918 eliminated the Church as a juridical entity. The state nationalized Church property—including buildings, land, and bank accounts—and assumed control of Church-operated schools.[16] Soldiers and Bolshevik hooligans invaded and desecrated churches, robbing them of precious icons and implements.[17] Patriarch Tikhon responded with defiance. In January 1918, he anathematized the Bolsheviks and in October accused them of being agents of the Antichrist.[18]

The campaign against the Church became more systematic and comprehensive after February 1919. The Bolsheviks closed churches and removed and uncovered relics of saints, seeking to demonstrate that they were merely dry bones or puppets.[19] In 1921, in the wake of famine precipitated by civil war and disastrous state agricultural policies, state authorities demanded that the Church hand over gold and silver implements in order to help the state raise money to feed the hungry, although their real aim was to attack the Church and enrich their own coffers.[20]

Tikhon himself had called for the sale of Church treasures to buy food for the famine victims. He forbade, however, relinquishment of implements needed for celebration of the liturgy. When parishioners in some places resisted the Bolsheviks' confiscations, bloody clashes ensued. The Bolsheviks soon concluded that their harsh measures were only hardening believers' resolve. State leaders implemented a second strategy: to destroy the Church from within by provoking schism.

In 1922–23, Patriarch Tikhon was placed under house arrest at Moscow's Donskoi Monastery. When the Renovationists, supporters of radical Church change, tried to seize power, Tikhon anathematized them.[21] But after harsh interrogations by the secret police in June 1923, Tikhon altered course. Believing that further confrontation with the state would only destroy the Church, he sought a modus vivendi. He publicly confessed his guilt before the nation for his previous opposition to the Bolshevik regime, declared that he no longer regarded it as his enemy, and made concessions demanded by the Renovationists but deeply opposed by most believers, such as abolishing the Old Style (Julian) calendar and commemorating the Bolshevik authorities in the liturgy.[22] The state hoped that Tikhon's apparent change of heart would discredit him in the eyes of the faithful and strengthen the state's hold on the Church. The authorities' calculations proved deeply mistaken. Upon his release, Tikhon was greeted wildly by his supporters. Deeply moved by his words, "Let my name be blotted out from history, if only the Church be built up," they were convinced that he had made his concessions only at great personal cost and for their sake.[23] State authorities soon found that Tikhon had gained, rather than lost, authority, and he was able to ignore some of the promised reforms.[24]

Tikhon spent the last months of his life serving the liturgy almost daily in different Moscow churches. He received as many as fifty visitors each day; most conversations had to be limited to five minutes. Although he was able to move about Moscow freely, he experienced constant harassment from state authorities. He was only sixty-one years old when he passed away late in the night of April 7, 1925. Rumors soon circulated that he had died of unnatural causes. On April 12, thousands of believers crowded into the grounds of the Donskoi Monastery as fifty hierarchs and as many as five hundred priests conducted his funeral and burial in the Small Cathedral.[25]

Tikhon had nominated three bishops as candidates to serve as patriarchal representative in the event that the Church was prohibited from calling a council to elect a new patriarch. The hierarchs who gathered for Tikhon's funeral immediately selected Petr (Polianskii). Although Tikhon had placed

Petr last in line, the other two candidates, Kirill (Smirnov) and Agafangel (Preobrazhenskii), were at that moment under arrest outside of Moscow. Metropolitan Sergii (Stragorodskii) of Nizhnii Novgorod played a leading role in promoting Petr's candidacy, and Petr subsequently appointed him as his deputy.

Petr was able to serve for only eight months before he, too, was arrested and sent into internal exile. The secret police relentlessly pressured him to renounce his position as patriarchal representative, but he refused. Meanwhile, Sergii took charge of Church affairs, assuming powers, such as episcopal appointments, that belonged properly only to a patriarch. After a brief period of imprisonment, Sergii issued, on July 29, 1927, a declaration that became infamous for its unreserved loyalty to the Soviet state: "We wish to be Orthodox believers and at the same time recognize the Soviet Union as our earthly home, whose joys and successes are our joys and successes, and whose misfortunes are our misfortunes." Sergii further called on the faithful to express their thanks to the state for attending generously to their "spiritual needs."[26]

The other two candidates for patriarchal representative, Kirill and Agafangel, accused Sergii of usurping Church power and compromising the Church politically. In response, Sergii excommunicated Kirill and several of Agafangel's supporters and made no effort to protect them from arrest and imprisonment. Sergii's opponents eventually relented, repented of their actions, and agreed to recognize Sergii's authority in order to maintain the unity of the Church, but they asserted a right to disobey any of his decisions that they regarded as illegitimate. The state's efforts to divide believers had failed; the Church remained united around its hierarchy. But the cost to the Church was tremendous.

Mazyrin argues that Tikhon and Sergii represent two fundamentally different approaches to the question of Church and state. Tikhon ultimately refused to ally the Church with any political party, to the great disappointment of both the Bolsheviks and the leaders of the White armies that fought the Bolsheviks from 1918 to 1920. In Mazyrin's understanding, Tikhon wanted the Church's children to regard every Russian as a brother or sister, even those Russians who wished to eliminate it. His proposed concessions in 1923 aimed not at submitting the Church to state control but rather at rescuing the Church from the Renovationists while demonstrating to the Bolsheviks that the Church was willing to recognize its authority in earthly matters.[27]

Sergii, in contrast, was willing to compromise the spiritual freedom of the Church in order to preserve it as a public institution. After his 1927 declaration of loyalty, the Bolsheviks briefly drew back from publicly ridiculing religion. The Church was permitted to operate a theological institute (1927–29) and publish an official journal (1931–35).[28] But the state, with Sergii's acquiescence, controlled appointment of hierarchs and priests, and went after those who opposed Sergii's leadership. Sergii, says Mazyrin, had reduced the Church to an earthly institution dependent on the goodwill of the state. Sergii's theology was wrong; moreover, his practical calculations to save the Church proved to be a colossal failure. New waves of church closings took place. By the end of Stalin's Great Terror in 1939, the institutional Church was nearly dead.

According to Mazyrin, those such as Petr who remained true to Tikhon's course understood the Church to be primarily a spiritual, sacramental reality, not a human, political institution. What united the Church was right doctrine and practice, not arrangements with the state. The Church did not even need a ruling hierarch in order to be the Church; its institutional life could be organized in any number of ways, as when Agafangel told bishops to manage diocesan affairs on their own if central Church authority collapsed. Mazyrin argues that, despite their opposition to Sergii, people such as Kirill and Agafangel remained loyal to the Church in a deeper sense. And Mazyrin notes that the Church today has canonized Kirill and Agafangel and their followers alongside martyred bishops and priests who did not challenge Sergii's authority.

What made Tikhon—and other new martyrs—so remarkable, in Mazyrin's judgment, was their faithfulness to Christ's command to love one's enemies. Their love was not, however, quiet and passive. Rather, it boldly claimed that the Bolsheviks, despite their militant atheism, belonged to God. The martyrs' and confessors' confidence in "speaking the truth in love" had a double implication.[29] On the one hand, Tikhon and his supporters did

not try to overthrow the Communist government. Even though it was perse-
cuting them, they acknowledged its earthly legitimacy, drawing on the
Apostle Paul's words that all authority comes from God.[30] On the other hand,
the Tikhonites refused to allow the Bolsheviks to define Christians as enemies
of the state. Rather, the Tikhonites treated their persecutors as divinely
created human beings who retained the freedom to change their ways and
accept the Church's offer of new life in Christ.

The Tikhonites tried to win over the Bolsheviks by exhibiting an inner,
spiritual freedom that Communist ideology could not provide. The
Tikhonites saw Christ's sacrificial love as the ultimate source and demon-
stration of human freedom. To Mazyrin, even though the witness of the
martyrs appeared hopeless at the time, it would ultimately bear fruit for both
the Church and the nation.

While Mazyrin is cautious about making applications to the present, his
interpretation of twentieth-century Russian history suggests that the Church
today, as for Tikhon, must be a Church for all of society. It must avoid taking
sides with particular political parties or interests. The Church's political
witness lies in cultivating a spiritual freedom that enables people to practice
and defend the Church's deepest moral values. Such a Church will have
the ability to resist those who oppose these values, even as it reaches out to
them in love.

A further implication would be that the Church will sustain its witness to
society only if it remains united. Church unity depends, however, neither
on institutional arrangements nor on the Church's relations with the state,
but rather on the Church's faithfulness to its liturgical and sacramental
life.[31] Today, as in the past, the Church must resist efforts by the state or
other social forces to dictate matters of belief or worship. Mazyrin approvingly quotes key, although controversial, words from the *Social Concept* that
the Church's bishops approved in 2000: "The Church maintains loyalty to
the state, but higher than the demand of loyalty is the Divine commandment: to act to save humans in whatever conditions and in whatever circumstances. If the government pressures Orthodox believers to abandon Christ
and His Church, or to undertake sinful, soul-corrupting activities, the

Church must refuse to obey."[32] Mazyrin believes that thanks to the faithful witness of such people as Tikhon, Petr, Kirill, and Agafangel, the Church has come back to life. And they show the way ahead as the Church, no longer persecuted, faces new temptations to yield to social pressures and deny moral values foundational to the Russian Church and nation.

As compelling as Mazyrin's narrative is, it leaves key questions unanswered. Are the contrasts between Tikhon and Sergii as sharp as Mazyrin makes them? How was Tikhon's declaration of loyalty to the state in 1923 different from Sergii's in 1927? Both Tikhon and Sergii were ready to compromise with the state in hopes of saving the Church's institutional existence. While they disagreed about whether centralized Church authority was necessary for the Church to be the Church, both leaders strove to preserve a public space for institutional Church life. Neither man wanted to see the Church condemned to a wholly underground existence.

Additional questions relate to Mazyrin's affirmation of a Church that stands above the political fray. Does such a Church inevitably tend to favor the political status quo rather than challenge the state to provide for a more just political order? How can the Church defend its moral values in society unless it enters into practical political alliances, sometimes with the state but at other times in opposition to the ruling authorities? How does the Church rightly participate in political life when it is no longer a persecuted body but rather makes claims, as does the Russian Church today, to represent the social majority? When do calls for Church unity obscure differences of opinion within the Church or even justify attacks on persons or groups that disagree with Church authorities?

The witness and legacy of the new martyrs are more ambiguous than Mazyrin acknowledges in his writings. Nevertheless, he helpfully identifies key moral values that today's Church wishes to instill in believers and more widely in the nation. In contrast to Western emphases on individual rights, Russian Orthodox thinking prioritizes social unity. The Church is most truly the Church, and the nation most truly the nation, when people are one in mind and spirit. Mazyrin's articulation of the values of the new martyrs also provides insight into differences between Western and Russian understandings of freedom. In the West, freedom is often understood as individual choice and self-determination, whereas Russian Orthodoxy thinks in terms of the individual's ability, with God's help, to remain faithful to the Church's moral values in the face of social opposition. This spiritual freedom is sustained by participation in the Church's liturgical, sacramental life.

Mazyrin's understanding of unity and freedom also has important implications for the Church's understanding of politics. In popular Western thinking, the state should be religiously neutral. It should not favor one religious group over another. The Russian Church also supports the disestablishment of religion in order to guard the Church from state interference in the Church's inner life, but believes that the state has the additional responsibility of preserving and promoting Orthodox Christianity. Just as Bolshevik efforts to destroy the Church once brought national disaster in their wake, a state that respects the Church and its values today will decisively strengthen the nation. Under Communism, the state martyred Christians; today the state should honor their legacy.

Few Russians will read Mazyrin's scholarly articles and books, and not all Church historians or leaders agree with Mazyrin that the unmerited suffering of Tikhon and the martyrs is the key to understanding Orthodox identity today. Nevertheless, the Church hierarchy has actively promoted their commemoration and regarded their achievements as significant not only for the Church but also for the nation as a whole.

In December 2012, the Church's Holy Synod established a commission for "the eternal memorialization of the new martyrs and confessors of the Russian Church" under the direction of Metropolitan Iuvenalii (Poiarkov) of Krutitsa and Kolomna, who had chaired the Church's canonization commission until 2012. In November 2014, Iuvenalii reported that a growing number of churches and chapels were being dedicated to the new martyrs and confessors. More parishes and dioceses than ever before were celebrating memorial services and processions; erecting commemorative crosses on sites of mass suffering and killing; organizing museums, publications, and educational activities; and identifying candidates for canonization. In some places, government officials had agreed to name public hospitals or streets in honor of local martyrs. The commission had concluded, however, that as of 2013 only 54 out of 147 dioceses had demonstrated satisfactory efforts. Iuvenalii called for intensification of their work prior to the Bishops Council scheduled for 2016.[33]

During the Soviet era, the Church could not canonize new martyrs. However, already in 1918, the All-Russian Local Council venerated the first of them.[34] In 1981, the Russian Orthodox Church Outside of Russia (ROCOR)—composed of Russian émigrés who regarded themselves as the true Russian Church, in contrast to a Moscow Patriarchate compromised by Sergianism (their term for Sergii's policy of political accommodation)—began canonizing new martyrs in anticipation of the millennium of Christianity in Rus' in 1988. In 1989, in the wake of *glasnost'* and the 1988 millennium celebrations, the Russian Church was able to canonize Patriarch Tikhon, although it could not publicly declare him a new confessor until the collapse of the Soviet Union two years later.

In 1992, the Church canonized seven of the earliest and most prominent new martyrs: Metropolitan Vladimir of Kiev (honored already in 1918 as the first martyred hierarch), Metropolitan Veniamin of Petrograd and three of his associates (falsely charged with withholding Church treasures demanded by the Bolsheviks), and Elizabeth Fedorovna Romanova and her personal attendant Barbara.[35] However, not until the Jubilee Council of Bishops in 2000 did commemoration of the new martyrs assume major proportions. On August 19 of that year, the Council of Bishops participated in the consecration of Moscow's Christ the Savior Cathedral, itself a symbol of the Church's death and resurrection. Russia's largest Orthodox church, it was constructed in the nineteenth century as a national memorial to the Russian people's victory over Napoleon, razed under Stalin, and rebuilt with President Yeltsin's vigorous support in the 1990s. The altar on the first level of the restored building (the "lower church") was dedicated to the new martyrs.

On the next day, the council established the Sobor (Council or Congregation) of the New Martyrs and Confessors of Russia Suffering for Christ, Both Known and Unknown, and canonized more than a thousand people who had suffered reprisals in the Communist era, including the royal family: Tsar Nicholas II and Alexandra; their daughters Olga, Tatiana, Maria, and Anastasia; and their son, Aleksei, whom the infamous Rasputin had tried to heal of hemophilia. The question of canonizing the royal family had proved controversial. On the one hand, many in the Church regard Nicholas as a pious believer. He and his wife had promoted construction of new churches, organization of Church social work, and the canonization and veneration of St. Serafim of Sarov, one of Russia's most popular saints. On the other hand, Church historians such as Mazyrin have seen Nicholas as an inept ruler. He had continued the synodal system that, to the thinking of many Church leaders today, had given the state too much control of the Church; he had allowed Rasputin, a self-proclaimed holy elder with no official Church credentials, into the royal family's inner circle; and his prosecution of the war against Germany had been disastrous. Mazyrin notes that Nicholas's abdication in February 1917 was widely welcomed, even in Church circles. And the Bolsheviks had executed Nicholas and his family as representatives of the old political order at a time that civil war was breaking out. They had not suffered specifically for their faith.

Patriarch Tikhon and other Church leaders had nevertheless continued to regard Nicholas as God's anointed protector of the Church, and the Bolsheviks' execution of him in July 1918 deeply shocked them. Patriarch Tikhon immediately ordered Church prayers for Nicholas's repose and spoke of his martyrdom.[36] In its 1981 canonizations, ROCOR designated Nicholas and the other members of his family martyrs and, after the fall of Communism, made canonization of the royal family a prerequisite for reunion with the Moscow Patriarchate.[37] After considerable research and discussion, the Russian Church's commission also approved their canonization—not, however, as "martyrs" but rather as "passion bearers." Commission members spoke of the remarkable piety that characterized Nicholas's final days: how he and his family prayed and sang hymns, accepted their fate as God's will, and showed love toward their captors.

Whatever the theological merits of canonizing the royal family, it was also a brilliant political compromise not only between ROCOR and the Moscow Patriarchate but also between conservative Church forces that idealized Orthodox tsars and those who called for guarding the Church's freedom from the state. Nicholas belonged to the new martyrs and confessors, but just barely.

In Orthodox Christianity, icons are more than illustrations; they are "windows into eternity." But they also reflect and communicate the Church's present-day self-understanding. The depiction of a saint—his or her posture and facial expression, clothing, and relation to other persons or objects in the icon—expresses moral ideals that the Church claims to embody and wishes to inculcate in its adherents. To be sure, icons are painted with a highly symbolic language that is subject to varying and sometimes conflicting interpretations. But the Church seeks to guard what it regards as a theologically correct interpretation. An icon should be commissioned and blessed by Church authorities; icon painters should work within historical canons; and the faithful should be guided by the official hymns and hagiographical accounts that the Church prepares to honor the saint in question.

The Jubilee Council icon of the new martyrs and confessors was commissioned by Metropolitan Iuvenalii and executed by leading representatives of St. Tikhon's University: rector Vladimir Vorob'ev, at the time a member of the Church's canonization commission; Aleksandr Saltykov, head of the department of art history; Maria Glebova, head of the department of icon painting; and three other women in her department. Vorob'ev and Saltykov personally presented the icon to Metropolitan Iuvenalii at the Jubilee Council. It now hangs in Christ the Savior Cathedral, and many other churches have commissioned copies.

The central section of the icon depicts 128 of the most prominent new martyrs and confessors against the backdrop of Christ the Savior Cathedral. Hierarchs stand around an altar table and cross. The altar table, its red cloths, and the cross symbolize Christ's passion, in which the martyrs participated. Tikhon, Petr, Kirill, and Agafangel are prominently placed at the center of the hierarchs and next to the altar table. Below them are the members of the royal family and several rows of parish priests, monks and nuns, laymen and laywomen, and even children and babies. Several rows in the rear include halos without faces as well as faces without names in the halos. They represent those martyrs not yet known to the Church or perhaps to be known only to

The *Icon of the New Martyrs and Confessors* (author's photograph)

God. The Church anticipated that more martyrs would be added by name to the great assembly in years to come, while others would never be identified.

The icon represents three categories of victims: those who were executed for their faith (martyrs), those who suffered severe persecution for their faith but were not executed (confessors), and those who, like the members of the royal family, did not suffer directly for their faith but nevertheless met execution in a Christian manner (passion bearers). Further, the icon demonstrates that all parts of the Church contributed martyrs. Whereas most Russian saints have been prominent rulers, hierarchs, or leaders of monasteries (and usually male), the new martyrs have been drawn primarily from the ranks of parish priests or deacons (60 percent), ordinary monks and nuns (9 percent), and laymen and laywomen (11 percent).

The word *sobor* can designate a cathedral building as well as a Church council. In the Nicene Creed, believers confess the *sobornuiu*—catholic, or universal—Church. In the nineteenth and twentieth centuries, great Russian thinkers debated the nature of *sobornost'*: the character of the Church as a living, organic body.[38] Today the new martyrs constitute a sobor because they represent the Church in its wholeness. Their suffering unites them in faithful witness to the God whose Son gave himself up on a cross, promising that life comes out of death for those who believe in him.

Christ heads this sobor, seated in glory at the top of the icon in the midst of a row of historic saints, among whom are representatives of the three kinds of political oppression experienced by the new martyrs: Metropolitan Philip, deposed and then killed by order of Ivan the Terrible in the sixteenth century (martyrs in the strict sense); Patriarch Job, who died in exile after being deposed by the False Dmitrii in the early seventeenth century (confessors); and Gleb and Boris, who were killed by a rival brother prince in the eleventh century (passion bearers—thereby providing historical precedent for canonizing the royal family). By including these historic saints, the icon places the new martyrs in a long history of suffering and witness.

The side panels depict fifteen scenes of Bolshevik persecution, including the arrest, trial, imprisonment, exile, and execution of Church leaders and the royal family; desecration of churches and relics; and suffering of ordinary believers. The faithful are depicted in bright colors and with peaceful expressions; in most of the panels, their persecutors appear as soldiers with the distinctive pointed caps of the revolutionary Red Army. The faithful offer signs of blessing, while the soldiers make threatening gestures and point their weapons at the helpless believers.

The inclusive character of the sobor is again apparent. While prominent Church leaders and the royal family are featured in eight panels, the other seven depict ordinary Church people. In one panel, soldiers fire on parishioners participating in a Church procession; in another, priests and laypeople stand before a firing squad at the Butovo killing field; in yet another, ordinary women are honored for their extraordinary efforts to preserve the faith while their bishops, priests, and sometimes husbands were being rounded up.

The icon painters adopted the distinctive style of the great fifteenth- and sixteenth-century iconographers Dionysius and Andrei Rublev, who strove to depict the saints as transfigured by eternity. The martyrs, while retaining their individual identity, have now been divinely glorified and are no longer subject to earthly decay. The icon only alludes to brutal persecution; nowhere does it depict blood or bodily decay. We see that the martyrs defied and defeated death. Their struggle against Communism belongs in the context of a larger historical, even cosmic battle between God and Satan, good and evil, in which God ultimately protects the Church.[39]

The renewal of the Church through the blood of the martyrs is closely related to the renewal of the nation. An official Church commentary on the icon of the new martyrs and confessors notes that the placement of Nicholas and his family beneath the altar table expresses the Orthodox understanding that civil authority is given by God through the Church. Rulers are account- able to God and should serve Church and society. By depicting the members of the royal family in the robes of ancient Byzantine royalty, the icon further represents the traditional Orthodox ideal of cooperation between Church and state for the good of the nation.

The theme of national renewal is further suggested by the thematic rela- tions between the icon of the new martyrs and the icon *The Feast of All Russian Saints*, composed in the 1930s by Maria Sokolova, a key figure in preserving ancient Russian canons of iconography.[40] The council of 1917–18 had established this holiday as a way to call the nation back to its great saints, past and present; it would need their guidance in the troubled days ahead. The Soviets responded by banning observance of the feast until Stalin's shift in religious policy in the 1940s.[41]

The Feast of All Russian Saints is dedicated to "the Most Blessed and Wise Ones Pleasing to God—All the Saints Shining Forth with Their Life in the Russian Land and Unceasingly Praying for Us." The icon of the new martyrs and confessors similarly suggests that the persecuted saints of the twentieth century illuminate the true Russia, a Holy Rus', in which all segments of the nation form a sobor of unity, peace, and mutual service. In the icon of the new martyrs, even the landscape participates in the nation's renewal. Rocks and trees radiate the same resplendent colors as the robes and vestments of the martyrs.[42]

The icon nevertheless reflects tensions in the Church's self-understanding. The whole Church is represented, yet the hierarchs are at the center and in robes more resplendent than those of the other martyrs. Moreover, the hierarchs are overrepresented proportionately (nearly 66 percent in the icon versus 11 percent of the canonizations of the Jubilee Council). The number of women in the icon, while corresponding to their percentage of the new martyrs (about 9 percent), cannot adequately represent their importance to Church life both during and after Communism.[43] Tension also lurks in the treatment of government. The icon sets forth both the ideal of the Christian ruler and the threat that evil rulers pose to the Church.

The icon's idealized picture of Church and national renewal is further complicated by what it omits. Only unintentionally does the icon allude to the Church's complicity with the Communist past; two of the hierarchs in the icon—Vasilii (Preobrazhenskii) and Iuvenalii (Maslovskii)—were "decanonized," that is, removed from the Church calendar in 2012, presumably because further research determined that they had made incriminating statements about themselves or others.[44] Moreover, the icon privileges Christian suffering; it omits reference to the millions of victims who died under Communism for reasons other than their faith, as when they resisted collectivization or succumbed to famine that resulted from the Bolsheviks' disastrous agricultural policies.

While dramatically representing values of Christian heroism and loyalty that the Church wishes to promote in Russian society today, the icon of the new martyrs obscures other lessons that I would draw from the Communist era. The icon emphasizes the traditional hierarchy of clergy and laity rather than democratic participation in Church affairs. By presenting the tsar as serving the Church, the icon fails to relate yet separate Church and state in a way that preserves the integrity of both. And the icon celebrates the Church as a victim of Communist oppression but leaves aside the Church's failures and mistakes, its compromises and fateful accommodations, in relating to the Soviet state.

The Church's hymns and hagiography in honor of the new martyrs, like the icon, tend toward Christian and Russian national triumphalism. A distinction is drawn between the (innocent, victimized) Russian people and those (betrayers of the people) who instigated evil. As in the icon, this struggle between good and evil is framed in cosmic terms. The persecutors are identified not specifically as Bolsheviks or Communists but rather as "the handymen of the devil," "godless ones," "godless rulers," or even "cruel wolves."[45]

Nevertheless, at key points the hymns and hagiography link national renewal to national repentance. In a hymn to the martyred Nicholas II, his venerators confess "our many departures from God in despising God's commandments and rebelling against the Lord and his anointed one [the tsar], which has brought God's wrath upon us. The blood of our brothers was spilled, the Russian people were banished to all ends of the earth, our churches were desecrated. . . . Taking all this to heart and with humble hearts of repentance, we cry out: Forgive us and have mercy on us, Lord, in your great mercy, purify us from our disobedience, and give our Russian land, which suffers because of its betrayal of the royal passion-bearers, forgiveness of sins, peace, and eternal mercy."[46]

Another hymn text asks Nicholas to intercede with God on the people's behalf. They need forgiveness for having allowed the tsar's murder.[47] Although God chose Russians to be his special people, they turned away from him. Here the Bolshevik victory is depicted not as the victimization of an innocent people but rather as divine punishment.[48] If Russians are truly repentant, they will cry out, "Lord, forgive the sinful Russian nation."[49]

The hymns express confidence that human repentance will be met by divine mercy. Sometimes they see national renewal as a matter of restoring an Orthodox monarch.[50] More generally, they ask God to save "the Russian land and its people . . . and glorify them for eternal praise of the Lord's name and true service to him."[51] The hymn in honor of the sobor of the new martyrs and confessors asks them to "preserve our nation in Orthodoxy until the end of the ages."[52] Similarly, the hymn to the new martyr Sergii (Lebedev) asks God "to confirm Holy Rus' in Orthodoxy to the end of the ages."[53] Renewal of the Church and the nation go hand in hand.

Historian Elizabeth Castelli has argued that Christian communities throughout the ages have venerated martyrs in order to create a collective memory and identity.[54] Recent studies of Russian saints have noted that up to the fifteenth century the Church primarily canonized princes, hierarchs, and abbots who established Orthodoxy's preeminent place among the eastern Slavs, such as Prince Vladimir (whose baptism in 988 traditionally marks the beginning of Orthodoxy in Rus') and Metropolitan Petr (who in 1325 expanded the power of the Russian Church by moving his see from Vladimir to Moscow).[55]

In the fifteenth century, canonizations were often associated with figures — such as Sergius of Radonezh (founder of the Holy Trinity–St. Sergius Lavra) and Metropolitan Aleksii (briefly, state regent) — who had blessed Russian princes in their battles against the Tatar occupiers. The rise of Muscovy and its Church in the sixteenth and seventeenth centuries was reflected in canonization of Russian abbots and monks who had enhanced the Church's spiritual and political authority, such as Zosima and Savatii, the founders of the famous Solovki Monastery.[56]

After Peter the Great replaced the Patriarchate with a Holy Synod in 1721, few canonizations took place, in part because state and Church authorities wanted to discourage popular practices of veneration that resisted Church control and that seemed "superstitious." Those figures who were canonized were primarily Church hierarchs whose relics, as in the case of Mitrofan of Voronezh (a seventeenth-century bishop), were determined by the synod to have genuine miracle-working powers.[57] This honoring of Church hierarchs of the past also reflected the hierarchs' close relationship to the state in the present.

With the rise of Communism, only a handful of uncontroversial canonizations took place, and even then not until the 1970s.[58] During the

Gorbachev years, however, and in conjunction with the 1988 celebration of the millennium of Christianity in Russia, the Church was able to canonize nine persons from the fourteenth to nineteenth centuries who had made major contributions to Russian culture and nationhood, including Dmitrii Donskoi (the fourteenth-century prince who defeated the Mongols), Andrei Rublev (the master icon painter), Amvrosii (one of the holy elders of the famous Optina Pustyn' Monastery), and Ksenia of St. Petersburg (a popular female "fool for Christ").[59]

The current canonization of martyrs under Communism reflects the Church's aspirations to exercise social influence today. The new martyrs are impressive not only for their individual achievements but also in their numbers. In the first thousand years of its existence, the Russian Orthodox Church canonized approximately four hundred saints.[60] The number of new martyrs and confessors is now about two thousand (the one thousand glorified at the Jubilee Council and another thousand since then). In just twelve years (2000–2012), the total number of Russian saints increased by five times.

Almost every day of the Church year now has new martyrs and confessors assigned to it; anyone attending services on a martyr's or confessor's memorial day (the anniversary of his or her death) will hear the person's name included in the Church's prayers for and to the saints. The number of new martyrs and confessors on a given day often exceeds that of older saints. A priest may devote his sermon to a martyr's or confessor's witness, especially if the person was a leading Church figure. Worshippers may venerate not only their icons but also their relics (if available, since the Bolsheviks typically buried their victims in unmarked mass graves).

The new martyrs and confessors shape Church life today also by their historical proximity. Beloved historic Orthodox saints such as St. Nicholas of Myra (the forebear of the West's jolly old St. Nicholas) or St. George belong to a distant and mythologized past. The new martyrs and confessors are closer, more real. They left behind photographs, diaries, and personal effects; their signatures appear at the bottom of protocols in the files of the secret police; and their descendants or spiritual children often initiate the process of canonization. Parishes and monasteries feature those new martyrs and confessors who are part of their specific history.

Although some of these saints are widely venerated, many are known only to a local community. The Church of the Mother of God, the Joy of All Sufferers, in St. Petersburg honors Father Georgii Serbarinov, who served as its priest from 1912 until his arrest and exile in 1922; he was martyred in 1938 and glorified in 2003.[61] Father Georgii's icon hangs on the church iconostasis, and the parish has turned his living quarters next to the church into a small museum. The iconostasis of Moscow's Church of Sophia, the Wisdom of God, includes Father Aleksandr Andreev, who served as the parish's priest from 1923 until his arrest in 1929; he was executed in 1937 and included in the sobor of 2000.[62]

The prominence not only of ordinary parish priests but also of women among the new martyrs and confessors reflects the Church's efforts to present itself today as a people's Church that comprehends every part of Russian society. There are twice as many women among the new martyrs and confessors as among traditional Russian saints. Among victims of Soviet repression included in Church research databases but not (yet?) canonized, the percentage of women is even higher; for example, eight times more nuns than monks suffered for their faith, corresponding roughly to the larger number of female monastics at that time.[63]

While Church power today remains concentrated in the hands of the male hierarchy, the new martyrs and confessors help the Church present itself as valuing women and their crucial role in renewing parishes and monasteries. Women not only constitute the majority of regular worshippers but also provide key leadership for Church educational and social initiatives, such as teaching Sunday school and visiting hospitalized parishioners. The Church seems to say that, if all parts of the Church contributed to the great congregation of new martyrs, all parts of the Church are now needed for its renewal.

Values that the Church wishes to bring into Russian society today are also reflected in the criteria that its canonization commission has established for identifying new martyrs and confessors. Especially important are moral uprightness, truth telling, and love of enemies. The canonization commission has emphasized that while the new martyrs and confessors gave their ultimate loyalty to God and the Church, they refused to allow the state to brand them as political opponents. This focus on the martyrs' freedom in spiritual matters together with their loyalty to the state in earthly affairs corresponds closely to Aleksandr Mazyrin's interpretation of Patriarch Tikhon's political course.

The protocol of March 22, 1938, included in the Church's official biography of the nun Maria (Tseitlin), is representative of many:

> —What are your convictions and views about the Soviet government?
> —As a believer, I understand every government to be from God, and it does not concern me who has power at the present moment in the Soviet Union.
> —As a monastic have you been subject to repression from the side of the Soviet government?
> —As a monastic I have been deprived of a right to vote.
> —You were arrested for counterrevolutionary activities that you undertook with other nuns of the Novodevichii Monastery. The interrogation requires a truthful response.
> —I went into an apartment with the nuns Evdokia (Golovanova) and Matrona (Lipatova). I said that a difficult time has arrived . . . [and] believers are discontent with the Soviet government. . . . The Soviet government is robbing monasteries [and] closing churches, but soon they will pay with their lives [and] everyone will then know that there is a God.[64]

The secretary of the canonization commission until 2015, Igumen Damaskin (Orlovskii), has written that evidence of a person's refusal to call the Church a counterrevolutionary organization is an essential criterion for canonization. A second and equally important criterion is a person's refusal to accuse other believers of being counterrevolutionary.[65] Orlovskii has argued that a person's ability to withstand interrogators' relentless pressure to implicate others was an indication of his or her extraordinary spiritual state. Conversely, those who succumbed to such pressures demonstrated that they still lacked spiritual discipline: "If a person fell, it was because of his problems with his own passions, not because of the agents of the secret police. . . . In his heart was an ideal other than Christ."[66]

A third criterion for canonization is the moral purity of a person over his or her lifetime. In the ancient church, people who led a sordid life before converting to Christianity could still be counted as martyrs if they died for their faith. Orlovskii argues that the victims of Bolshevik persecution, in contrast, had been baptized and raised in a Christian culture. They had no excuse for severe moral lapses. The canonization commission therefore considers not only secret police archives but also diocesan records, letters, journals, and testimonies of acquaintances that testify to person's general character.[67] Orlovskii cites the example of a bishop who died heroically but will not be canonized because he was known to have a drinking problem.[68]

Moral perfection, however, is not a prerequisite for canonization. Indeed, only Christ and his Mother are regarded by the Church as never having sinned.[69] In some cases, a martyr may have incorrectly represented Church dogma but, because he or she did not promote heresy or schism, is not disqualified from canonization. In other cases, people such as Kirill (Smirnov), who briefly broke eucharistic fellowship with Sergii, could nevertheless be canonized because they had worked ultimately not to divide the Church but rather to call it back to its true spiritual unity. In still other cases, persons have been canonized who implicated themselves or others in counterrevolutionary activities but later repented.[70]

It is striking to me that the Russian Orthodox Church in the past often canonized warrior saints, such as Alexander Nevskii and Dmitrii Donskoi, who fought with arms to save the nation from foreign invaders. In contrast, the new martyrs and confessors rejected violent resistance. They distinguished themselves by their love for their persecutors. The new martyrs saw the Bolsheviks not as enemies but rather as brothers and sisters who in many cases had been baptized and had attended Church schools or seminaries, as did Lenin and Stalin. The new martyrs and confessors called the Bolsheviks back to their true identity as Russians shaped by an Orthodox culture and its moral values.[71]

I have often heard Church leaders say that the new martyrs teach the Church similar lessons today. Active believers sometimes wonder what to

think of the many Russians who call themselves Orthodox but do not participate in Church life, perhaps living according to secular values that are
contrary to Church teaching or even opposing the Church and its new
social influence. The new martyrs teach today's believers that they will best
win their neighbors to the Church and the nation's Orthodox legacy by
defending the truth of Orthodox belief and practice while reaching out to
society in love. And so, in their prayers to Nicholas II, believers ask for the
strength not to return evil with evil but rather to grow in humility, meek-
ness, and love.[72]

As with its efforts in education and social ministries, the Church's veneration of the martyrs is a matter not simply of internal ecclesiastical affairs but
also of shaping contemporary social life and national identity.[73] Nicholas II,
whom Metropolitan Hilarion of the Church's Department of External
Church Relations regards as one of the most important of the new martyrs,
represents a prerevolutionary Russia in which Orthodoxy was an essential
part of the nation's identity.[74] Nicholas's venerators call for a Russian government that will support the Church and Orthodox moral values.[75] They hope
for restoration of Holy Rus'.

The royal family represents the Orthodox ideal of Church-state cooperation. But veneration of Patriarch Tikhon—whose body was hidden after his
death and then rediscovered and declared incorrupt in 1992, an event that
Bishop Tikhon (Shevkunov) of the Sretenskii Monastery witnessed (and
recounts in *Everyday Saints*)—lifts up a different ideal: the restoration of
Church authority and tradition in the face of state domination and secularization. Tikhon reminds the Church that it must be prepared to defend its
values against state and society if they turn against it.

Other martyrs remind the Church of other moral ideals. Bishop Hilarion
(Troitskii) is honored for his theological acumen and political courage. A
member of the 1917–18 council and a strong advocate for restoring the
Patriarchate and electing Tikhon, Hilarion in 1923 drove out the
Renovationists who had seized control of the Sretenskii Monastery, and
Tikhon appointed him abbot.[76] Soon afterward, however, Hilarion was
arrested and exiled, and six years later he died under the harsh conditions of

imprisonment. On his feast day in 2011, I attended the Divine Liturgy in the Sretenskii Monastery. Although it was a weekday, the church was packed. The priests were dressed in resplendent red vestments symbolizing the blood of the martyrs; parishioners also wore red; and Hilarion's icon and relics were framed by dark red roses.[77]

Although the royal family, Tikhon, and Hilarion all have their faithful venerators, the most popular new martyr is Elizabeth Fedorovna Romanova. The royal family stands in the center of the icon of the new martyrs and confessors, but Elizabeth and Barbara, immediately to their left, command visual prominence by virtue of their bright white robes. Elizabeth is honored

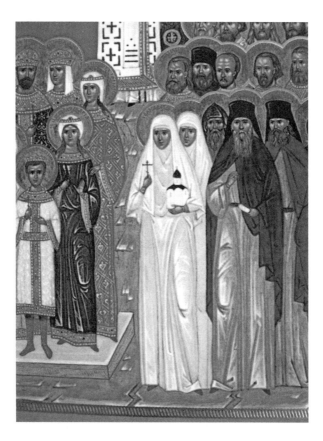

St. Elizabeth and the royal family, detail from the *Icon of the New Martyrs and Confessors* (author's photograph)

across the Church, as demonstrated by the prominent place of her icon on the iconostasis both in the conservative parish of St. Nicholas in Pyzhakh and in the Church of Cosmas and Damian, which aligns itself with the progressive legacy of Father Aleksandr Men'. Moreover, Elizabeth's is one of only a handful of icons of new martyrs available from Sofrino, the Church-operated firm that produces high-quality paper icons for a mass market. On my visits to Moscow, I have often seen in believers' homes not only icons of Elizabeth but also framed colored photographs that feature her as a highly attractive young princess—my Russian Orthodox friends like to say that she was one of Europe's most beautiful women.

Arrested soon after the Revolution and transported to the Urals, Elizabeth and Barbara reportedly met their deaths with deep confidence in God's providential care. On July 18, 1918, only a day after the execution of the royal family, they and several nobles were thrown into a mine shaft to die. Elizabeth and Barbara were still wearing their white habits. Though wounded by the fall, Elizabeth survived for a time. She is reputed to have sung hymns as she cared for another of the victims. When members of the White Army recovered her body several months later, they reported that the fingers of her right hand were joined together for making the sign of the cross. In 2005, thousands of people lined up to venerate these fingers when they went "on tour" to several cities in Russia.

Like Nicholas II, Tikhon, and Hilarion, Elizabeth represents key Orthodox values to both Church and nation. Her loyalty to Russia, even though she was German by birth and upbringing, exemplifies the patriotism that Russians should have for their native land. Just as she converted from Lutheranism to Orthodoxy by personal choice and persuasion, so, too, Russians today should consciously understand, practice, and affirm their Orthodoxy rather than treat it as merely an inherited national-cultural identity. In giving her life for others, Elizabeth represents a faith that goes beyond performing religious rituals to demonstrating loving service to those on the margins of society. Her innocent suffering at the hands of the Bolsheviks reminds believers today to expect social rejection and even persecution. She forgave her enemies; so, too, should believers today forgive their opponents. Elizabeth was beautiful, and her venerators should also cultivate earthly beauty rather than retreating into the gloomy introspection that sometimes seems to be the mark of Russian Orthodox piety.

Elizabeth does not fit the stereotypical picture of a Russian Orthodox woman. In the Soviet era, the popular imagination in both East and West associated Orthodoxy with impoverished old women, *babushki*, in drab clothes who came to church to light candles. Elizabeth, in contrast, was attractive, self-confident, and professionally talented, and she organized and managed a major church institution. She reflects the important role of Russian Orthodox women today as active, initiating Church leaders, even if only men serve as priests and hierarchs.[78]

When Elizabeth's admirers examine themselves against her purity, they see how far they fall short. She—along with Nicholas II, Tikhon, Hilarion, and other new martyrs and confessors—is a great historic example that inspires and admonishes. But, like all the Church's saints, she is also somehow still live today. When I asked the abbess at the Martha and Mary Monastery what it was like to work and worship where Elizabeth herself once did, she replied, "As we walk the halls, clean the rooms, and gather in her church, we hear her voice and feel her presence."[79]

I have come to see the Church's exhibitions, historical research, icons, hymns, and hagiography as part of a cohesive understanding of Church and society in the new Russia. The Church memorializes the new martyrs, it seems to me, as innocent victims of worldly evil. Their inner freedom and selfless love stand in pointed contrast to a prerevolutionary Church that had become too concerned with earthly matters, a Sergiian Church that traded away spiritual freedom for institutional survival, and a secular Soviet Russia that turned against the Church and rejected the nation's historic Orthodox identity. Even in death, the new martyrs and confessors seem to call Church and nation to reform themselves—to honor the martyrs' and confessors' sacrifice by recovering Orthodoxy.

The presence and witness of the new martyrs is most poignant to me at sites of suffering that have become Church memorials. Like other means of honoring the new martyrs, these memorial sites lift up values of truth telling and love that I see the Church asking post-Communist society to embody.[80]

The Church's commemorative efforts do not replace the state's honoring of the nation's sacrifices in World War II or the memorialization work of Memorial and other nongovernmental organizations. But the Church adds to them a narrative of suffering that it believes to be an essential part of the nation's identity today.

Ground drenched in the blood of the saints exudes holiness. One major memorial site is the Butovo killing field on the southern outskirts of Moscow, where in the 1930s the secret police executed tens of thousands of people, including at least one thousand Church leaders. In the 1990s the Ministry of Security, uncertain what to do with the territory, offered it to the Church. In 1995–96, a small wooden chapel was erected on the site; in 2007, a large two-story stone church was completed and dedicated to the new martyrs and confessors.[81] The Divine Liturgy, with its commemoration of the new martyrs and confessors, is celebrated daily.

The lower church of the new edifice is dedicated to the suffering of the new martyrs. Visitors descend a staircase into a narthex. On the walls are the victims' mug shots, and glass cases hold personal items recovered from the mass graves: shoes, shreds of clothing, and bullets. In the nave hang more than fifty icons with the 320 victims of Butovo who have been canonized; the saints are arranged in groups according to the date of their execution. The upper church is dedicated to the spiritual victory of the new martyrs. A copy of the *Icon of the New Martyrs and Confessors* is complemented by icons dedicated specifically to the Butovo martyrs, the royal family, and Patriarch Tikhon. Scenes of Bolshevik persecution frame the icons of Christ and Mary, the Mother of God, on the iconostasis before the central altar.

Across the road from the stone church lies the killing field. At its gates, large tablets display mug shots and document how many victims died each year. When pilgrims enter the grounds, they walk among the thirteen mounds that mark the mass graves. Huge memorial crosses rise above sites where excavations of the graves have taken place. Since 2000, the patriarch has annually celebrated an outdoor liturgy. I was among the approximately three thousand faithful worshippers on a rainy day in May 2012. The place of suffering had been momentarily transformed by springtime. Daffodils were blooming on the mass graves. Apple trees with white blossoms stood on their perimeter. In his sermon, Patriarch Kirill declared that the new martyrs remind us that God strengthens us just when we feel most weak and helpless.

A second major memorial site is at the Solovetskii Monastery in Russia's far north. Founded in the fifteenth century, the monastery was transformed in the 1920s into the first Soviet gulag. In tragic irony, Solovki specialized in holding Christians. Thousands of prisoners were executed or died of broken health. In the summer, some were tied naked to trees and eaten alive by mosquitoes. In the winter, others were left to freeze to death. Today monastic life has been reestablished. Pilgrims pray with the monks and visit the sites of suffering. An exhibit in the major monastery complex and a small museum in the nearby village trace life in the gulag.[82] The nearby island of Anzer offers additional sites of commemoration: a chapel in honor of the martyred Bishop Peter (Sverev), the Church of the Crucifixion, the Church of the Resurrection, and the tree that has grown into the shape of a cross.[83]

A third major area for memorialization lies in and around Ekaterinburg, where the royal family spent its final days. The Church on the Blood stands on the site of the house in which Nicholas and his family were held prisoner and in whose basement they were executed on July 17, 1918. Every year, tens of thousands of believers travel to the city on the eve of the anniversary. When the memorial liturgy in the Church on the Blood concludes in the wee hours of the morning, the pilgrims walk, banners and crosses in hand, nearly five hours and twenty-five miles to a monastery on the site of the mine shafts in which the bodies were first dumped. And there again they pray and sing.

Other memorial sites have local significance. At Levashova, near St. Petersburg, the secret police secretly buried thousands of their victims. Since the fall of Communism, various religious groups, local government authorities, and nongovernmental organizations have cooperated in turning it into a memorial site. Dozens of crosses have been placed in the ground or attached to trees. Orthodox believers regularly gather to offer prayers for the dead.[84] In Moscow, the Sretenskii Monastery is building a huge cathedral "on the blood of the martyrs," those unknown believers whom the secret police tortured and killed on the monastery grounds near the secret police headquarters on the Lubianka.[85]

Like the Church's 2011 exhibition in Moscow's Manezh, these memorial sites bring the new martyrs before a wider public. The Church seems to be asking Russians to acknowledge the magnitude of the nation's crimes under Communism—unprecedented in Christian history—and ensure that such things never happen again.[86] The state has the duty to protect and honor the Church. Perhaps the Church hopes, however, for something even more: that the new martyrs and confessors will inspire Russians to enter actively into its life. If people today will embrace the Church and receive its sacraments, they will acquire the spiritual freedom of the new martyrs and confessors. I would add that only this kind of freedom can ultimately sustain Russians individually and as a nation.

The Orthodox Church is one of the few voices in contemporary Russia that tells people not to repress this difficult era of their national history but rather to examine it and draw lessons for today. Nevertheless, as with its initiatives in education and social work, the Church's commemoration of the new martyrs is more limited in impact than some Church leaders—or I—might like. The Church's narrative of faithful suffering easily disappears amid the wider turmoil and chaos of twentieth-century Russia that secular historians write about. Even within the Church, many believers know or care little about the Church's history of suffering. As several Church historians told me, interest in the new martyrs and confessors is mostly for a few "enthusiasts."

One problem is that commemoration of the new martyrs and confessors has been initiated from above, in contrast to canonizing a saint only after a long period of popular veneration. In traditional practice, a person was initially honored locally, especially for miracles that he or she performed during his or her lifetime or at his or her gravesite after death. Often, what was decisive for securing the cult was the discovery after a period of time that a holy person's body had not decayed but remained "incorruptible." Eventually, a local parish or monastery would commemorate the person in its liturgical services. If the cult of the saint spread in popularity, the local bishop would sanction it and even propose to the patriarch or the Holy Synod that the person be formally canonized. The cult of the new martyrs and confessors, however, has been driven primarily by Church hierarchs and especially the Church's canonization commission, some of whose members have had privileged access to secret police archives. Popular experience of a saint's miracle-working power or veneration of an incorrupt body has rarely played a role. And although the body of Patriarch Tikhon is reputed to be incorruptible, Tikhon was canonized prior to discovery of his body.

While some of the new martyrs have won popular veneration, traditional saints with a reputation for helping people with a particular need receive much more attention. St. Nicholas of Myra is especially popular because he helps with financial matters, as does St. Panteleimon with illness and physical disability. When I venerate the relics of Patriarch Tikhon at the Donskoi Monastery or those of Elizabeth at the Martha and Mary Monastery, I rarely see anyone else. The story is different at the women's Monastery of the Holy Intercession of the Mother of God in Moscow. People often wait for hours to venerate the relics of Matrona, a blind and crippled peasant woman who lived through the Soviet era; became famous for her piety, clairvoyance, and ability to heal people; and, by some popular accounts, received Stalin as a visitor and persuaded him to repent of his religious persecutions. In St. Petersburg, people line up for St. Ksenia.[87] Both of these female saints are beloved for their assistance especially to women in need of work, love, housing, or resolution of other practical problems.

Few of the new martyrs or confessors have such a reputation. An exception is Luke (Voino-Iasenetskii) of Crimea, a skillful surgeon who eventually became a priest and monk and in 1923 was secretly ordained as a bishop. Arrested and exiled three times, Luke won a reputation for his medical care of fellow prisoners, his inspiring preaching, and his deep spiritual counsel. Today St. Elizabeth inspires by her moral example, but people are more apt to turn to Luke the physician (like the Evangelist Luke) when they need healing.[88] Andrei Kuraev's school textbook *The Foundations of Orthodox Culture* mentions the Church's suffering under Communism only in relation to Bishop Luke, although Kuraev values him more for his life "free of egoism" than for his powers of healing.[89] Kuraev makes no mention of other new martyrs or confessors.

While the memorial sites in Ekaterinburg elicit popular devotion, Solovki and Butovo have other profiles. For centuries Solovki has been renowned for its powerful spiritual life in a remote location with extraordinary natural beauty. The years of suffering under Communism are just one small episode in its glorious and tragic history. Today, pilgrims from Moscow and St. Petersburg again make the arduous journey north by train to the town of Kem', and by boat across the sometimes rough waters of the White Sea. As pilgrims approach the main island, they crowd onto the deck and watch the huge monastery walls rise up out of the water. Butovo, in contrast, is easily accessible from Moscow, but Orthodox believers more often make pilgrimage to a major working monastery, where they can pray before miracle-working icons and relics, labor with the monks or nuns in the gardens, and briefly glimpse heaven on earth. Butovo, which Patriarch Aleksii II once called "the Russian Golgotha," perhaps repels as much as it attracts.[90] Even the annual patriarchal worship service draws fewer people than a major liturgy at Christ the Savior Cathedral. Those who care about Butovo are often relatives of the people who lie in its mass graves; some descendants learned of parents' or grandparents' fate only when Church researchers identified them as being among Butovo's victims. Butovo also draws as many Western visitors as Russians, as evidenced by its website, which offers information in Russian, English, French, German, Italian, and Spanish.

It will take many years, if ever, for veneration of the new martyrs and confessors to embed itself in popular devotional practice. My friend Valia regularly attends services at the Church of the Dormition in the Novodevichii Monastery and venerates its miracle-working icon of the Theotokos. When I read that the church also had an icon of the monastery's new martyrs from the Soviet era, I asked her to guide me to it. But she had never noticed it and could not help me.[91] Other believers honor the new martyrs and confessors but assign them a minor place within a much longer history of Church suffering and triumph, as at the Holy Trinity–St. Sergius Monastery in Sergiev Posad, where great monks of the past are venerated and the relics of the fourteenth-century founder, St. Sergius, attract thousands of pilgrims. Still others see the new martyrs and confessors as essential to Orthodox identity, as at the monasteries dedicated to St. Elizabeth or at St. Tikhon's University, where the new martyrs orient a new generation of Orthodox leaders in Church and society.

Nevertheless, even those who honor the new martyrs do not always agree about their moral significance. Patriarch Kirill has declared that the new martyrs teach Church and nation to stand against new idols of "wealth, consumption, power, money and pleasure." Just as the nation suffered for worshipping the false gods of Bolshevism, Russians today are destroying their lives by losing "their chastity, purity, their righteousness and inner integrity." The new martyrs and confessors challenge Russia not to abandon "faith and the Christian tradition. . . . As a nation, we must have spiritual strength—we do not have a right not to, not in the face of the sacrifices of our fathers and grandfathers."[92]

Father Aleksandr Shargunov at St. Nicholas in Pyzhakh interprets this battle against secularism in more apocalyptic terms. While the Church is currently not persecuted as it was in the 1920s and 1930s, he sees a new era of martyrdom approaching. Father Aleksandr argues that post-Communist Russian society suffers under mass violence, alcoholism, and sexual deviation because it has never truly repented of the crimes of the Communist era. The forces of secularity reject the notion of a divine moral order, reduce religion to a private affair, and oppose the Church's efforts to influence society.[93] For Father Aleksandr, only if the Church cultivates love, peace, joy, and unity in its inner life will it succeed in representing the values of the new martyrs to a hostile society.[94]

For priest and historian Georgii Mitrofanov, the major lesson of the twentieth century is the importance of clearly separating Church and state. He argues that many Russians turned against the Church in the early twentieth century because of its close alliance with the state. Today, he believes, the principal problem facing the Church is not persecution from antireligious forces but rather the temptation once again to seek a privileged status in society at the cost of dependence on the state or simply satisfying "consumer demand" for miracles. For Father Georgii, the martyrs and confessors of the underground church of the Soviet era teach the Church today not to compromise itself with state or society but rather to cultivate intimate, caring community in its life.[95]

In 1931, Russian historian Georgii Fedotov presciently wrote words that at the time could not be published in his own country: "The revolution ignited by the fire of Russia's sins has called forth an unprecedented flowering of holiness: the holiness of the martyrs. . . . Today the persecuted little flock of the Russian Church has been driven out of Russian life. . . . But a time is coming when the Russian Church will stand before the task of baptizing a godless Russia anew. Then the Church will have the responsibility for the nation's destiny . . . and our experience of the service of the ancient Russian saints to society will have unexpected relevance."[96]

Today leading Church figures such as Patriarch Kirill, Father Shargunov, and Father Mitrofanov, like Fedotov, see the new martyrs and confessors as key to Russian identity, even if most Russians—and most Russian believers— do not. For these Church leaders, the Church's experience of persecution under Communism frames a way of viewing the world and politics that has implications for the Church and the nation. The broad contours of what I would call a distinctive Russian Orthodox "theology of culture" is emerging.

In my view, the new martyrs and confessors have taught the Russian Church to see the world as a place in which powerful social forces seek to displace God. These powers—sometimes carelessly labeled "secularism"— deny the existence of any transcendent spiritual or moral order. They tell humans that they and their earthly well-being are all that matter. Communism demonstrated, however, that the result of such an ideology is a chaotic world in which people fight for material prosperity and harm themselves by sensual self-indulgence. Violence and enmity undermine social and national life.

To my thinking, the Russian Church offers an alternative. It calls people into intimate fellowship and cultivates their spiritual freedom. Through the Church and especially its liturgical life, people learn to transcend selfish desires, to care for each other, and to live in truth and love. The Church's different members become one body. While the Church has a hierarchical order in which bishops, priests, monastics, and laypeople play different roles, no one part should dominate the others in a way that denies their essential place in the whole. But the Church can offer people this kind of freedom only if it remains free in itself. Whenever the Church has allowed the state to dictate its doctrines, practices, or clerical appointments—as under Sergii—the Church has inevitably compromised itself. The Church cannot be the Church if it becomes a mere agent of the state.

To be sure, I agree with the traditional Orthodox affirmation that secular government has been divinely instituted to provide for earthly peace and justice. But it must do so in correspondence with the moral order that God has established and to which the Church points. Rulers, moreover, have no sacred status. Bolshevism demonstrated how secular government can become demonic. I believe that the new martyrs ask the Church continually to determine where it may have contributed to, or failed to prevent, such evils. Such a Church will confront rulers with the truth about their misdeeds, warn them of God's judgment, and therefore be prepared for the state to persecute it.

At the same time, I hope for a Church that will take the path of long-suffering love. Rather than seeking to overthrow oppressive rulers by violent means, such a Church will do all that it can to remind them that they, too, are children of God whom the Church seeks to win back to their true identity. This kind of Church will commit itself to every member of society. It will strive to establish its loving presence in every area of social life—education, social work, the arts, the military, business, and politics. Rather than aligning itself with one party or group, such a Church will welcome all.

For me, the new martyrs deserve the nation's veneration because they represent the highest values of Russian culture as shaped by Orthodoxy: love, honesty, and moral integrity. Whether the nation—or even the broader Church—will offer this veneration is another matter. And will the Church propagate the "spiritual freedom" that I have described, or will it choose instead to try to manipulate people and what they believe and do? The question remains as relevant today as when it was raised by Dostoyevsky in his parable of the Grand Inquisitor. For the Church is never simply a spiritual reality but also an earthly institution constantly tempted to worship itself, a

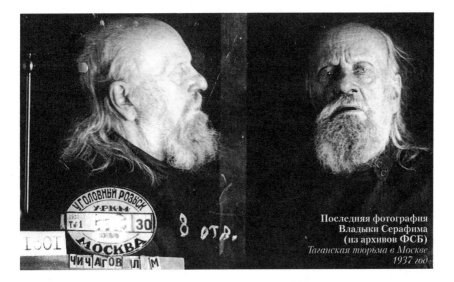

Последняя фотография
Владыки Серафима
(из архивов ФСБ)
Таганская тюрьма в Москве
1937 год

Bishop Serafim Chichagov shortly before his execution (WikiCommons, from the files of the Soviet secret police)

truth that the Russian Orthodox Church does not often acknowledge in its rush to blame "secularism" or "the West" for Russia's problems.

Nevertheless, the witness of the new martyrs and confessors defies my Western temptation to become cynical about Russia and its Church. The mug shots that the secret police left behind forbid it. When I look into the eyes of Butovo's victims—Bishop Serafim (Chichagov) (d. December 11, 1937), the nun Anna Makandina (d. March 14, 1938), or the priest Sergii (Lebedev) (d. March 22, 1938)—I see terror and exhaustion but also confidence that a higher, better reality will ultimately triumph.[97] The new martyrs challenge me to think carefully again about the ancient Christian adage of "in but not of the world" and what it might mean for a Russian Church that so often links itself to the nation yet claims a destiny beyond it.

SIX

Parish Life

While Moscow's Church of Sophia, the Wisdom of God, in the Middle Gardens cannot represent every Russian parish, it nevertheless illustrates the remarkable development of Church life since the collapse of Communism.[1] Under the leadership of a talented priest, Father Vladimir Volgin, the Church of Sophia has today become one of Moscow's leading parishes. The parish's story is also his.[2]

Father Vladimir represents a generation of Church leaders that emerged as Communism gasped its last breaths in the 1980s. Volgin was born in 1949 in Moscow. His parents were nonbelievers, but his grandfather, a schoolteacher, had served as a lay overseer of an Orthodox parish.[3] The grandfather was nearly executed in the early 1920s when he refused to hand over Church treasures. He escaped only because the Soviet *troika* (three-member kangaroo court) that heard his case included a former pupil who had mercy on him.

Volgin reports that he began to have a sense of God when he was a boy. Because he was sickly and unable to play with other children, he spent a great deal of time alone thinking about questions of life and death. When he was six, he saw a dead body at a funeral and began wondering what was on the other side of life. By the time he was eighteen, he was thinking about becoming a priest, and two years later he was baptized, although, he says, he continued to struggle with his worldly ambitions to be a writer and poet. During these years, Volgin neither wore his faith on his sleeve nor hid it. He was a member of the local *komsomol*, the Communist youth organization, and even served as editor of its newspaper. He barely escaped trouble, however. Once he left behind on his school desk a piece of paper on which he had written about his Easter faith. When a classmate found it and turned it in, the school director ordered Volgin to his office. Only because a highly placed friend quickly intervened did the threatened conversation never take place.

Volgin's spiritual development was deeply influenced by his interaction with some of Russia's last great holy elders. In the late 1960s, Volgin began visiting the Pskov-Pecherskii Monastery and became a spiritual son of Ioann (Krest'iankin). Father Ioann foresaw that Volgin would eventually marry and enter the priesthood, and Volgin regularly consulted him until Ioann's death in 2006.[4] Volgin initially studied film production in Moscow, but in 1972 began to serve as an altar helper in several churches, including that of Aleksandr Men'. In 1979, the bishop of Kursk and Belgorod, Khrizostom (Martishkin), ordained Volgin and assigned him to a small village church. Volgin remembers well the antireligious mood of the time. If he went outside in his priestly robes on May 1, International Workers' Day, people looked at him with disdain.

State authorities did not allow Volgin to attend seminary. Eventually, however, he was able to enroll in correspondence courses at the Theological Seminary and Academy in the Holy Trinity–St. Sergius Monastery north of Moscow. In 1995, Patriarch Aleksii II assigned him to the Church of Sophia, one of Moscow's great historic churches. Located just south of the Kremlin along the Moscow River, the church had been closed by the Bolsheviks in the 1920s and used alternately as a drinking club, dormitory, and scientific laboratory. In the 1960s, the state designated the building a historical monument and began but never completed restoration work. When the property was returned to the Church in 1992, it was in such poor condition that for nearly a decade services had to be held in a small church in the nearby bell tower.[5]

Today Volgin is almost speechless when he thinks of all that has transpired. Only eighty-five people gathered for the first Easter Vigil in 1995. In recent years more than two thousand have attended, and over eight hundred have received the Eucharist. In 1995, Father Volgin was the sole priest. Today the parish has six priests, four deacons, and a full schedule of weekly services. And while renovation work continues inside, the exterior of the church again stands in glory, with its tall bell tower proudly proclaiming the Church's public presence in the new Moscow.

The Church of Sophia's many programs are impressive. Since 2013, a Sunday school in the parish house behind the church has attracted fifty or more children. A group of young people meets every Thursday evening. Thirty to forty participants regularly gather around tables in a side aisle of the church nave, drink tea, play games, and discuss questions of faith. Until 2015, Father Boris Potapov led the group; now he and many of his youth group members have helped reestablish parish life in the Church of the Transfiguration in northeast Moscow.

While no adult classes have been taking place weekly, the parish has regularly organized evening meetings with speakers on such topics as Orthodox missionary work in other countries or Orthodox understandings of marriage and family. An English-language club has been meeting on Monday evenings. Father Vladimir's commitment to religious education is further evident in his practice of distributing theological books to parishioners after the liturgy on special holy days. His recent gifts have included a volume of writings by St. John of Kronstadt and a Church Slavonic dictionary. In 2012, the parish began offering a fellowship time after the Sunday liturgy; people gather outside, drink hot tea, and eat freshly baked *pirozhki*, even in subzero winter temperatures. Social ministries are still developing, such as gathering winter clothing for the poor and homeless. Talented laypeople assist with the church website.

Father Volgin has oversight of not only the Church of Sophia but also Moscow's Church of the Holy Martyr Antipa, five local chapels, and a new church in a gated community on the outskirts of Moscow with a resort hotel and exclusive residences for government officials and wealthy businesspeople. This new church is modeled after a famous twelfth-century edifice in the town of Pereslavl-Zaleskii, northwest of Moscow, and is named after the three greatest Orthodox theologians of the fourth century, Basil, Gregory, and John Chrysostom, because, in Father Volgin's words, "They were great preachers, and Russia needs great preachers today."[6] Volgin also led efforts to rebuild the Church of the Transfiguration; recently, Church hierarchs have asked him to help redevelop several other parishes.

Volgin's lectures on theology and Church life are regularly broadcast on Orthodox radio and television stations, and he moves easily in powerful Church, state, and social circles. Nevertheless, Father Volgin's first love is priestly service in his home parish. Those who attend the Church of Sophia do not for the most part come from the immediate neighborhood. Many of them are young, well-educated professionals, Russia's new intelligentsia. They have children, drive to church from the "suburbs," and enjoy each other's company. But it is especially Father Volgin's charismatic preaching and gracious spiritual counsel that attracts them.

Father Volgin's understanding of parish life is informed by the religious vision of culture that I see as characteristic of the Russian Orthodox Church as a whole today. Like many other Church leaders, Volgin regards the Russian "soul" as essentially Orthodox. He says that even in the early 1980s, when he experienced public ridicule, local bureaucrats would quietly ask him to baptize their children. The Church never died under Communism.

Father Vladimir believes that God has guided Russia throughout its long but tragic history. Volgin notes that after Stalin changed his antireligious policies in 1941–43, the Church was able to conduct public processions with its famous icons around Moscow, St. Petersburg, Stalingrad, and other cities. The Germans, he says, suddenly sensed that a new power was arrayed against them, and the tides of war shifted. Later, Khrushchev persecuted the Church, but in 1964, three months after he ordered the destruction of Moscow's Church of the Transfiguration, he was deposed, an act of divine justice, says Volgin. Today the church has been rebuilt on its historic site.

According to Father Vladimir, God used Communism to punish Russia for its faithlessness to its Orthodox heritage. But now a new era has dawned. Having brought Russia and its Church back to life, God is asking Russian Orthodox believers to call the whole world to repentance and spiritual renewal. Volgin is not concerned that many Russians seem to be Orthodox in name only. For him it is enough that they are sympathetic to the Church, and that the Church now has the opportunity to invite them into its life.

Volgin sees himself—and other leading priests today—as heirs of Russia's great tradition of holy elders, although he in no way claims to manifest their extraordinary holiness. The holy elders once communicated God's blessing to the nation through visions and miracles; today, as in the past, the Church's priests also offer Russians divine blessing but in more modest ways, such as through faithfully celebrating the sacraments. The holy elders called the nation back to its Orthodox foundations; priests do so today through their preaching. The greatest of the holy elders have passed away, but those priests, such as Father Volgin, who knew them personally, explicate their writings and promote their example.

In Volgin's view, the locus of Russia's salvation has moved from the remote monastery to the city parish, from the holy elder to the priest-preacher, and from individuals with extraordinary spiritual abilities to religious communities that sustain everyday life together. Volgin especially wants to draw Russians into Eucharist fellowship. In a world that is increasingly secular and even antireligious, it is remarkable to him that people come to church at all, and he uses the sacrament of confession, which the Russian Church normally requires of people prior to each reception of Communion, as an opportunity to show forth the Church's mercy rather than to throw up roadblocks to their participation in Church life. Volgin longs for people to experience the divine love and power that, he believes, communion with Christ alone can give. He tells people, in the traditional language of Orthodoxy, that the Eucharist unites them not only with Christ's humanity but also with his divinity. Those who receive the Church's sacraments enter a process of deification. Volgin himself celebrates the Divine Liturgy and receives the Eucharist at least three times a week.

According to Volgin, deeper eucharistic fellowship will renew not only the Church but also the entire nation. In recent years, Father Volgin has celebrated a midnight liturgy in the Church of Sophia on New Year's Eve. When I attended in 2011–12, an extraordinary conjunction of events occurred. In the midst of the Eucharist prayers, just as Volgin began to declare Christ's words of institution—"This is my body, broken for you"—a huge fireworks display went off across the river on Red Square, and the entire church shook. Two Russias seemed momentarily to collide—the one was holy, quiet, and prayerful; the other seemed shrill, demanding, and secular.

Volgin hoped that as his parishioners partook of the Eucharist, they would show forth their distinctive spiritual and moral values to a society that would otherwise spend the night in drunken revelry. In his sermon at the end of the liturgy, he noted that the Soviets had once used the New Year's celebrations to replace Christmas (January 7 in the Orthodox calendar). He added that the December 31–January 1 celebration poses difficulties to Orthodox believers, because it falls during Advent, when they are fasting from meat, dairy products, and alcohol. Raising his voice to a crescendo, Volgin publicly called on the government to move the national celebration of New Year's to January 14, which is January 1 in the Old Style calendar that Russian Orthodox believers use.

Two other examples further underline Volgin's hope that eucharistic fellowship will transform Church and nation. Volgin told me that establishing a parish in the gated community would help bring Orthodox values into the lives of the policy makers and business leaders who live in the area. And he spoke in a similar way about the Church's presence in the television broadcasting center in Ostankino. In 2006, Mikhail Shubin, the general manager of the Ostankino complex, approached Volgin about constructing a chapel.[7] Russia has a long tradition of housing chapels in schools, universities, hospitals, prisons, factories, and public buildings. As many as twenty-five thousand such chapels once existed in the Russian Empire.[8] Today many older buildings in Moscow or St. Petersburg still have large halls or meeting rooms that once served as chapels, but only a few have been reclaimed for their original purpose. In some cases, as in St. Petersburg's Mariinskii Theatre complex, the Church has been allowed to erect a temporary iconostasis in the former chapel space and celebrate the liturgy on Sundays or holy days, while the room serves secular purposes during the week.

As a Soviet project, however, Ostankino had never had a chapel, and Shubin's proposal initially met considerable opposition. As in many Western nations, people who work in the media industry often prize artistic and journalistic freedom and creativity, regarding religious bodies with suspicion.

Moreover, some people questioned why the Orthodox Church should be privileged with an official presence in what is a secular entity. Nevertheless, four hundred employees eventually signed a petition in support of a chapel. Shubin speaks of the constant stress that people in the television industry experience: immediate deadlines and heavy workloads that they carry late into the night. Ostankino provides for their material well-being with shops, cafeterias, and beauty salons—and now ministers to their spiritual needs as well. The church was consecrated in September 2010 and is open around the clock for people to light candles and pray. Father Volgin and his staff provide leadership for the liturgy, which is celebrated at 9:30 a.m. five days a week. While attendance at the liturgy when I visited in 2012 was small, only twenty to thirty people, the very existence of the church was of tremendous importance to Father Volgin as a symbol of the new Russia. He greeted several people by name, and they asked his blessing.

Father Volgin has lived through a period of tremendous growth in Church numbers and influence in Russian society. Despite low rates of active participation in Church life, he sees impressive progress. "A decade ago, it was 2 percent of the population, now it is already 5 percent," he once told me. He seems confident that the upward trend will continue as more and more Russians claim Orthodoxy as an essential dimension of their personal and national identity. Volgin places this renewal of the Russian Church in an apocalyptic framework, however. He remembers that the holy elders, like some conservative Christians in other parts of the world, believed that the end-time was approaching. They pointed to the gathering of Jews into Israel, the movement toward a world government, and growing immorality in Western societies. And for Father Volgin, the cessation of holy eldership may be yet another sign that the end is near. China may soon invade Siberia. Christians may face new persecutions. He wants the Church to welcome every person who comes to it, and to strengthen pepole through confession and Eucharist to make the same kind of faithful witness to Christ and his way of life as did the Russian martyrs of the twentieth century.

Father Volgin and the Church of Sophia represent key aspects of parish life in Russia's major churches today. Many rural parishes are in decline while large city parishes are growing. The fastest-growing cohort in the Russian Orthodox Church consists of young, well-educated, urban professionals, as at Moscow's Church of Sophia.⁹ And even though the word *parish* (*prikhod*) continues to be used, the parish principle has broken down in urban areas. People once attended the church in their immediate neighborhood. Today they select a church on the basis of what appeals to them, such as the personality of the priest, an atmosphere of love and compassion, or attractive programs in education or social work.

While the figure of the "charismatic priest" has never been absent from Russian Orthodoxy, it has become increasingly prominent in post-Communist Russia and especially Moscow. The canonization of John of Kronstadt in 1990 lifted up the Church's contemporary ideal of parish life. John won fame as an inspiring preacher, spiritual counselor, and organizer of Church social work. He had so many spiritual children that he often offered a general confession and absolution of sins in the Divine Liturgy immediately before the celebration of the Eucharist, because he did not have time to confess all of them personally.¹⁰

Like Volgin, some of Moscow's other "charismatic priests" claim authority from holy elders. Vladimir Vorob'ev, Bishop Panteleimon (Shatov), and Dmitrii Smirnov were spiritual children of Father Pavel (Troitskii), whom they regard as a holy man of extraordinary prophetic vision and spiritual wisdom.¹¹ Bishop Tikhon (Shevkunov) and Aleksei Uminskii, like Father Volgin, received spiritual guidance from Ioann (Krest'iankin). Aleksandr Shargunov at the Church of St. Nicholas in Pyzhakh had brief contact with other holy elders and proudly notes his parish's historic connections to St. Elizabeth (Romanova), who herself sought counsel from several of Russia's great holy elders.¹²

The charismatic priest typically has major responsibilities beyond the parish: Vorob'ev is rector of St. Tikhon's University; Shatov is head of the Church's department of social ministries; Smirnov is head of the patriarchal department for relations with the armed forces; Bishop Tikhon is head of the patriarchal department for culture; Shargunov is a professor at the Moscow Theological Seminary and Academy; and Uminskii is the spiritual father of a prestigious Orthodox high school in Moscow.

Their charisma attracts not only an older generation of Russians that remained faithful to Orthodoxy during Soviet times but also the nation's new intelligentsia: business and political leaders, educators and artists. These people are used to taking personal initiative in their secular work and often seek out a talented priest to help them organize Church-related projects. A woman in Father Volgin's parish asked him to help her organize a school for girls. The head of an antiabortion organization turned to Dmitrii Smirnov for help in finding office space.

These charismatic priests are remarkable not only as Church leaders but also for their commitment to two major liturgical changes that increasingly characterize the post-Soviet Church. The first is the emphasis on inspirational preaching. With important exceptions, such as Father Aleksandr Men', Russian Orthodoxy has not been known for great preachers. It has rarely produced someone of the stature of Billy Graham or Martin Luther King Jr. Russian Orthodox priests sometimes give no sermon at all. If they do, it may come at the end of the service, almost as an afterthought. Careful biblical exegesis and application of biblical insights to contemporary life, so central to Western Protestantism, seem less important in Russian Orthodox preaching, where the focus more often is on the saints and their moral example. Today, however, seminary training emphasizes biblical interpretation and homiletics. And young priests tell me that every liturgy should include a sermon.

The charismatic priests in Moscow demonstrate this new prominence of preaching in Church life. Audio recordings of Father Volgin's sermons are posted on the parish website; collections of Aleksandr Shargunov's sermons are regularly published, such as his Lenten meditations entitled *Before the Cross and the Gospel*.[13] An Orthodox calendar with spiritual readings for each day of the year uses selections from Dmitrii Smirnov's sermons.[14] And as we have noted, many of the stories in *Everyday Saints* first appeared in sermons that Bishop Tikhon preached at Sretenskii.

An emphasis on frequent reception of the Eucharist is the second major liturgical change in Russian Orthodox Church life. Prior to the revolution, many Russians communed only once a year. Today long lines form in these model parishes both for making confession of sin and for receiving the eucharistic elements afterward. Parishioners are encouraged to think of Communion not simply as a matter of the individual's relationship to God but also as a way of life in a community of believers.

Because the Orthodox Church has traditionally understood the liturgy as the principal means of transmitting Christian faith, these new emphases on preaching and frequent Communion signal important changes within the Church's very self-conception. The Church becomes more than an institution that dispenses sacramental grace to individual believers. It is a communion of "ordinary saints" who share each other's everyday joys and concerns and reach out in love to a needy, suffering world.

Some conservative Orthodox "dissenters" view these new emphases as an effort by the hierarchy to "Protestantize" the Church. They prefer an Orthodoxy characterized by personal spirituality or "mystical" experiences with holy items—such as miracle-working icons or sacred springs. While Father Volgin and others regard preaching and the Eucharist as central to Christian faith, they do not deny the legitimacy of a "popular Orthodoxy" outside of the Church's walls. Preaching and the Eucharist, however, are key for shaping a community of believers who can relate the Church's faith to contemporary social realities. In urban areas in Russia, as in other parts of the world, people increasingly look to the Church for a supportive community that will help them overcome the anonymity and moral confusion of everyday life. Preaching and the Eucharist have become central to Church life because they draw people together into a common vision of life. These believers want to help each other live in an Orthodox way amid a world in which identity and moral values seem up for grabs.

The emphasis on the Eucharist and eucharistic community has raised anew basic questions about how a person should prepare for Communion. Prior to the October Revolution and during the Soviet era, infrequent reception of the Eucharist was matched by extensive preparation beforehand: sacramental confession of sin before a spiritual father, a three-day (or longer) fast (from meat and dairy products), a complete fast from food and drink from midnight until reception, and recitation of a long series of prayers.[15] These practices arose in part because of the strong influence of monasticism on

Church life historically, and continued during the Soviet era with the added concern that priests could not assume that parishioners had basic grounding in Church teaching and practice.[16] Since the fall of Communism, priests such as Father Vladimir Vorob'ev have argued that Orthodox believers should recover the earliest Christian ideal: reception of the Eucharist every Lord's Day. In the ancient church, confession of sin before a priest was not a prerequisite for receiving the Eucharist except in cases where a person had committed a severe ("mortal") sin.

Vorob'ev contends that those members of a parish who with the guidance of a spiritual father are striving faithfully to live as Christians, including receiving the Eucharist regularly, need not make sacramental confession of their sins prior to each Communion. The Eucharist itself offers forgiveness of sin. Faithful believers will make regular sacramental confession of sin, but at a frequency agreed upon with their spiritual father.[17] Vorob'ev, however, supports stricter measures for people who have not been educated and nurtured in the Orthodox faith and have not learned how to examine their sins carefully. He rejects the practice in some large parishes of reading a general confession of sin when time does not permit individual confession. He insists that eucharistic fellowship demands serious preparation and discipline.

Other Church leaders, such as Metropolitan Hilarion (Alfeev), have joined Vorob'ev in encouraging a rethinking of the relation of confession and Eucharist. Hilarion cites North American Orthodox theologian Alexander Schmemann, who observed that the sacrament of confession of sin has too often been reduced to "a ticket to Communion." Hilarion also notes that the different autocephalous (that is, self-governing) Orthodox Churches handle preparation for, and frequency of, receiving the Eucharist differently. The traditional Russian pattern is not the only one.[18]

In 2015, after several years of discussion, the Church's bishops approved the document "The Participation of the Faithful in the Eucharist."[19] The document acknowledges that many believers today wish to receive the Eucharist more frequently. Although the work emphasizes the continuing need for careful preparation with help of a spiritual father, including confession of sin prior to reception of each Eucharist, it calls for making this preparation more meaningful. Believers should have one spiritual father rather than moving around from one to another. Confession should take place prior to the worship service rather than in the course of it. Those wishing to commune should participate in the entire service rather than arriving late or leaving early. Moreover, confession should be sincere and reach deep into one's conscience rather than obsessing about trivialities. As a priest once said to me, "Ninety percent of what I hear is sheer 'rubbish.' People confess about eating meat on Friday or momentarily losing their cool with a spouse. They don't know how to recognize deeper problems, such as trusting more in power and money than in God, or getting so busy that they no longer notice others' needs."

At two points, the 2015 document allows greater flexibility than was typical in prerevolutionary practice. Believers who are observing all of the Church's regular fast days may, but are not required to, observe an additional fast prior to receiving the Eucharist. And in the case of someone who wishes to partake of Communion several times in the course of one week, for example, during Bright Week (that is, Easter week), a priest may require only one sacramental confession.

Father Vorob'ev has argued that the inability of many baptized believers in 1917 to resist Communism was a result of not regularly receiving the Eucharist. Today, he says, believers who live a deeply eucharistic life and experience the parish as a eucharistic fellowship live differently from people who merely call themselves Orthodox. The Eucharist strengthens them in sexual purity and marital faithfulness, a desire for children and therefore a rejection of abortion, and a concern for the physical well-being of themselves and others.[20] And those values are good not only for Christians but also for the nation as a whole.

Nevertheless, the challenges to shaping a parish as a eucharistic fellowship are significant, even in Moscow's model parishes. "Community" remains elusive, even where preaching is strong and people regularly receive Communion. In response, a Church commission has been established to examine "contemporary problems of parish and community life." At a theology conference at St. Tikhon's University in 2011, the commission's director, Archbishop Mitrofan (Iurchuk), chaired sessions on such topics as "lessons for parish life from Russian Orthodox churches in western Europe," "the relation of parish life to Church social ministry," "the efforts of the 1917–18 Local Church Council to renew parish life," and "the continuing impact of state-imposed parish reform during the Khrushchev era on parish life today."

Conference participants identified three crises in contemporary parish life. First, many people have a commercial relationship to the Church. What they want from the Church is not fellowship but rather "religious services"—baptisms, weddings, funerals, prayers for deceased loved ones, and priestly blessings—for which the parish has a set charge. This commercial relationship is exacerbated by the limited financial resources of most parishes. They receive no money from the Patriarchate or diocese; on the contrary, they are required to direct a considerable part of their income to the hierarchy. Fees for priestly services are a major source of revenue for everyday parish expenses. And for major renovation projects, priests have to find wealthy sponsors.

As I listened to the discussion, I remembered my Protestant fascination in seeing Russians drive their cars into church courtyards and pay the priests to pray over the machines and sprinkle them with holy water. I had also noticed that most churches have a counter at the back where candles are organized according to size and price. Although the Church hierarchy has asked parishes to provide candles without charge, most churches communicate that a "donation" is nevertheless expected.

The second crisis in parish life that the conference identified is the breakdown of family life. Father Vorob'ev expressed concern at the widespread use of abortion and birth control in Russian society as well as the high rates of divorce. He noted that one rarely sees families at the Divine Liturgy, and that few families sustain an Orthodox way of life at home. A related problem is that parishioners typically do not regard the church as a spiritual family. They may attend the Divine Liturgy for years yet never get to know the people around them. Especially in large city parishes, people are constantly dropping in and out of Church life. Or they may move from one church to another. Moreover, parishes do not maintain membership rolls, and priests often have little sense of who belongs to the parish or who is missing.

The third crisis relates to the persistence of a "Soviet mentality" in many parishes. During the Soviet era, parish life became individualistic. Parishioners often avoided socializing with each other because they did not know who might be an informant. Conference participants also noted that until recent reforms in parish governance, the priest, despite his central importance to parish life, was banned from the parish council. Under Khrushchev, power was concentrated in the hands of a lay elder, often friendly to the state—a measure that enabled state authorities to keep priests under surveillance, close parishes, or divert parish monies into their own pockets.[21]

Even with greater control over parish decisions today, priests encounter other remnants of "Soviet" thinking. Conference participants said that parishioners typically look to the priest to make major or even minor life decisions for them rather than taking responsibility for themselves. At the end of a liturgy, people line up to speak to the priest to request financial assistance, exceptions to fasting during Lent, help in casting out demons from mentally disturbed family members, or resolution of other practical problems. And I had noticed that people were often willing to wait for an hour or longer to have two or three minutes with the priest; it was not unusual for the line to be so long that he had to leave before everyone had gotten a turn.

Conference participants also saw a "Soviet mentality" in popular grumbling about the Church. Despite deference to the clergy in public, many people are critical of the Church in private. I, too, had heard Russians complain that priests are wealthy, privileged, and indifferent to the financial plight of ordinary believers. While these charges were often unjustified, they did reflect resentment about the social and political connections that separate priests from many of their parishioners. Someone such as Vladimir Volgin lives modestly but nevertheless has a car and private driver—in part because Moscow traffic is so bad that he would otherwise spend an inordinate amount of time just getting from one place to another. He has two apartments—one in central Moscow; the other, a gift from friends, in the gated community with the new church—again, not because he lives profligately but in order to retreat from the city after a long day of pastoral service. And while priests in smaller city parishes have more modest resources, they, too, can count on a steady stream of income, unlike many of their parishioners.

Conference participants noted that the gap between priest and parishioner manifests itself in decision-making processes. The model parishes in Moscow in which talented parishioners work closely with their priest to shape parish life are still the exception. Too often priests seem remote, inaccessible, and unfriendly. Especially in large city parishes, they carry heavy administrative loads. Those priests who successfully rebuild parish life are frequently assigned additional churches and diocesan responsibilities that allow them even less time with their parishioners.

Mark (Arndt), the Church's archbishop of Berlin-Germany and Great Britain, elicited great interest from the audience when he described the active leadership role that laypeople assume in Orthodox parishes in the West. Conference participants peppered him with questions about how to realize such ideals as "shared governance" in Russian parishes. The priests in attendance did not seem concerned about guarding their power. Rather, they expressed how desperately they sought fuller lay involvement.

The vision of parish life that I have been sketching out involves more than having people show up for the Eucharist. Rather, they will participate actively in all aspects of worship, develop bonds of Christian friendship and service, and work together to order a parish's life and mission. An associate to the head of the Church's department of missionary work told me that formation of genuine "community" was the Church's most pressing need in contemporary Russia. This man spoke admiringly of the work of the late Father Alexander Schmemann, the famous rector of St. Vladimir's Orthodox Seminary in New York and a prolific author. Although Schmemann has sometimes been the object of fundamentalist Orthodox ire in Russia—several years ago, extremist monks publicly burned his books—other Orthodox believers have admired his efforts to save the Church from an excessively legalistic, ritualistic, and otherworldly spirit. The publication of his diaries in Russia in 2005 was welcomed by a younger generation of Orthodox intellectuals, who found his honesty about the institutional

Church and its flaws refreshing. They long for their Church leaders to be as forthright as was Schmemann about the need to reform Orthodoxy.[22]

In addition, these Russians have been attracted to Schmemann's vision of an Orthodoxy that cultivates the divine transfiguration of all reality. For Schmemann the liturgy and especially the Eucharist invite the worshipper to experience the mystical intersection of eternity with time, what Schmemann calls the redemption of time. In such moments, he says, ordinary time seems to stop and be filled with an extraordinary "presence" that awakens people to wonder and thanksgiving at the very gift of life. Schmemann believes the Church should be a community that continually draws people together out of everyday, secular experience into this alternative way of seeing the world around them.[23]

Young Church intellectuals have also been inspired by the example of the catacomb or underground church of the Soviet era, whose members seemed to shape and experience authentic Christian community. If the Church today were oriented by such figures as Aleksandr Men', it might not be large and powerful, say his admirers, but it would be vital, because its priests and laypeople would be dedicated to catechization, social outreach, theological reflection, and eucharistic fellowship.[24]

For the Church to transform itself from a "religious services" provider for individual consumers into a "communion of saints" freely encouraging each other's spiritual growth inevitably raises the question of the language of the liturgy. Whereas most Christians today celebrate worship in the vernacular, many Orthodox churches still use ancient liturgical languages— in Russia Church Slavonic, rooted in the translation work of the Greek missionaries to the Slavs, Cyril and Methodius, in the ninth century. Church Slavonic last received extensive revision in the seventeenth century under the controversial Patriarch Nikon. While Church Slavonic has deeply influenced Russian literary language, it has significant differences from spoken Russian. My Russian friends tell me that in Church worship services they can generally follow the chanted gospel readings but little of the Apostolic Letters, Psalms, selections from the Old Testament, or ancient hymns. Some parishes offer instruction in Church Slavonic, but only a few enthusiasts devote the time and energy needed for mastering it.[25] And I discovered that Church people in both past and present have had different attitudes toward Church Slavonic.

The great Local Council of 1917–18 in Moscow was considering liturgical reforms that might have resulted in establishing Russian as a liturgical language, but the revolution brought an abrupt end to the council's work.[26] In the following years, the so-called Renovationists promoted use of Russian in the liturgy but discredited themselves and their agenda in the eyes of many because of their alliance with the Bolsheviks.[27] To this day, proposals to translate and celebrate the liturgy into Russian meet popular resistance. A Moscow priest told me that Patriarch Kirill quietly approached him and other leading priests several years ago with a proposal to allow parishes to use a Russian liturgy. They advised him against it on the grounds that parishioners would rise up in arms, and the proposal was never made public. As one scholar has noted, popular religious culture appreciates antiquated language because it nostalgically calls "to mind a period of more secure religious and linguistic norms."[28]

Some Orthodox believers still remember the scandal around a liberal Moscow priest, Father Georgii Kochetkov, who after the fall of Communism introduced a Russian liturgy and other reforms into his parish.[29] An opposition group from Bishop Tikhon's Sretenskii Monastery and Father Shargunov's Church of St. Nicholas in Pyzhakh invaded Kochetkov's church and confronted him and his supporters during the Sunday Divine Liturgy. In the aftermath of the incident, Kochetkov was transferred to the church at the Novodevichii Monastery, where he was prohibited from preaching but allowed to help celebrate the Eucharist. Some of his supporters followed him. While he would use Church Slavonic in the liturgy, they would follow along with a Russian translation in their hands. More traditional worshippers resented the newcomers and avoided the service.

I discovered that Church people have differing attitudes toward Church Slavonic. Some Russian Orthodox believers assert that they do not have to understand the words of the liturgy in order to participate in it. They say that a Russian liturgy would distract them. For them, the Church Slavonic contributes to a mystical atmosphere that draws them into deep inner prayer.

Other believers, often intellectuals, value the beauty and precision of this ancient language, perhaps in the way that some Catholics regard the Latin Mass—or some Anglicans the *Book of Common Prayer*. For these Orthodox believers, Russian translations fail to capture the richness of the Church Slavonic. Still other Orthodox worshippers see Church Slavonic as an indispensable part of Church tradition. The liturgy just would not sound right to them in another language, even if they do not understand the Church Slavonic.

A growing number of Church leaders argue, however, that the language of the liturgy must change if the Church is to reach Russians today. These "reformers" do not regard themselves as opposing Church tradition or authority. Rather, they want to recover liturgy in its root meaning as "the work of the people." Moreover, as several priests told me, change need not be disruptive if it takes place gradually and incrementally. As a first step priests could read the gospel in contemporary Russian while leaving the rest of the liturgy in Church Slavonic. Even those who love Church Slavonic acknowledge a need for modest revisions to render it more understandable to contemporary Russians. They support modernizing older texts, particularly Church Slavonic words that are confusing or unfamiliar to contemporary Russians. And they approve a recent trend in hymn writing to use a simplified and Russified form of Church Slavonic.

Some parishes are adopting measures to promote fuller congregational participation in the Divine Liturgy. Up to now, the pattern in most parishes has been for a choir to take the lead in singing the people's responses. Worshippers join in only for the Symbol of Faith (the Nicene Creed), the Lord's Prayer, and perhaps the hymns of magnification at the end of the Divine Liturgy. However, at the Church of the Annunciation in Mytishshy, just north of Moscow, parish helpers hand out copies of the day's hymns to worshippers and invite them to sing along. In other parishes, priests encourage people to bring along prayer books in which the Church Slavonic and the Russian translation are printed in parallel.

The goal of greater congregational participation raises practical questions about acoustics and sight lines. The situation in Father Volgin's

Church of Sophia was typical. Several hundred people typically attended the Sunday Divine Liturgy. Those in the rear could see little of what was happening at the front and had a hard time hearing the priests. The church has now installed loudspeakers, but many people prefer the purity of the naked human voice, and not all believe that laypeople should hear what their tradition has called the priest's "secret prayers," which are recited behind the iconostasis. Solutions remain elusive, and the sermon at the Church of Sophia continues to take place without amplification.

Other aspects of Orthodox worship further complicate congregational participation. Churches with more than one priest typically offer worshippers the opportunity to make confession of sin as the Sunday Divine Liturgy is taking place. In the Church of Sophia, long lines would form, and as people waited their turn, they could hear the liturgy but not actively participate in it. The length of Orthodox worship may also discourage full participation. The Divine Liturgy in Russia is typically two and a half hours. Saturday night vespers last three to four hours. It is not surprising that people feel free to drop in or leave as they will. Sometimes even a priest will not stay to the very end of a service if other priests can cover for him.

The greatest challenge to congregational participation, however, is the seeming indifference of many believers. Some come to church primarily to receive the Eucharist and leave immediately afterward. For others, worship is less a communal event than the backdrop for their personal prayers. And in other cases, people are distracted from worship because they are more interested in buying candles, lighting them before icons, or ordering prayers for loved ones at the rear counter. During a Divine Liturgy, they may insist on elbowing their way through a crowded church to a particular icon that they wish to venerate. As my wife once said, Russian Orthodox worship can be a contact sport.

On a typical Sunday morning in a large Moscow parish, babies are crying, and mothers are trying to keep young children busy with coloring books and stuffed animals. People cannot resist the temptation to chat, especially when they are waiting for the priests to finish their Communion behind the iconostasis. More than once, Father Volgin expressed frustration at people's lack of reverence. He would send a young deacon out to announce in his resonant baritone voice, "Brothers and sisters, please do not talk during the service. You should be praying, not socializing."

Sociologist Robert Wuthnow has written of the importance of small groups for North American church life.[30] In post-Soviet Russia, Orthodox parishes, too, are organizing fellowship opportunities. Coffee hours and discussion groups are just the beginning; some parishes have developed innovative programs of pastoral care, such as Moscow's Church of St. Nicholas in Novokuznetsakh, headed by Father Vorob'ev, which has a fund to help parishioners if they need a surgery that they cannot afford.

The Church's educational and social initiatives are often as important for the bonds of friendship that they create among participants as for their primary goals of intellectual formation or social outreach. I think again of the thirty regular participants in the Friday evening Bible study at Sretenskii Monastery or the sisterhood in St. Petersburg whose members support each other emotionally in their difficult and sometimes unpleasant tasks in the hospital. I could say the same thing about the Orthodox youth groups that I have visited. In Russia, as in the West, people are looking to the Church for loving community.

And, as anywhere in the world, people seeking community tend to gather around strong personalities—in Russian Orthodoxy, this is often a charismatic priest, monk, or nun. Perhaps because priests and monastics seem closer to God and somehow different from the rest of us, they fascinate ordinary believers, who seek a holy person who will give them time, attention, and counsel. Father Volgin told me that in a large parish such as his, each priest has his own following. People come to that particular priest to confess their sins and ask for advice. Again and again, I saw how a personal relationship to a priest, monk, or nun could be decisive for a person's connection to the Church. Father Iosaf (Shvetsov), a monk at the famous Pskov-Pecherskii Monastery, does not live in cloistered isolation from the world but rather reaches out actively to people in the wider community. While he has a cell within the monastery walls, he often hosts guests in a nearby house, where his mother lived until her death. When I visited, he was cooking a big meal for members of a local soccer club for which he has become an unofficial chaplain.

In Darna, a small town east of Moscow, I became acquainted with Father Konstantin Volkov. Father Konstantin serves on his diocese's commission for relations with the armed forces and has a special interest in veteran affairs. A group of former army officers, including veterans of the Afghanistan conflict, have found their way to him and become key benefactors of the parish. Some regularly drive all the way from Moscow, a couple hours' drive. Darna, like many Russian Orthodox parishes, has a small dining room and kitchen for the priest and his staff. It is a special honor for the priest to invite others to the table, as does Father Konstantin when his army friends arrive.

I experienced the same kind of hospitality from Father Volgin. I had known his personal assistant for several years, and when my family moved to Moscow for a year, she offered to try to set up a meeting with him. A couple of weeks later, she reported with delight, "Father Vladimir wants to invite you to his apartment in the gated community." When my wife and I arrived, Father Volgin greeted us with a traditional threefold Russian kiss on the cheeks. The combined living and dining area was crammed full of old furniture, oversized scholarly books, and beautiful icons. His cook had prepared a wonderful Russian meal with soup, several fresh salads, fish, potatoes, and wine. Father Volgin listened carefully to me and gave an extensive answer to each of my questions. At the end of the evening, he went back to his bedroom and rummaged through boxes of gifts that he has received over the years but now passes on to special guests. His present to us was a magnificent hand-painted icon of St. Panteleimon. Then he kissed us again, blessed us with the sign of the cross, and sent us on our way home.

Personal contact with a priest and experience of loving community among parishioners are difficult to achieve in large parishes. Since the fall of Communism, a major priority for the Church has been building more churches and training more priests. A related concern has been to divide large dioceses into smaller ones, so that bishops will have more time for personal contact with their priests and parishes and be honored as pastoral leaders rather than be viewed as mere Church bureaucrats. One significant effort to expand parish life is an initiative announced in 2011, in cooperation with the mayor's office, to construct two hundred new churches in Moscow. Smaller building programs are also under way in St. Petersburg and other cities.

One of the great if ambiguous achievements of the Soviet Union was the extraordinarily rapid transformation of the nation into an urban industrial society. If at the beginning of the century, 80 percent of Russians were rural peasants, by 1985, 70 percent were city dwellers.[31] In 1900, Moscow had just under 1 million inhabitants. By 2000, the number had risen to nearly 10 million—and stands at 12–15 million today.[32] St. Petersburg grew from 1.4 million to nearly 5 million (and 8 million today).[33] In both cities, hundreds of square miles of empty fields were turned into residential apartment complexes. While the growing cities sometimes swallowed up villages that had an old church, most of the new suburbs had no church at all. The few churches that remained open were in the old city center, distant—sometimes ten to twelve miles—from where most people now lived.

With the fall of Communism, the Church moved quickly to reestablish parishes. The challenges, however, were formidable. Historic churches that had been used for other purposes—as gymnasiums, factories, museums, or schools—often required extensive renovation and reconstruction, as in the case of the Church of Sophia. In other cases, reestablishing Church life was complicated by property disputes. The Bolsheviks had often given away the historic property of a parish, and the new occupants resisted Church efforts to move them out after the end of Communism. The Sretenskii Monastery spent years recovering land on which the Soviets had built a school. The challenges involved in building new churches have been equally formidable. Cities such as Moscow are tightly zoned. Most land within the city is already taken for one purpose or another. Vacant lots are rare. Any land that is available is extremely expensive and coveted by commercial interests. Only close cooperation with city officials has enabled the Church to develop new parishes in urban areas.

The town of Reutov, on the southeastern outskirts of Moscow, illustrates the political dynamics of new church construction. Before the October Revolution, Reutov was a small factory town with only thirty-three hundred inhabitants. During the Soviet era, it grew rapidly and became a center of arms production.[34] Today Reutov has more than eighty-four thousand residents and continues to boom. The town has attracted research and development firms while also becoming a bedroom community to Moscow. For most of its history, Reutov had only a small Orthodox house of prayer, and because it lacked a consecrated altar, the Eucharist could not be celebrated. Since the fall of Communism, however, two large churches have been constructed. In both cases, the mayor at the time, Aleksandr Khodyrev, played a key role. As he surveyed local needs for housing, schools, healthcare facilities, and cultural centers, he argued that the city administration should also support people's religious interests.

Khodyrev, who identifies himself as an Orthodox believer, although he does not often attend services, took the initiative in planning and supporting construction of both of Reutov's churches: in 1999, the Church of the Kazan Icon of the Mother of God and, a decade later, the Trinity Church. In 2008, Khodyrev led a procession of fifteen hundred people from the Church of the Kazan Icon to the site on which the Trinity Church would be built.[35] In 2012, he attended the first Divine Liturgy in Trinity's lower church while construction continued on the upper church.[36] To provide enough land for the Trinity Church, the city administration donated a section of the central city square and rerouted a major street. Ironically, the square includes a statue of Lenin, who now seems to gesture approvingly toward the church. Not all of Reutov's citizens, however, were amused. An adjoining property owner has refused to sell his building to the church for conversion into a parish house. Nor has the parish been able to recover the former prayer house across the street from the Trinity Church.

Because the Russian Constitution forbids state establishment of religion, government officials such as Khodyrev understand themselves to be prohibited from directly funding Church building projects except in the case of restoration of edifices of special historical or cultural value. Nevertheless, state endorsement is key to almost every project's success. Private firms implicitly understand that if they wish to do business with the state, they should donate materials and money for new church construction that the state has approved.[37] In many a new or restored church, visitors will find a large memorial tablet that identifies these sponsors.

The priest at the Trinity Church, Father Maksim Belikov, fits the Church's bill for bright, well-educated men who will serve as dynamic parish leaders. He was not yet thirty-five when he helped bring the Trinity Church to birth. Even before the church opened, he was conducting services, sometimes in the rain or snow, on the plaza next to it. He negotiated construction details with the mayor, who sometimes had his own ideas of how the church should look; helped design its iconostasis and frescoes; and energetically raised money for completing them, even traveling to talk to potential donors abroad. Father Maksim has also tried to root the parish in its distinctive history. In 2015, he helped the parish organize a major exhibition about Patriarch Tikhon, who in 1919 conducted prayers in the former prayer house across the street. Like Father Volgin, Father Maksim has the gift of quickly establishing trust and an emotional bond with people. Whenever we meet, he greets me warmly and thanks me for taking so much interest in him and the parish.

At first glance, developments since the fall of Communism support the Church's assertions about "rebirth" and "re-Christianization." The number of Orthodox parishes in the Russian Federation has grown nearly fivefold to approximately eighteen thousand.[38] In many urban areas, a church building is now as much a part of the local neighborhood as a shopping mall or bank. And Russians increasingly experience the Church not just as a building with onion domes and icons but also as a community of faith in which people gather for worship, education, service, and fellowship.

But as with religious education, social ministry, and commemoration of the new martyrs, efforts to develop parish life face profound limitations. One Church leader has estimated that Moscow needs not two hundred new churches but five thousand if priests are truly going to come close to the people and serve as personal spiritual counselors.[39] However, even the plan to build just two hundred has met opposition. Local citizen groups frequently resist government proposals to return Church properties that since the Soviet era have housed kindergartens, senior citizen facilities, or other social services. Neighbors sometimes resent the way in which the state privileges the Church by giving it precious green space that they thought was protected.[40] It is not unusual for people to wake up one morning to discover that a corner of a park in Moscow or St. Petersburg has been cordoned off, and that bulldozers are moving in to raze trees. Moreover, the pattern of financing major church projects from companies that do business with the state raises popular concerns about corruption. Some Church leaders themselves question the current wave of construction of huge cathedral-like edifices, as in Reutov. As one priest said to me, "The truth is, we don't need a lot more churches. The ones that we already have are empty most of the time." I experienced for myself how on major holy days crowds could pack the churches so tightly that I could hardly breathe, but on a normal workday most people regarded the church more as a place to "drop in" for a couple of minutes when they had prayers for personal needs than as a community whose members had obligations to each other.

To be sure, it is still too early to judge in-churching a failure. Building new buildings will always be easier than helping people abandon destructive behaviors and cultivate a vision of "heaven on earth." The Church's efforts in parish life, as in education and social work, are still new and developing. And some of the statistical evidence suggests that the Church is making headway. Russia is among a handful of countries in the world in which interest in religion appears to have grown in recent decades. The number of Russians identifying themselves as Orthodox rose from 31 percent in 1991 to 72 percent in 2008. Those who call themselves "somewhat," "very," or "extremely" religious increased from 11 percent in 1991 to 54 percent in 2008.[41]

Nevertheless, surveys of Orthodox affiliation are sufficiently inconsistent as to raise doubts about their reliability. A major survey in 2011–12 pegged it not at 70–80 percent but rather at just below 50 percent.[42] And despite a decade of intensive efforts to in-church Russians, active participation remains low. In 1993, according to one study, about 60 percent of Russians reported never attending church. By 2007, that number had declined to 32 percent, with nearly 58 percent attending occasionally. However, growth in frequent attendance, defined as at least once a month, was more modest: from 6 percent of the population in 1997 to 10 percent in 2007. And among those people who explicitly identified themselves as Orthodox, the percentage of frequent attendees had in the course of fourteen years remained within the range of 9–11 percent.[43] Other surveys saw dramatic growth in frequent church attendance during the 1990s but a modest decline in recent years: 2 percent of Russians had attended religious services at least once a month in 1991, 9 percent in 1998, and 7 percent between 2008 and 2012.[44] In 2012, only 3 percent of Russians were attending Church services weekly.[45]

Surveys indicate widespread lack of familiarity with basic Orthodox teaching, and rates of religious practice are no different.[46] In recent years, no more than 5 percent of Russians, regardless of religious affiliation, have been observing the Great Fast of Lent, the Church's most important liturgical season. Even among those people self-consciously identifying themselves as Orthodox, only 10 percent fast during Lent.[47] Far fewer, 1–2 percent, have been keeping both the Great Fast and the Church's other prescribed fasting periods (a total of more than two hundred days of the year).[48] And only 14 percent of Russians—and 19 percent of self-identified Orthodox—have reported praying daily.[49]

The formation of eucharistic fellowship seems even more elusive. In 2011–12, only 8.2 percent of Russian believers were participating regularly in the life of a specific parish. Only 2 percent were receiving the Eucharist at least once a month, while 43.2 percent reported never receiving Communion, and another 35 percent were receiving it once a year or even less frequently.[50] Russians overall said that they looked to the family, not the Church, to form their moral values.[51] As Elena Mchedlova, a Russian sociologist, has observed, "A significant percentage of believers are not 'in-churched.' They are passive believers. It is entirely possible that a certain religiosity manifests itself, but far from the Church. For them, belonging to a community and going to church are not important. The main thing, rather, is what is in your heart."[52] Sociological analysis, says Mchedlova, can demonstrate only that since the fall of Communism more Russians call themselves Orthodox, not that they really are.[53]

According to traditional Orthodox teaching, the Church calls people into its life because it believes that they will find salvation for their souls when they receive the sacraments, which unite them to the resurrected Christ.

Their unity with this divine-human Christ will be further strengthened if they work at overcoming destructive passions, participate in the Church's worship and prayer, and love and care for others. Christian community—such as a parish or a monastery—is so important because believers need each other's encouragement and support to grow in this way of life.

For Orthodoxy, the Christian Scriptures and Church tradition help make the demands of the Christian life concrete. Today's Russian Orthodox Church places particular emphasis on faithfulness in marriage, protection of unborn children, respect for the national culture to which a person belongs, and the cultivation of beauty, fairness, and social harmony. In the Church's thinking, those who practice these values not only draw closer to eternal life—life beyond death—but also shape the present-day world for the better. As they progress toward deification, believers simultaneously promote the moral foundations that make society possible. Human sin has distorted human relationships, but even now believers can make a witness, however limited and incomplete, to the world as they believe God created it to be and that God promises someday to restore.

Sociologists will tell us whether efforts at in-churching eventually bring more Russians into the Church's life. Numbers, however, are of limited value in questions of the spiritual life. As Sergei Chapnin, former editor of the Patriarchate's official journal and a frequent critic of Church policies, has argued, the "experience of Christian life is not exhausted by 'in-churching' in the narrow sense of the word, i.e., attention to morality, Church regulations, and the structure of liturgical life. Without communion with God and knowledge of God, the experience of 'Christian life' limits a person, fails to lead him to freedom in Christ, and ultimately deprives him of the possibility of recognizing and grasping the purpose of the Christian life." What mattered most to Christ, says Chapnin, was not outer formal religiosity but rather the quality of relationships among his disciples: "that they have love among one another."[54] As Igumen Nektarii (Morozov) has written, the Church will want to know whether people who regularly attend the liturgy, receive the Eucharist, study the Church's teachings, and live in Christian community are actually making progress in the long, slow process of moral and spiritual self-transformation.[55]

Nevertheless, long experience has taught me that Christians everywhere, even though they should know better, are perpetually tempted to make observance of rituals and affirmation of formulas of faith the key markers of a "good" Christian life.[56] The temptation is perhaps inescapable because measuring "repentance" and "transformation" of the self is much more difficult than counting how many people attend the Divine Liturgy or participate in educational or social activities. I believe that the Russian Orthodox Church today can be thankful for its new opportunities after Communism. It can take genuine satisfaction in the fact that so many parishes are vital because of new educational and diaconal initiatives. But the Church for all of its wisdom will never have access to a person's innermost thoughts and motivations. People come to church for all kinds of complicated and not always consistent reasons: social habit, family pressure, personal crisis, a longing for life meaning, or a hope for moral orientation for themselves or their children. And people remain in church for all kinds of reasons: because of a priest whom they like, friends that they make, a glimpse of something beautiful and transcendent, or a sense that the Church has precious wisdom that they need if they are to live well. Those who call themselves Christian (or Orthodox) sometimes seem to make great strides in faith; at other times, they relapse into old destructive behaviors. The Church can only invite people to grow toward eternal life; whether they actually do or not remains beyond human comprehension or quantification.

The mystery of faith is compounded by the Church's own fragile life. According to Orthodox theology, the Church is a divine creation. But it is also a human institution composed of people who are weak, limited, and never entirely free of self-interest and selfishness. Priests may be motivated not just by genuine concern for their parishioners but also by love of power and prestige. They may demand obedience to the Church's precepts not only because they care about people's eternal destiny but also because they want to control what people do here and now.

Two of Father Volgin's favorite sayings illustrate his awareness of these temptations and the need to resist them. The first was a piece of advice from his spiritual father, Ioann (Krest'iankin): "Be as strict as possible with yourself but as generous as possible with others." Volgin says that a priest must continually examine himself and repent of his sins while being as open and loving as possible to those who come to the Church. Father Volgin's second saying comes from the great eighteenth- and nineteenth-century Russian saint Serafim of Sarov: "Save yourself, and thousands around you will be saved." Father Volgin regularly encourages his parishioners not to judge others but rather to focus on their own salvation.

Over the past twenty-five years, the Russian Orthodox Church has grown at a rate that most traditional Protestant churches in the West can only dream about. And its parishes are doing many good things. People are finding joy and comfort in the Church's rituals. They are caring for each other and reaching out to society in love and service. A Church that was once pushed to the margins again has a home in Russian society.

As new churches appear against the horizon, I would describe the Orthodox hope in this way: an unchurched Russian may walk around the exterior of an ancient Orthodox monastery and value its architecture as a national historical treasure, regardless of whether he or she is a Christian believer. However, once a person has been moved by such otherworldly beauty, he or she may wish to learn more about the history of the monastery and even to understand the way of life that has been cultivated within its walls over the centuries. If such a person then steps into the monastery church, he or she may discover that this way of life continues to be cultivated today. Monks or nuns are chanting prayers while laypeople light candles and venerate icons. What an outsider took at first to be mere history proves to be living reality. And he or she may be moved to take yet another step into this world: to learn about its way of life and even to begin to practice it. From this perspective, just reestablishing the Church's physical presence in Russian society makes a witness to the possibility of Holy Rus'.

Over the course of an entire year, my family and I rode the metro forty-five minutes every Sunday morning from our apartment house on the southern edge of Moscow to the Tret'iakov Gallery stop, just south of the city center. When we emerged from under ground, the first landmark that we passed was a McDonald's. It was always overflowing with customers; in Russia McDonald's is popular not only for its food but also for its free toilets, and more than once when we stopped in I encountered men shaving and even taking sponge baths in the restroom.

After McDonald's, we would turn north and make our way on foot through the charming architecture of the old Moscow and the gaudy glass-clad banks, restaurants, and business centers of the new. The towers of the Kremlin rose up ahead of us. Beneath the bridge that crosses the Moscow River to Red Square—the very bridge on which the political dissident Boris Nemtsov would be assassinated on February 27, 2015—we would turn left, follow the banks of the river, pass through the arch of the bell tower, and enter the courtyard of the parish that we had come to call ours: the Church of Sophia, the Wisdom of God. From the time we passed McDonald's, church bells had been ringing—those from our parish in the distance as well as those of the other half dozen churches along the way. Sometimes they tolled deeply, slowly, and steadily; at other times they were a cacophony—a wild, clashing frenzy—as in Rimsky-Korsakov's *Easter Festival Overture*. For a few magical minutes, eternity was again breaking into ordinary human time.

Whether Russia has become a more moral nation—or, to put it more sharply, whether, because of the Church and its many new parishes, Russia is becoming more like Holy Rus'—is impossible to determine. Moreover, the Church will never be able to answer that question with sociological evidence. But the Church does not have to. It is enough that its priests and parishes cultivate, however faintly and imperfectly, a glimpse of what Orthodox believers call a new heaven and earth. Russians cannot fail to notice. Something has changed against the horizon of the city. The Church again beckons; the bells again resound.

SEVEN

The Future

In the fall of 2011, 3.5 million Russians, beginning with Vladimir Putin, venerated holy relics from a monastery on Mt. Athos said to be the belt that the Virgin Mary wore more than two thousand years ago when she was pregnant with Jesus. Over the course of seven weeks, the relics traveled to five different cities in Russia; nearly 1 million people in Moscow alone lined up, sometimes waiting up to twenty-four hours in damp, chilly weather to be admitted to Christ the Savior Cathedral. Nearby were warm buses provided by city officials where people could sit for a few minutes or get a cup of hot tea. Hundreds of police officers and medics provided logistical support.[1]

As people stood outside the cathedral, they sang hymns to the Virgin Mary and venerated small, inexpensive icons that they had brought along. My friend Elena later compared the long night in line to one of Orthodoxy's ascetical disciplines. As she and her friends stood miles distant from the cathedral, they wondered whether they would survive the demands on their bodies and emotions. The experience was pushing them to their limits. But, as she told me later, just when they thought they could endure no longer, a power from beyond themselves propped them up. They reached the church, fell down, and venerated the relics. Elena and her friends had truly accomplished a spiritual feat.

Orthodox believers normally spend a few minutes venerating relics: they cross themselves, bow, and kiss the reliquary. As the crowds grew larger and larger, however, Church authorities had to speed up the process. At one point, they considered placing the relics in an airplane that would fly the belt over Moscow, distributing its power to those who reverently waited below. In the end, they kept the relics on earth but placed them on a canopy beneath which venerators walked, one after another, at a steady pace. All who wished would eventually make it into the cathedral.

Patriarch Kirill declared that this public outpouring of religious piety confirmed that Russia was truly Orthodox. But skeptics noted that other relics of the Virgin's Belt are permanently on display in another Moscow church; there is no media frenzy about them, and no one lines up day after day to venerate them. The Virgin's Belt reflects all the possibilities and ambiguities of Russia's Orthodoxy today—and, perhaps, of religion in general. Russia is somehow Orthodox, and yet this "somehow" is difficult to define and measure. Church, society, and state interact in complex, unpredictable ways to produce different kinds of Orthodoxy, each of which has adherents and detractors.[2]

Political scientist Irina Papkova speaks of three major groups in the Russian Orthodox Church: the traditionalists, the liberals, and the fundamentalists.[3] Building on her work, I suggest five kinds of Orthodoxy: an "official" Orthodoxy represented by the patriarch and the institutional Church, with its exclusive claims to administering the sacraments and ordaining clergy; a moderate Orthodoxy, which supports modest Church reform for the sake of securing the institutional Church; a liberal Orthodoxy loyal to the institutional Church while calling for democratic reform; a conservative Orthodoxy, also within the institutional Church but critical of its accommodations to a liberal culture; and a "popular" or "unofficial" Orthodoxy that thrives outside of the institutional Church yet draws on its key symbols, narratives, and rituals. Like Papkova, I acknowledge that any such categorizations are inexact, with a range of positions within and across types.

Official Orthodoxy is based on the principle of cooperative Church-state relations and symphonia. In Russia, as anywhere in the world, religious organizations have to work closely with government officials. To erect a church, synagogue, mosque, or religious school involves building permits and zoning regulations. Religious organizations face government mandates with which they must comply or for which they must seek exemptions. In a highly centralized state such as the new Russia, the Church has all the more need to work cooperatively with the government, especially in relation to religious education and social ministry. But this cooperation has come at a price. A public image of privilege and wealth has made the Church fair game for criticism. Much of the Russian media—and some parts of the Russian population—have come to regard Orthodoxy as a corrupt, wealthy, and authoritarian institution that is concerned with self-preservation, not advancement of a religious vision of deification and transfiguration.

Official Orthodoxy might have hoped that it would be otherwise. When Kirill was enthroned as patriarch in 2009, he appeared to be the perfect person to lead the Church into a new era of in-churching.[4] During the Soviet period, he had been associated with the Church's more liberal wing under the leadership of Metropolitan Nikodim of Leningrad. In that context, "liberal" had especially meant openness to ecumenical dialogue with Western Protestants and Catholics and their concerns for human rights and social justice. In 1989, Kirill was appointed head of the Church's Department of External Church Relations. His prominence grew as he directed the writing of the *Social Concept* and then a major Church document on human rights. Rumors regularly surfaced about Kirill's moral integrity—cooperation with the KGB during the Soviet era, expensive personal tastes, and even shady business dealings. He nevertheless successfully projected the image of a dynamic, reform-minded leader. An eloquent speaker, he had been publicly commended for his command of the Russian language. His public charisma reminded some Orthodox, especially in more intellectual and progressive circles, of Pope John Paul II.

Kirill's election to the Patriarchate seemed to signal that the institutional Church would no longer hide behind rules and traditions but rather demonstrate its openness to society. As a headline in the *New York Times* declared, "Russian Orthodox Church Elects Outspoken Patriarch."[5] Kirill immediately called on the Church to see all of society as its mission field, even atheists and aggressive, Hell's Angels–type bikers. His popularity was such that he could fill a huge stadium in St. Petersburg with enthusiastic Orthodox young people.[6]

But such exuberance did not last long. By 2011, the institutional Church no longer seemed to represent national rebirth but rather repressive power politics.[7] In the fall, the patriarch's representative for relations with society, Father Vsevolod Chaplin, provoked media ridicule when he called for instituting a national dress code (because women's skirts were too short) and for removing certain literary classics from the high school curriculum, such as Vladimir Nabokov's *Lolita* (because they supposedly exhibited pedophilia).

In December 2011, large anti-Putin demonstrations took place in Moscow and other cities, further complicating the Church's public image. Chaplin initially adopted a conciliatory stance, calling for the state to enter into dialogue with its opponents.[8] Soon afterward, however, Kirill gave full-fledged support to Putin's candidacy for the presidency, declaring that the Putin era had been a "miracle of God." Moreover, Kirill asserted that Orthodox believers "would stay home and pray," not attend protest demonstrations.

In February 2012, another incident cast harsh light on the Church. Five members of a feminist art collective known as Pussy Riot slipped into Christ the Savior Cathedral, donned brightly colored ski masks, and kicked their legs and pumped their fists in front of the iconostasis as they performed a song accusing the patriarch of believing in Putin, not God. Guards quickly escorted the women out of the church, but a video recording of the event went viral on the Internet. Church authorities insisted that the women either repent publicly or be prosecuted. Three of the women were eventually sentenced to two-year terms in prison colonies.

Not long afterward, the media revealed that Kirill, despite his monastic vows, owned a luxury apartment on the Moscow River in which he housed a rare book collection. Kirill had reportedly received nearly $700,000 in compensation from an upstairs neighbor whose renovation work caused extensive damage to the books. A second event proved even more embarrassing. In 2009, critics had spotted a $30,000 Swiss Breguet timepiece on Kirill's wrist when he lifted his arms during church prayers on a visit to Kiev.[9] Kirill vehemently denied the accusations. In April 2012, however, the issue surfaced again, when the patriarch's website published a photo of him sitting with the federal minister of justice at a table. In the photo the Patriarch wears no watch—yet a reflection of the controversial timepiece appears on the highly polished tabletop. Kirill's Photoshop doctors had apparently overlooked it in their haste to rescue his public image.[10]

Church leaders began to speak of a new "anticlericalism" in Russian society. Some loyal supporters of official Orthodoxy saw an organized conspiracy, perhaps even directed by Western intelligence agencies, to discredit the Church. As one priest said to me, "They know that Russia's strength comes from the Church. If they weaken the Church, they weaken Russia." Church authorities called for a mass prayer service in support of the patriarch. Publicity flyers displayed a dramatic photograph of the implosion

Leaflet calling for prayer service to defend the Church, featuring
the implosion at Stalin's order of Christ the Savior Cathedral in 1931
(author's photograph)

of Christ the Savior Cathedral on December 5, 1931. The headline beneath the photo read, "This Must Not Repeat Itself! With Prayer and Unity We Will Defend the Faith, the Church, and Our Holy Things." On the back of the flyer, in an appeal that would also be read from the ambo of every parish, the Highest Church Council declared: "Anti-Church forces fear the growing power of Orthodoxy in the nation. . . . To these forces are joined others that promote the false values of an aggressive liberalism, for the Church is unbending in its opposition to such anti-Christian phenomena as the recognition of same-sex unions, the freedom to express all desires, unbridled consumption, and the propaganda of 'anything goes' and licentiousness. In addition, these attacks on the Church are useful to those whose business interests are being hurt by the program to erect new churches."

The declaration went on to list several recent incidents in which churches and icons had been desecrated, beginning with the Pussy Riot action, and compared the current "campaign" against the Church with Bolshevik attacks on the Church in the early twentieth century. On April 22, an estimated sixty-five thousand believers gathered for the prayer service on the square outside Christ the Savior Cathedral. Parked nearby were rows of buses that had transported thousands of people from outside Moscow to the event, an operation organized so quickly and efficiently that it had clearly required state assistance.

A year later, events in Ukraine posed additional challenges to Russia and official Orthodoxy. When Putin moved to annex Crimea and support separatists in eastern Ukraine, Patriarch Kirill sought to stay above the political fray, repeatedly calling on both Ukrainian government forces and the rebels to lay down their arms and negotiate a peace. However, in failing to support the EuroMaidan Revolution or condemn Russian intervention in Ukraine loudly and clearly, Kirill appeared to ally himself with Russian state interests. Chaplin stoked further suspicions about the Church's position when he criticized the West for trying to impose on other countries a brand of democracy that results in moral and religious decay.[11] In December 2015, the patriarch abruptly dismissed Chaplin, who had earlier called Russia's intervention in Syria in support of President Bashar al-Assad a "holy war," but there was no sign of a change of course in Church-state relations.

If the patriarch and official Orthodoxy have spoken confidently of in-churching Russia, other Church people openly admit that efforts at re-Christianization have fallen short. To their mind, Russian society is not moving toward "in-churching" but rather toward "de-churching." Some of these voices are moderate; others are liberal or conservative. What they share in common is a deep concern that Russian Orthodoxy has failed to win a new generation to the Church and a living faith.

Father Vladimir Vorob'ev, rector of St. Tikhon's Orthodox University, is a thoughtful "moderate," well connected in the institutional Church but also able to pose critical questions about it. He notes that too many people who turned to the Church at the end of the Soviet period did not know how to raise their children in Orthodoxy. Because the Bolshevik state had torn people away from Russia's organic Orthodox traditions, parents were unable to offer their children an example of personal faith won through repentance and suffering. Instead, they thought that their children would become Orthodox if they simply forced their children to go to church or an Orthodox school.

Vorob'ev also cites the problem of priests whose personal behavior put up barriers to active lay Church participation. The priests whom the Church hastily ordained in the 1990s often raised money to renovate churches and pay their salaries by charging exorbitant rates for basic Church services to individuals, such as baptisms and funerals.[12] People began to regard the Church as a business enterprise rather than a community of faith. An additional problem was that many of these priests were young and lacked spiritual maturity. They were unable to hear confessions properly or offer genuine spiritual guidance.

The effects of de-churching are increasingly apparent at St. Tikhon's, says Vorob'ev. Today's students lack basic grounding in Orthodoxy and Russian culture, and often show little interest in acquiring them. Vorob'ev suggests that the Church must do much more to become a genuine community of mutual support and care if it is to attract young people and incorporate them into its life.[13]

Igumen Petr (Meshcherinov), who served for many years as head of the Patriarchal Center for the Spiritual Development of Children and Young People, is another "moderate" voice, although his analysis is more stinging. Petr notes that as many as two-thirds of children raised in the Church will eventually leave it: "For contemporary post-Soviet families, being 'churched' has been stripped of any genuine Christian content. It has become a peculiar mix of ideology, magic, and a 'Soviet' complex mimicking an Orthodox way of life: irresponsibility being presented as 'obedience'; disrespect for oneself and others as 'humility'; contentiousness and spite as 'the struggle for the purity of Orthodoxy.' "

Petr argues that the Orthodox Church has reduced itself to a social subculture that is obsessed with enforcing certain traditions—the Old Style calendar, Church Slavonic in the liturgy, and rules about fasting—even though all these practices are historically conditioned and not divinely mandated. Moreover, says Petr, too many Russians have concluded that because of their Orthodox identity they are morally superior to other peoples, and that to be Christian means to enjoy worldly power and success. He refers to popular Orthodox media outlets that are obsessed with Russia's special spiritual path in contrast to a decadent West, or that long for a return of empire and monarchy. He adds that even many people who have entered deeply into Orthodox life now feel alienated from the Church. They do not experience freedom and encouragement to grow in faith. Instead, the Church constantly communicates an anxiety that its adherents may fall into heresy if they think too much for themselves. A spirit of moral judgmentalism has replaced the joy and mercy that should characterize the Christian life. Ritualism has taken the place of faith.

Like Vorob'ev, Petr calls for the Church to be a eucharistic community in which people experience solidarity in love. The Russian Church today needs a new language and a "pastoral pedagogy" that points people away from worldly privilege and power to heaven on earth. In-churching in the sense of attending the Divine Liturgy is not enough. Ritual and tradition matter only if they lead to life in Christ.[14] People associated with the Church's department for work with young people made a similar point to me: a younger generation of Orthodox believers is searching in the Church for life meaning and spiritual fellowship, not rules. They are interested in such people as Aleksandr Men', who had the courage to think deeply and critically about Christian faith.[15]

Other critiques of the official Church go even farther, calling for "liberal, democratic" reform. In 2011, Russia's major Russian cultural television station (Channel 24) broadcast a documentary film, *Heat* (*Zhara*), which traces the history of the catacomb church of the 1960s–80s and several of its leading priests, including Aleksandr Men'. The title refers to the huge peat moss fires that burned in the summer of 1972 in drained swamps outside of Moscow—at a time in which some Russians began quietly turning to Orthodoxy, away from Marxist-Leninist ideology. The film has resonated among many of my Orthodox friends who feel that the Church has lost its way since emerging from the underground and acquiring social prestige and political influence. They see a repetition of the Soviet era, when the official Church yielded to state control in order to secure a measure of public institutional life—including the ability openly to celebrate the liturgy and the Eucharist—but compromised its freedom and integrity.

I remember sitting with a group of theologians and philosophers discussing an open letter that had been quietly circulating in Orthodox intellectual circles in Moscow in early 2012. Signed by O. Bugoslavskaia and entitled "Reason to Doubt," the letter accused the Church of cultivating a smug moral and religious arrogance. Orthodox believers were being told to avoid non-Christian art and literature rather than to learn from them and assess them thoughtfully. Some believers were refusing to think for themselves, consulting instead their spiritual father even for the simplest of matters. And, Bugoslavskaia added, when Church authorities asserted that all power comes from God, they were simply supporting the political status quo rather than motivating people to work for a more just, humane world.

Other Orthodox figures have directly challenged the Church hierarchy. Sergei Chapnin, dismissed in December 2015 from his position as editor of the Patriarchate's official journal, has drawn a sharp contrast between the Soviet "dissident" church and today's official Church. Chapnin talks about how he loves to contemplate photographs of Aleksandr Men'—as other

believers, it seems to me, might peer at icons of a saint—because in Men'
he sees someone of "depth, wholeness, concentration and, at the same time,
simplicity, lightheartedness, and inspiration."[16] Father Aleksandr, according
to Chapnin, maintained a deep and clear sense of "privateness." What
Chapnin has in mind is Father Aleksandr's ability to live "without the
government." "Privateness" does not mean a privatized or individualistic
faith but rather the freedom that comes from being oriented by God, not by
any social or political authority.

Chapnin worries that the Church today has not overcome a "Soviet
mentality" that concerns itself only with how the state will support or undermine the institutional Church. "Post-Soviet civil religion" is focused on
Orthodoxy's contributions to Russian national identity rather than humans'
ultimate ends before God. For Chapnin, a Church that in the 1990s represented hope with its vision of an alternative society has become a "Church
of empire," a civil religion "without God," that consistently supports the
political status quo and never places it under divine judgment.[17] Such a
Church, says Chapnin, fails to represent the true values of Christian faith
to society.

Cyril Hovorun, a Ukrainian priest-monk of the Moscow Patriarchate, has
argued along similar lines. For Hovorun, the events on Kiev's Maidan in
2013–14 now challenge the Russian Orthodox Church to develop a political
theology that focuses on society rather than the state. Such a Church would
offer a free space for people to develop democratic habits of critical thinking
about, and deliberative negotiation of, social problems. Such a Church
would not seek to preserve, with government assistance, an Orthodox identity over and against the West but rather forge alliances with other religious
groups and social forces to promote a more just society. Hovorun contrasts
the Russian Church with those churches in Ukraine that won the people's
trust by supporting the EuroMaidan and are now able to contribute to a
vital civil society.[18]

Notwithstanding these sharp critiques of the official Church, I have seen
how some Russian parishes do cautiously nurture a progressive vision of
Church and society. The Feodorovskii Cathedral in St. Petersburg has skillfully negotiated Russian political and ecclesiastical realities while offering

an alternative to them.[19] The glorious edifice, constructed in the early twentieth century in honor of the three hundredth anniversary of the Romanov
family's ascension to state power, was turned into a milk factory during the
Soviet era. By the time the Church regained ownership in 2005, thirteen
years after the state promised to return it, only a dilapidated, brick/concrete
shell remained. Restoration efforts would take another decade of sophisticated planning, negotiating, and fund-raising. Boris Gryzlov, head of the
Russian Duma and chairman of Putin's United Russia Party, headed up a
board of directors. Among the chief financial sponsors was Vladimir Iakunin,
the country's railroad magnate until 2015 and a close associate of President
Putin. Rededicated on September 15, 2013, the four hundredth anniversary
of the Romanov ascension to power, the cathedral is again an architectural
wonder—and more.

The new edifice includes a lower church for which funds had failed
when the cathedral first opened in 1913, on the brink of the First World War.
The spatial arrangement, frescoes, and icons are the work of Father Zinon
(Teodor), one of Russia's most creative icon painters—and a monk who has
been criticized and even punished for his criticism of a narrow-minded
Church. When I first walked into the lower church, I was stunned by its
beauty. The space, filled with light, is open and welcoming. Rather than a
traditional multistoried Russian iconostasis, only a low barrier marks the
separation of nave and altar. Worshippers can see and hear all the liturgy.
The space invites not clerical control but rather a liturgy that is the work of
both the priests and the laypeople. And I saw for myself how hundreds of
parishioners—men and women, adults and children, clergy and laity, and
conservatives and liberals—feel like family here, despite their social and
political differences.

At the Feodorovskii Cathedral, Orthodox symbols have inspired a partici-
patory, even democratic vision of Church and society. One of the cathedral's assistant priests is a student of contemporary Western philosophy of
science and is writing a dissertation on Theodor Adorno and the Frankfurt
School of social theory. Another assistant priest serves as a vice rector at the
St. Petersburg Theological Seminary and Academy, and regularly travels
abroad to lecture about icons and Orthodox theology. The head priest,

Father Aleksandr Sorokin, welcomes ecumenical dialogue and cooperation with Catholics and Protestants in matters of social ministry. And parish members vigorously discuss and debate contemporary political issues—and even Russian military actions in Crimea and eastern Ukraine.

Another kind of Russian Orthodoxy joins in the call for Church reform, but along "conservative" or "fundamentalist" lines and therefore in sharp contrast to Chapnin's or Hovorun's admiration of Western democracy. Adherents of this conservative Orthodoxy typically anticipate an apocalyptic battle between true and false believers—and relegate Church and state leaders to the anti-Orthodox camp. Some political observers judge these conservative circles to be larger and more powerful than the Church's liberal wing.[20] But just as those Orthodox believers who seek a more progressive Orthodoxy interact in different ways with state, society, and official Orthodoxy, so, too, do these conservatives. Some remain firmly within the bounds of the institutional Church, while others exist on its outer fringes.

Conservative Orthodoxy finds one of its representative centers in a historic Moscow church, St. Nicholas in Pyzhakh, just down the street from St. Elizabeth's Martha and Mary Monastery. In the 1920s, one of the monastery's last priests briefly served at St. Nicholas after the Bolsheviks closed St. Elizabeth's community. Today at St. Nicholas, icons of St. Elizabeth and Patriarch Tikhon have prominent places on the iconostasis before the chief altar. The head priest, Father Aleksandr Shargunov, translates classic Western poetry into Russian, publishes widely on theological and spiritual topics, and teaches at the Moscow Theological Seminary and Academy.

After the collapse of Communism, Father Shargunov gained notoriety for his conservative politics. During the 1993 constitutional crisis, he called on Orthodox believers to defend the Parliament when President Yeltsin used military force to quash opposition to his program of democratization, and Shargunov's parish played an active role not only in opposing liberal Orthodox priest Georgii Kochetkov but also in shutting down the 2003 Sakharov Center art exhibition *Danger, Religion*.[21] During these same years, Shargunov became well known for promoting canonization of the new martyrs and especially Tsar Nicholas II. The parish commissioned an icon of Nicholas that thousands of people lined up to venerate after the Bishops Council glorified him in 2000. Father Aleksandr began regularly celebrating an akathist (special Orthodox hymn) to Nicholas II and added his icon to the iconostasis of a side church altar dedicated to the ancient St. Nicholas of Myra.

For the parish, as for conservative Orthodoxy more generally, Tsar Nicholas represents a prerevolutionary Russia in which Orthodoxy shaped all aspects of public life. In contrast to some Orthodox conservatives, Father Shargunov does not look for a restoration of a God-anointed tsar today. But he does appeal to Nicholas II to call both Church and state to account for their failure to protect Orthodox values in Russian society. Shargunov's criticisms of the Church's worldly compromises with the Putin government can be as sharp as those that politically liberal Orthodox believers make.

Father Aleksandr and his parish demonstrate how religious symbols help not only liberals but also conservatives imagine an alternative political order. Shargunov, no less than Chapnin and Hovorun, argues that the Church should be a community of love and peace. No less than "progressive" Orthodox believers, he appeals to the new martyrs when he calls believers to remain faithful to Christ in the face of social opposition. Where he differs from the liberals is in his definition of the kind of political order that follows from these shared symbols, narratives, and rituals. For him and his parish, the issues are not human rights and liberal democracy but rather pornography, abortion, and homosexuality.

Father Shargunov remains firmly within the institutional Church, but other conservative Orthodox believers take a more militant stance against it and its "liberals." These fundamentalists have physically attacked people publicly demonstrating for civil rights for homosexual persons in Russia. Some of these Orthodox reactionaries regard as saints dubious historical figures whom a supposedly corrupt, politically accommodated institutional Church has refused to canonize. Ivan the Terrible is said to have defended "true Orthodoxy." Rasputin was martyred for his faith in Holy Russia and his loyalty to its divinely anointed monarch, Nicholas. Even Stalin claims their admiration because at the beginning of the war he supposedly visited the holy elder Matrona and became a believer. And while Church officials do not publicly support these reactionary groups, they have failed to condemn them, perhaps fearing that they could become even more aggressive or schismatic. Not only I as a Western theologian but also many liberal and even moderate Russian Orthodox believers whom I know fault the official Church for its silence.

Nevertheless, Orthodoxy—whether in its official, moderate, liberal, or conservative forms—is more limited in social and political influence than we might expect. Anyone who spends years among Orthodox believers can forget that the Church is only one social organization among many. We can too easily accept the official Church's assertion that most Russians are Orthodox. But, as we have seen, very few Russians are actually in-churched. Although honoring the Church in principle, they keep their distance from it in everyday life. And even those who do regularly attend the Divine Liturgy or observe the Church calendar are not necessarily interested in matters of deification, transfiguration, or Holy Rus'. Yes, Orthodoxy has shaped historic Russian culture, but in my more sociological moments, I see a Church that is barely noticeable in a pluralistic society—even if contemporary Russia appears less pluralistic than western Europe or North America. In a post-Communist world, Orthodoxy competes with many other social identities to define Russia. The Virgin's Belt changed Moscow for only a few days.

No, not the long lines in front of Christ the Savior Cathedral but rather something else stays in my mind when I think about everyday Russian life. When my family and I lived in Moscow, I walked every morning from our fifteen-story Soviet-era apartment building to the metro through an underground pedestrian passageway lined with small kiosks. They offered everything from shoe repair to key copying to sale of inexpensive souvenirs and clothing. Next to the shop selling women's underwear of various sizes, colors, and shapes was a tiny Church kiosk with a limited supply of Orthodox crosses, icons, calendars, and books. Orthodoxy, it struck me, has a firm place in Russian society again—but to the tens of thousands of people who passed those kiosks every day, it was just one more consumer option in a crowded marketplace.

What is perhaps more significant than trying to describe different types of Orthodoxy—symphonic, moderate, liberal, or conservative—is the phenomenon of different Orthodoxies that merge and diverge, wax and wane, and mean different things to different people at different times. I have argued in this book that something in all of these Orthodoxies holds forth a vision of the transfiguration of reality. This heaven on earth is not the material comfort or proletarian liberation that Soviet Marxism once taught. Rather, Orthodoxy promises intimate, trusting relationship between divinity and humanity and among humans. Here and now, even if fragmentarily and incompletely, people are able to pursue holiness and deification. They begin to take wonder at existence and overcome alienation and enmity.

I have further argued that this traditional Orthodox view of ultimate reality has assumed a special form in Russia, what I call Holy Rus'.[22] In Russia, the longing for beauty, deification, and moral and spiritual transformation has been not only individual and personal but also social and national. Russians have believed that as a people and land they can shine with the divine light that has enlightened their greatest saints, such as St. Serafim of Sarov in the nineteenth century. As one of his companions reported, "I looked in his face and there came over me an even greater reverential awe. Imagine in the center of the sun, in the dazzling brilliance of its midday rays, the face of the man who talks with you. You see the movement of his lips and the changing expression of his eyes, you hear his voice, you feel someone grasp your shoulders; yet you do not see his hands, you do not even see yourself or his figure, but only a blinding light spreading several yards around and throwing a sparkling radiance across the snow blanket on the glade and into the snowflakes."[23]

I have described how Church initiatives in religious education, social work, commemoration of the new martyrs, and parish life have the potential to draw people into this vision of Holy Rus'. And Russia, I have argued, is indeed a healthier, more vital society today because of these efforts. Russians are learning more about their nation's historical roots in Orthodoxy; persons in physical and emotional need or on the margins of society are receiving love and practical assistance; new generations are honoring the victims of Bolshevism; and parishes are helping people experience genuine fellowship with God and each other. To be sure, the Church faces real limitations in each area. Russians are not always Orthodox, and they are not always Orthodox in ways that the Church would like. But because of the public revival of Orthodox symbols, narratives, and rituals, Russians at least have the opportunity to glimpse Orthodoxy's vision of transcendent beauty and become aware of a different dimension of their existence.

For me, then, the place of Orthodoxy in the new Russia goes far beyond questions of Putin and the patriarch. As parishes and monasteries, lay brotherhoods and sisterhoods, and Church social service programs bring Orthodoxy closer to everyday Russian life, the Church has again become part of the nation's cultural and physical landscape. Russia is slowly being "reenchanted" with the help of Orthodox symbols, narratives, and rituals. Orthodox life in all of its complexity is no longer hidden in catacomb churches or private corners of people's lives but rather manifests itself in full public view.[24] As the Church becomes a comprehensive social presence, reminders of divine mystery are never far away, shaping not only institutional Church life but also a popular unofficial Orthodoxy outside of its walls—as apparent on Kreshchenie, perhaps the most popular of all the Church's holy days.

Kreshchenie (literally, Baptism) is celebrated twelve days after Orthodox Christmas. It is associated both with Christ's baptism in the Jordan River by John the Baptist and with Theophany (in Western Christianity, Epiphany), the manifestation of God as Trinity: Father, Son, and Holy Spirit. On this day, Orthodox churches bless the waters of the earth, a blessing that for the Church points to the salvation and transfiguration of all reality through Christ. Kreshchenie offers more than a guarantee of personal blessedness beyond death; it points to the divine glory that already fills the earth.

Several years ago, I traveled to a historic monastery several hours outside Moscow to participate in the celebrations. I arrived on the eve of Kreshchenie, and the monastery church was already packed. I could barely squeeze my way to the front. "There must be even more people here than at Christmas or Easter," I thought to myself. The service was long but spectacular, with a procession of the clergy in splendid robes. The singing of the monastery choir was heavenly, and worshippers participated enthusiastically in the Church's prayers. The high point came when the priests and monks gathered in the back of the church around four huge stainless steel vats of water, each perhaps twelve feet high and twelve feet in diameter, to perform the "Great Blessing of the Waters." After chanting prayers and dipping a large gold cross three times into each vat, the priests drew water into bowls, walked through the church, dipped long brushes into the bowls, and wildly threw drops of water over the icons and the worshippers. People pushed closer, hoping to get as wet as possible—and I was struck by the joy and delight that filled their faces.

When the service ended near 2 a.m., hundreds of people lined up with plastic bottles of all sizes and shapes to take water home with them. They would carefully guard it over the rest of the year, adding it to their food and drink or even their mop water, to sanctify themselves and their homes. The Church regularly performs blessings of water and teaches that the blessing at Kreshchenie is not different from or superior to the others. But many people believe that *kreshchenskaia voda* (baptism water) has a different molecular composition than regular water, endowing it with special healing and protective properties.

Outside the church, I met my friend Father Vasilii, a young, energetic monk and rising star in the official Church. His twenty-something face sported a few straggly chin hairs, the only beard that he could grow. "Let's go," he said. "Another blessing of the waters will take place down by the creek." We followed the clergy and a large group of laypeople through the huge monastery gates, around the high, thick, white monastery walls, to a narrow path leading to a small wooden hut over the tumbling stream. People had lined up to enter the structure—one side for men, the other for women—and dip into a pool that had been carved into the riverbanks. Other people were filling their bottles from a spring next to the path.

Kreshchenie falls on January 19, usually the coldest time of the year; Russians even refer to the phenomenon of the *kreshchenskii moroz* (baptismal deep freeze). This year was no different. The night sky was crystal clear, the stars shone bright, and temperatures had plunged to zero degrees Fahrenheit. Out here the crowd was rowdier than in the church. A number of men were sharing bottles of vodka. People were laughing, talking loudly, and stamping their feet to try to stay warm. A hush came over them as the priests blessed the waters in the stream and the spring, but immediately afterward the noise started up again. In an effort to restore some semblance of pious order, one of the monks began chastising the drunken revelers. Other monks distributed flyers articulating a theologically correct understanding of Kreshchenie and cautioning people against popular superstitions. A few crumpled sheets already lay on the ground.

In recent years, the Church's blessing of the waters has merged with the Soviet tradition of a January "polar bear" swim. On Kreshchenie, Church people often carve a hole in the shape of a cross into the surface of a frozen lake or river, the priest dips a cross into the icy waters below, and members of the public plunge in. My friends Evgenii and Natalia—faithful, in-churched Orthodox believers—spoke with delight about the hundreds of Muscovites who every year on Kreshchenie line up along the river that runs by their church outside Moscow. On Kreshchenie in 2015, the bishop of St. Petersburg joined other polar bears in the Neva River near the famous Peter and Paul Fortress.[25]

This combination of different Orthodoxies leaves me feeling conflicted. On the one hand, I appreciate Orthodoxy's ability to embed itself in popular culture. That kind of popular Orthodoxy enabled the Church to survive the Soviet era. Even though parishes and monasteries were closed, ordinary believers continued to keep icons in their homes, draw water from holy springs, baptize their children (or grandchildren), and observe rituals connected to holy days and seasons. And today, too, the Church depends on a "people's Orthodoxy." Their piety permits the Church to imagine that it is stronger than ever in Russian society. Moreover, monasteries and parishes raise much of their money from people who come to venerate their holy things and places, even though many of these pilgrims are not in-churched.

On the other hand, I worry about "believing without belonging," however much it now characterizes not only Russia but also much of the historically Christian West.[26] In that kind of Christianity, personal rituals become more important than Church doctrine or practices—matters that I as a theologian regard as central to Christian faith. And I know thoughtful Russian Orthodox

Church leaders who share my concern that some kinds of popular Orthodoxy tend toward superstition. When that happens, venerators of holy things and places look for a practical payoff—say, a miraculous healing when all else has failed—rather than the transformed way of life that the Church calls salvation. Extraordinary "spiritual" experiences take the place of attending the Divine Liturgy, receiving the Eucharist, doing charitable works, and participating in parish life. The bishop of St. Petersburg undoubtedly wished to make a personal connection with those Russians who celebrate Kreshchenie but do not regularly go to church. But I agree with those Church leaders who worry that combining "the blessing" with "the swim" just further confuses the popular mind about the true meaning of Kreshchenie.[27]

The problem, as I see it, is not that the Church tolerates and sometimes even encourages this kind of popular religiosity. Over the course of Russian history, official Orthodoxy has never been able to monopolize sacrality within its own walls. As historian Gregory Freeze notes, the institutional Church has regularly had to recognize believers' need for "direct access to the power of the sacred."[28] But as a theologian, I wish that the Church's authoritative teachers would speak more openly about just how ambiguous a phenomenon this "popular Orthodoxy" really is. While it offers powerful glimpses of the transfiguration of reality, it also easily distorts or truncates the Christian message of personal sacrifice and self-giving love.

But, again, Russia has taught me to be cautious about my judgments. The line that I would like to draw between religious faith and social custom, Church and nation, or deification and superstition is not so clear. Popular unofficial Orthodoxy intersects in complicated ways with official Orthodoxy, Russia's other Orthodoxies, and state efforts to use Orthodoxy for its own purposes.[29] The result is still other ways of being Orthodox that draw upon yet go beyond either institutional Church life or the popular Orthodox religiosity characterized by Kreshchenie. And there are also people who have consciously left official Orthodoxy for something that they regard as more authentically "Orthodox."

On the boat from Solovki back to the mainland, I met Tanya. As we traveled across the choppy waters of the White Sea on a glorious summer afternoon, she spoke with me in the way that only Russians can to a complete stranger who has mysteriously won their trust. As she told me her story, I slowly came to see all the complexities and contradictions of Orthodoxy in today's Russia.

Tanya is a professionally successful, middle-class Muscovite who lives in a comfortable apartment and has enough money to travel extensively both within Russia and abroad. In the 1990s, she and her husband explored various Eastern and Western spiritualities but never settled into a religious community. Tanya nevertheless decided to be baptized in an Orthodox church. Several years later, she agreed to be godmother to her niece. Although she has heard of Aleksandr Men' and says that he fascinates her, she has never read his books. She does not attend church services in Moscow, even though she keeps telling herself that she should. As she confessed to me, she is not even sure that she believes in God.

Tanya had nevertheless taken ten days of precious vacation to make the arduous journey to Solovki, where she had worshipped every day with the monks, made pilgrimage to Anzer and other remote sketes, walked in the expansive birch tree forests, and watched the sun set over the sea. She told me that she had glimpsed something precious there: a holy world. Never before in her life had she experienced such peace and joy. "I'm afraid that I will lose all of that," she lamented, "once I'm back in Moscow."

Tanya is not very interested in politics. If she bothered to vote, she would likely cast her ballot for Putin and his party United Russia, but she does not expect much of him or any other politician. She would rather devote her time and energy to her professional work and her two sons, now grown and looking for jobs. While she respects the patriarch, she does not pay attention to his public pronouncements. "The Church," she told me, "should focus less on itself and more on doing good for others."

I doubt that Tanya will ever return to Solovki, but when I visited her several years later in Moscow, we went for a stroll in the gardens next to the Danilov Monastery, where the Patriarchate has its offices. It was a winter evening, and night had fallen. A light snow swirled around us as we walked along the monastery walls and talked about our work and families. The setting again seemed to draw out our wonder and perplexity about life, where it takes a person, why we are who we are. Is Tanya Orthodox? She is not in-churched, but Orthodox symbols, narratives, and rituals touch her deeply. They somehow connect her to what it means to be Russian.

I got to know Marina and Sergii more than ten years ago in Kronstadt. Like Tanya, they live their Orthodoxy outside of the institutional Church. But while Tanya finds Orthodoxy to be elusive, if fascinating, Sergii and Marina regard themselves as serious believers—so serious, in fact, that they are willing, like the new martyrs, to suffer for their faith.

For many years, Sergii worked on a ship and was gone for weeks on end. Marina worked part-time as a translator and cared for their only child, Natasha. She was their "miracle child," the child for whom Marina had prayed so fervently for so many years in front of miracle-working icons and relics. In her desperation, she finally sought out a man reputed to be a holy elder. Before she could explain her situation to him, he blurted out that she would indeed have a child. A few days later, Marina became pregnant.

In 2009, Sergii was seriously injured at work and had to go on disability. About the same time, he and Marina began attending a house church of the renegade Russian Orthodox Church Abroad under Metropolitan Agafangel (Pashkovskii), which consists of a handful of priests and congregations both within and outside Russia that have refused to recognize the 2007 union of the Moscow Patriarchate and the Russian Orthodox Church Outside of Russia. A couple of years later, Sergii, Marina, and Natasha moved to the village of Dudachkino, a hundred miles east of St. Petersburg.

Dudachkino lies in an almost forgotten corner of post-Soviet Russia.[30] Away from the main highway, roads quickly turn to dirt. Thick birch and pine forests are slowly taking over the unplowed fields. Villages are few and far between, and their small wooden houses tilt to one side. Many have been abandoned to the elements, as people move away in search of work. Dudachkino no longer has a school, a store, or even a bar. The "official" church, closed under the Communists in 1937, is now just an empty, rotting wooden shell. A few hungry, filthy dogs wander the street.

Perhaps because of its relative isolation, the village lent itself to a utopian project. In the late 1980s, as the Soviet Union was collapsing, Father Aleksandr Sukhov came here to organize an Orthodox community whose members would live and worship together while preparing for the end of time. Born in Siberia in 1955, Sukhov, like many of his generation, was baptized in infancy by his grandmother but grew up with no living connection to Orthodox belief or practice. When he came to St. Petersburg in the early 1980s to study law, he began, like many other intellectuals of that time, a deep spiritual search that brought him into the Orthodox Church.

Another turning point came several years later when he visited Nikolai (Gur'ianov), the renowned holy elder. To Sukhov's astonishment, Father Nikolai blessed him to become a priest, although he warned Sukhov that he would have few friends or assistants. Four years later, Sukhov was ordained in St. Petersburg's grand Kazanskii Cathedral and sent to Dudachkino to reestablish a parish. Father Aleksandr knew the area well. He had often come to its forests and swamps to pick berries and mushrooms. The sparsely inhabited expanses reminded him of Siberia. Land was cheap, and he bought twenty acres at the top of the hill near the village. A person of great energy and charisma, he soon attracted more than a hundred followers, many of whom would travel three or four hours by car or bus from St. Petersburg just to spend the weekend in the parish.

Almost thirty people eventually moved to the community. Living conditions were primitive. The wooden houses had electricity but no indoor plumbing. A nearby spring provided water. The only bathing was on Fridays in a Russian *bania* (bathhouse). The community strove to be self-sufficient, raising its own food. Father Aleksandr even cultivated grapes in a makeshift greenhouse so that the community could supply its own wine for the Eucharist. A cook prepared the community's midday and evening meals. A young woman gave daily school lessons to the community's only two children. Parishioners donated whatever financial resources they had to Father Aleksandr and accepted his spiritual authority. He assigned their work, heard their confessions, determined the daily schedule, handled money, and made community decisions.

One autumn several years ago, Sergii and Marina invited me to visit them. I felt as though I had suddenly stepped into Nesterov's Holy Rus'. As we walked down the road, a tiny rose-colored chapel rose up to the left, and behind it a large wooden church, both dedicated to St. Michael the

Archangel. One of its icons was miraculously exuding oil. On a ridge on the other side of the road stood two slender chapels painted in bright green and dedicated to the warriors who fought for Dmitrii Donskoi in his fourteenth-century battles against the Mongols. Farther up the road, we came to a small chapel in honor of the prophet Elijah, to whom the original village church had been dedicated. A miraculous apparition of the Mother of God had appeared in one of the chapel windows. Marina said that she could still trace it out; if I looked the right way, I could perhaps see it too. Next door was a parish house with a chapel on the first floor dedicated to St. John the Clairvoyant, an Egyptian anchorite of the fourth century. Across the road stood a church and bell tower painted in pale yellow and dedicated to St. Nicholas of Myra. The church was being used primarily by the sisters of a small monastery that Father Aleksandr had founded. Behind the Church of St. Nicholas—and still in the process of being constructed—was a large cathedral-like edifice. It would be dedicated to the Protection of the Most Holy Theotokos.

Sergii and Marina took their turns in the parish's continuous reading of the Psalter, day and night, in the Chapel of St. John the Clairvoyant, something that otherwise takes place only in a few monasteries. Father Aleksandr celebrated the Divine Liturgy every morning in the Church of St. Michael the Archangel and vespers every evening, also usually in the Church of St. Michael. On the iconostasis, next to Mary with the baby Jesus, was a kind, motherly Rasputin holding the Tsarevich Aleksei on his lap. What kind of Orthodoxy was I now encountering? Several strands of religious belief had merged: conservative apocalypticism with utopian communitarianism, a rejection of official Orthodoxy with a popular Orthodoxy that finds the holy in everything around it, and the creation of a lonely lifestyle niche with the effort to be true to deep religious convictions in a modern, pluralistic society.

The community at Dudachkino has suffered for its uncompromising faith. Moscow Patriarchate officials excommunicated Father Aleksandr after he rejected their oversight because, he said, they were corrupt and had accommodated themselves to the state. Local residents and authorities have accused him of running a cult, even of planning terrorist attacks. The FSB

(Russian secret police) has raided the community. Father Aleksandr has been physically threatened and taken to court—and has hired lawyers to defend his constitutional rights. Church buildings have been set on fire. Dudachkino's Holy Rus' does not fit with dominant official visions of Church, state, and society. Even some of his followers have worried that Father Aleksandr can be controlling, even abusive; he is known for bringing women to tears when they make confession before him.

On my last evening in Dudachkino, the solitary bell at St. Nicholas began to toll; the bells in the Church of St. Michael across the valley responded. The tempo started slowly but steadily accelerated over the next twenty minutes as the hour of evening prayer approached. Whether at home or in the fields, the members of the community put their work aside and walked across the fields or down the road to the church. When we arrived, only a few candles illuminated the dark space; the iconostasis glowed like burnished gold against their flames.

The beleaguered Orthodox believers of Dudachkino ushered me into a holy world in, yet not of, the hostile, secular world that surrounds them. Father Aleksandr began gently intoning the Church's prayers. His followers bowed and crossed themselves. Sergii's baritone and Natasha's soprano voice constituted the entirety of the church choir in the balcony. I looked out the window. Night had fallen, and the everyday world was silent. All that I could hear now were Sergii's and Natasha's plaintive and haunting voices—"Lord, have mercy; Lord have mercy"—as though they were calling out with their deepest longings for a Dudachkino, a Holy Rus', in which everything would finally be made good and right.

In the 1960s, famed sociologist of religion Robert Bellah argued that every people needs a civil religion: religious symbols, narratives, and rituals that unify it and anchor its identity in transcendent moral and spiritual values. He observed that in the United States, great national commemorative sites along the National Mall in Washington or widely observed national rituals such as Thanksgiving Day help the nation regularly remember and rehearse its highest, most noble identity.[31] Although Bellah was later more cautious about the term *civil religion*—he saw how it could easily be misused for narrow sectarian purposes or to justify oppressive social-political arrangements—he continued to believe that transcendent symbols, narratives, and rituals can both elevate a people and call it to repentance. This kind of civil religion need not simply sacralize existing social arrangements; it can also judge these arrangements in terms of ultimate ideals of justice, freedom, and peace.[32]

I have often hoped that Holy Rus' would play a similar function in Russia, that a religious vision of a transfigured people and place would bring Russians together and help them understand their unique value and purpose among the peoples of the world. Moreover, I have hoped that this Orthodoxy would retain a critical potential rather than simply endorsing symphonia and the current political order in Russia. And I have indeed seen how not only a progressive Orthodoxy at the Feodorovskii Cathedral in St. Petersburg but also an unofficial Orthodoxy in Dudachkino, which to a Western Protestant so easily distorts Christian faith, draw on the Church's symbols, narratives, and rituals to nurture alternative social spaces. Wherever Church, state, and society negotiate the meaning of Orthodox symbols, narratives, and rituals, there is the potential for new visions of life together to appear. Remember, when it comes to social reform, never rule religion out.[33]

There is another reason not to count religion out. Western political scientists often remark on the importance of a vibrant civil society for the development of democratic politics. As people organize and participate in voluntary associations—clubs, political parties, social welfare societies, and churches—they learn democratic skills of negotiation and compromise. Those abilities enable them to participate in government, as well as to resist its excesses.[34]

Today civil society in Russia appears to be far less developed than in Ukraine or the Baltic states, despite a common Soviet legacy. The Putin government has increased state control in every area of social life—from the Internet to motorcycle gangs to university accreditation. The prospects for democracy appear poor because the space for civil society is so constricted.[35] But Russia is not fated to despotism. In the early twentieth century, Russia experienced an explosive growth of voluntary associations that stepped into the breach as the tsarist regime crumbled under the burdens of the First World War and popular discontent. When the state proved unable to solve pressing social tasks on the ground, Russians successfully organized trade unions, local governments, and civic movements.[36] And today the Orthodox Church provides a critically important space, however limited and imperfect, for this kind of civil society.[37]

Russians who enter deeply into Orthodox belief and practice envision a God who gives them the freedom to work for moral and spiritual transformation of themselves and their society. A profound commitment to human dignity undergirds that freedom.[38] It is possible that some of Russia's Orthodoxies will inspire people to think about what kind of political order can best protect human dignity and whether a democracy may do so better than centralized authoritarian rule.[39] When Orthodox believers personally participate in the Church's social ministries, they get to know people who suffer not only because of personal sinful choices but also because of unemployment, inadequate access to medical care, and social marginalization due to illness or disability. As the Russian Church endeavors to conduct its ministries more effectively, it learns from Western models of social care. We wait to see whether Orthodox believers will eventually develop social analyses that suggest the value of democratic arrangements for addressing these problems.

The icon of the new martyrs, as we noted, can be read as sacralizing the political order—or, alternatively, as holding rulers accountable to transcendent ideals of justice. The icon supports traditional Orthodox notions of a symphonia between Church and state—but also warns the Church that the state can quickly become demonic and turn against it, as happened under Communism. A Church that recognizes the dangers of a totalitarian state retains the potential not only to criticize Western individualism and consumerism but also to question an insufficient commitment to human rights at home.

The development of parish life and eucharistic fellowship depends on Orthodox believers who take responsibility for parish affairs. As they organize Sunday schools, social outreach to the needy, or building projects, they debate strategies, negotiate differences of opinion, and come to consensus. They practice democratic virtues, even if they do not use the word *democracy* or think of themselves as Western liberals. Even while respecting the authority of the clergy, they draw from their own experience in business and social life. A Church that is increasingly characterized by young urban professionals will also be shaped by their entrepreneurial skills and ways of thinking.

While greater democracy is possible in Russia, it is not inevitable. And even if democratic impulses do develop, Russia's social-political order is apt to look very different from American, French, or German systems of government. We cannot yet say what role the Orthodox Church will play in advancing or restraining a distinctively Russian kind of democracy. Next to my principle "Never count religion out as a source of social reform" lies a second: "Religious phenomena are always ambiguous." They can be socially repressive or liberating; they can stabilize existing arrangements or call them into question.

As Father Vasilii and I returned from the creek to the monastery, he told me that the previous year he had gathered the monastery's youth group late in the night after the vigil. They went into the countryside, built a bonfire, and looked at the stars. The young men in the group stripped and jumped into a nearby pond. The two young women in the group, however, were hesitant. They were not active Church members and had never before celebrated Kreshchenie. Father Vasilii gently encouraged them. Finally, they, too, stripped off their clothes and dove into the icy waters. When they returned they were changed, he says. The polar bear swim had become their initiation into the Church.

The next morning Father Vasilii invited me to travel with him and his monastic brothers to a neighboring town, where they would bless the waters again. When we arrived, I waited with the fifty people who had gathered in the church while the monks organized themselves behind the iconostasis. Suddenly, one of the brothers came out and handed me a heavy gold robe. "Father Vasilii says that you can assist." I did not have time to protest that I, a Protestant theologian, had no business wearing an Orthodox robe. As the other brothers appeared, one handed me a long pole to carry; atop it was an icon of Christ. Together the monks and I processed out of the church, down the steps, along the street, and across the nearby fields to a small spring, where the monastery's abbot lowered his cross into a well and blessed the waters.

Celebration of Theophany along a river near the Pafnutii-Borovsk
Monastery (with permission of Father Makarii Komogorov)

When we had finished, Father Vasilii invited me to join him and the
brothers in dipping into a pool fed by the spring. Air temperatures were in
the low teens, but something about the moment swept me up beyond immediate time and space. I stripped and plunged—but just one time, not three
(Father, Son, and Holy Spirit)—into the body-numbing waters. As I was
drying off afterward—the droplets of water were quickly turning to crystals
of ice on my bare skin—two of the young monks exclaimed, "Now you are
truly Orthodox!"

Yes, it is true, I have experienced on my own body the power of Orthodox
symbols, narratives, and rituals. I have joined thousands of Russian pilgrims
surging through the courtyards of the Holy Trinity–St. Sergius Monastery
on a holy day; stood with a handful of monks through a long summer night
in one of Solovki's wooden churches—as dusk turned to dawn but dark
never fell—wrapping myself in the chanting of the All-Night Vigils; lined
up to venerate the incorruptible bodies of St. Aleksandr of Svirsk and

St. Ioasaf of Belgorod; faithfully attended the Sunday liturgy in the Church of Sophia, the Wisdom of God; strictly observed the Church's fasts; climbed the long, steep hill to glorious Easter morning; and passed through the frigid waters of Theophany. I have been—and have not been—"Orthodox" in many different ways, and each has given me a glimpse of heaven on earth.

Moreover, after a decade among Russian Orthodox believers, I have learned to pay more attention to ways in which Christianity has shaped—and will continue to shape—not only their nation but also Western societies for the better.[40] "Christian America" or even "Judeo-Christian America" is no less problematic a proposition than Holy Rus'. But American commitments to justice and freedom are arguably fruits of the nation's deep Christian heritage. *Re-Christianization* is a misleading term, but the effort to remind a nation of those Christian ideals that have embedded themselves in it may be a valid enterprise if it means not imposing a sectarian ideology on those who believe differently or not at all, but rather the effort to ground in everyday life a vision of the divine transfiguration of a people and place—the hope for a more just and beautiful world even within the real limitations of a particular society.

And yet . . . as much as I have entered into Russia and its Church, I finally decided not to venerate the Virgin's Belt during those cool, wet November days in Moscow. I could not overcome my nagging doubts that Holy Rus' could ever really include me. As much as I love and respect Russian Orthodoxy, I am still an American and a Protestant theologian. The social vision and program of the Russian Orthodox Church contrast dramatically with my assumptions about the separation of Church and state, the limited place of the Church in pluralistic societies, and the rightful "secularization" of the physical and cultural landscape. I agree with those North American theologians who argue that social privilege and cultural dominance too often cause churches to neglect their first task, which is to call people to a distinctive way of life shaped by the gospel, not general social norms. And I believe that the Russian Orthodox Church would benefit by attending to these insights.

My questions about Holy Rus' haunt not only me as an outsider but also a new generation of Russians who relate to religion and society so differently from many of the Church's hierarchs. These young Russians have never known Communism, only President Putin. They have enjoyed access to the Internet and travel to the West—and seen a people's revolution in Ukraine. They have gotten used to a steady rise in their standard of living but now worry that the future will bring political and economic insecurity. And while all of their lives they have heard that they are Orthodox, they struggle—like young people everywhere—to know who they really are and where they fit. Will re-Christianization make sense to them, or will they seek a different kind of Orthodox Russia?

Late one evening, Pavel knocks on the door of the dormitory room at a small seminary where my wife and I have been staying, a few hundred miles outside Moscow. He shyly asks if he can invite us up for a cup of tea. In his simple, sparsely furnished room, we take the two available chairs while he sits on the bed. Pavel hopes to become a priest, but he also wants to marry, and the Church will not allow a priest to marry after he is ordained. So far, he admits, he has no marriage prospects in sight. He is working on a master's degree in Church history but confesses that he lacks motivation. His salary at the seminary amounts to $130 a month, a pittance even in Russia, and he is thankful that he does not have to pay for room and board. His cat recently escaped and has not returned. We talk a little about America, and then he takes out his guitar, and as he plays, he squeezes his eyes together and his soft voice takes on an edge of urgency. "They call Rus' holy," he sings.[41] And for a moment, he sweeps us up into a magical world of vast forests and endless steppes, big skies and deep lakes, and bleached white monastery walls and tolling church bells.

A few days later, I sit with Dmitrii and Sophia, two young friends in St. Petersburg who are just beginning adult life. They have scraped together enough money to rent a small apartment in a new high-rise on the outskirts of the city, and six months ago Sophia gave birth to Ivan, their first child. Dmitrii studied theology at one of the country's premier Orthodox institutions but now works for a technology startup. "I was a pious believer when I began my studies," he says, "but ironically my Orthodox university taught me to think for myself." When Sophia speaks of her education in Orthodox primary and secondary schools, she is only bitter: "They constantly berated us for not being religious enough." Today Dmitrii and Sophia are more apt to read Deacon Andrei Kuraev's blog than attend church.[42] They say that he is one of the few independent voices in the Church—and they sadly note that he himself has been pushed to its margins. "How can you name your book *Holy Rus'*, they ask, "when you see the Church's obsession with power and control?"

As we take our seats at a small table in their kitchen, I change the subject. What will their life be like now with a son? What are their hopes for him? When they tell me that they are planning to have him baptized on Sunday, I cannot contain my astonishment. "But that makes no sense to me," I finally blurt out. "Why baptize him if you aren't committed to the Orthodox Church?" Calmly but firmly, they respond, "Because we want him to know who he is, where he comes from. When we walk into a church or stand during the Divine Liturgy, when we look at the icons and hear the choir's chanting, when we make pilgrimage to a great monastery or a holy spring, something ineffable touches us—something that should be a part of his life, too. It's not about the Church. No, it's about goodness and love, beauty and justice." Sophia graciously offers me another cup of tea, and I look at Ivan— so tiny, so miraculous—and silently ponder their words.

NOTES

Chapter One. Envisioning Holy Rus'

1. The Russian term is *votserkovlenie*.

2. See Masha Gessen, *The Man Without a Face* (New York: Riverhead Books, 2012); Fiona Hill and Clifford Gaddy, *Mr. Putin*, rev. ed. (Washington, DC: Brookings Institution Press, 2015); Karen Dawisha, *Putin's Kleptocracy* (New York: Simon and Schuster, 2014); and Ben Judah, *Fragile Empire: How Russia Fell in and out of Love with Vladimir Putin* (New Haven: Yale University Press, 2013).

3. Stephen Kotkin, "The Resistible Rise of Vladimir Putin," *Foreign Affairs*, March–April 2015, https://www.foreignaffairs.com/reviews/2015-02-16/resistible-rise-vladimir -putin.

4. For the concept of "national identity," see Eric J. Hobsbawm, *Nations and Nationalism since 1780* (New York: Cambridge University Press, 1990); Benedict Anderson, *Imagined Communities: Reflections on the Origin and Spread of Nationalism*, rev. ed. (New York: Verso, 2006); and Adrian Hastings, *The Construction of Nationhood: Ethnicity, Religion, and Nationalism* (New York: Cambridge University Press, 1997). For the emergence of national identity in Russia, see James H. Billington, *Russia in Search of Itself* (Washington, DC: Woodrow Wilson Center Press / Baltimore: John Hopkins University Press, 2004).

5. "Zapad otdaliaetsia ot Rossii iz za ee vozvrata k pravoslaviiu, schitaet Lavrov," *Interfax-religion.ru*, June 5, 2014, http://www.interfax-religion.ru/?act=news&div=55525.

6. For typical Western media presentations of Church and state in Russia, see Joshua Keating, "Russia Gets Religion: Is Vladimir Putin Trying to Build a New Orthodox Empire?" *Slate*, November 11, 2014, http://www.slate.com/articles/news_and_politics /foreigners/2014/11/russia_orthodox_church_will_vladimir_putin_eradicate_all_ boundaries_between.html; Peter Pomerantsev, "Putin's God Squad: The Orthodox Church and Russian Politics," *Newsweek*, September 10, 2012, http://www.newsweek.

com/putins-god-squad-orthodox-church-and-russian-politics-64649; and Tim
Neshitov, "Die unheilige Allianz," *Süddeutsche Zeitung*, March 15, 2015, http://
www.sueddeutsche.de/kultur/kirche-und-staat-in-russland-die-unheilige-allianz-
1.2391936/.

7. Metropolitan Kirill, "Blagovestie i kul'tura," *Tserkov' i vremia* 1/4 (1998): 31, as
   quoted in O. E. Kaz'mina, *Russkaia Pravoslavnaia Tserkov' i novaia religioznaia
   situatsiia v Rossii* (Moscow: Moscow State University Press, 2009), 271–72. See
   also Metropolitan Kirill, "Gospel and Culture," in *Proselytism and Orthodoxy in
   Russia*, ed. John Witte Jr. and Michael Bourdeaux (Maryknoll, NY: Orbis, 1999),
   66–76.

8. For the term *second Christianization*, see *Kontseptsiia missionerskoi deiatel'nosti
   Russkoi Pravoslavnoi Tserkvi*, March 27, 2007, *Patriarchia.ru*, http://www.
   patriarchia.ru/db/text/220922.html.

9. See Stanley Hauerwas and William H. Willimon, *Resident Aliens* (Nashville:
   Abingdon, 1989); and Martin Reppenhagen and Darrell Guder, "The Continuing
   Transformation of Mission," in David Bosch, *Transforming Mission: Paradigm
   Shifts in Theology of Mission*, rev. ed. (Maryknoll, NY: Orbis, 2011), 543–51.

10. For a review of key literature on secularization, see Geoffrey Evans and Ksenia
    Northmore-Ball, "The Limits of Secularization? The Resurgence of Orthodoxy in
    Post-Soviet Russia," *Journal for the Scientific Study of Religion* 51/4 (2012): 796–97.
    Recent scholarship speaks of different kinds of secularization. See David Martin,
    On Secularization: Towards a Revised General Theory (Burlington, VT: Ashgate,
    2005); and *Rethinking Secularism*, ed. Craig Calhoun et al. (New York: Oxford
    University Press, 2011).

11. See Peter Berger, "Desecularization," *American Interest*, May 13, 2015, http://www.
    the-american-interest.com/2015/05/13/desecularization/.

12. For estimates of church attendance, see Igor' Riazantsev and Tat'iana Veselkina,
    "Sotsial'nyi portret 'molchalivogo bol'shinstva Rossii,' " *Pravoslavie.ru*, April 10,
    2014, http://www.pravoslavie.ru/put/print69702.htm; and Hans-Christian Diedrich,
    *"Wohin sollen wir gehen . . ." Der Weg der Christen durch die sowjetische
    Religionsverfolgung* (Erlangen: Martin-Luther Verlag, 2007), 339–40. For Lenten
    observance, see Vserossiiskii Tsentr Izucheniia Obshchestvennogo Mneniia, press
    release no. 938, April 21, 2008, http://wciom.ru/index.php?id=236&uid=10035. See
    also *SEIA Newsletter on the Eastern Churches and Ecumenism* 166 (2009): 11–12;
    and Erzpriester Georgij Mitrofanov, "Wir sind heute eine Gesellschaft von
    getauften Gottlosen," *G2W. Ökumenisches Forum für Glauben, Religion und
    Gesellschaft in Ost und West* 7/8 (July–August 2010): 42–43.

13. See Zoe Knox, *Russian Society and the Orthodox Church: Religion in Russia after
    Communism* (New York: RoutledgeCurzon, 2005), 186.

14. Forty-three percent of Russians support instruction in the foundations of Orthodox

culture in public school, whereas only 19 percent prefer secular ethics. Fifty-three percent "highly" value Patriarch Kirill's social activity. See *Rossiiane—2011: rezul'taty oprosov* (Moscow: Sluzhba "Sreda," 2011), 154–57. See also E. M. Mchedlova, "Religioznost' rossiian: pervye rezul'taty vserossiiskogo issledovaniia 2010–12 gg.," in *Sotsiologiia religii v obshchestve pozdnego moderna* (Belgorod: Belgorod State University Press, 2012), 246; and Christopher Marsh, *Religion and the State in Russia and China* (New York: Continuum, 2011), 121–22. According to Marsh, "Surveys regularly find that the church is the most trusted institution in Russian society, with around 60 percent of all Russians expressing their confidence in it" (121).

15. Katja Richters, *The Post-Soviet Russian Orthodox Church: Politics, Culture and Greater Russia* (New York: Routledge, 2013).

16. Irina Papkova, *The Orthodox Church and Russian Politics* (New York: Oxford University Press, 2011), 71–117.

17. A recent collection of essays on contemporary Russian politics does not even mention the Church as a political factor. See Leon Aron, ed., *Putin's Russia: How It Rose, How It Is Maintained, and How It Might End* (Washington, DC: American Enterprise Institute, 2015).

18. See Martin Malia, *The Soviet Tragedy: A History of Socialism in Russia, 1917–1991* (New York: Free Press, 1994), 227; and Edvard Radzinsky, *Stalin*, trans. H. T. Willetts (New York: Doubleday, 1996), 237.

19. Robert N. Bellah, "Civil Religion in America," *Dædalus: Journal of the American Academy of Arts and Sciences* 96/1 (1967): 1–21.

20. See Olga Kazmina, "The Russian Orthodox Church in a New Situation in Russia: Challenges and Responses," in *Eastern Orthodox Encounters of Identity and Otherness*, ed. Andrii Krawchuk and Thomas Bremer (New York: Palgrave Macmillan, 2014), 228–29. For an expanded treatment, see Kaz'mina, *Russkaia Pravoslavnaia Tserkov'*, 261–69.

21. Especially influential representatives of this position have been North American theologians John Howard Yoder and Stanley Hauerwas and German theologian Wolf Krötke.

22. See Robin W. Lovin, *Christian Realism and the New Realities* (New York: Cambridge University Press, 2008); and William Schweiker, *Dust That Breathes: Christian Faith and the New Humanisms* (Malden, MA: Wiley-Blackwell, 2010).

23. Georgii Mitrofanov, "My dolzhny izvlech' dukovnye uroki iz opyta novomuchenikov," *Blagovest-info.ru*, April 5, 2012, http://www.blagovest-info.ru/index.php?ss=2&s= 4&id=46412. For an English-language description of Mitrofanov's position, see Anna Briskina-Müller, "The Search for a New Church Consciousness in Current Russian Orthodox Discourse," in *Eastern Orthodox Encounters of Identity and Otherness*, 76–77.

24. Vsevolod Chaplin, head of the Church's department for cooperation with society until 2015, has strongly represented these positions. For an earlier collection of his essays, see Vsevolod Chaplin, *Tserkov' v Rossii: obstoiatel'stva mesta i vremeni* (Moscow: Arefa, 2008). Critics of current Church-state relations cite state legislation in 1997 that restricted the ability of foreign and minority religious groups to proselytize in Russia; state prosecution in 2012 of members of a feminist art collective (Pussy Riot) for their intrusion into Christ the Savior Cathedral in Moscow; and joint appearances of Putin and Kirill at major national celebrations, such as the 865th anniversary (2012) of the founding of Moscow.

25. See John P. Burgess, "Minority Report: Lutherans and Methodists in Russia," *Christian Century*, October 2, 2013, 28–30; and Karrie J. Koesel, *Religion and Authoritarianism: Cooperation, Conflict, and Consequences* (New York: Cambridge University Press, 2014), 145.

26. Sergei Chapnin, "Sovetskoe i postsovetskoe v sovremennoi tserkovnoi kul'ture: obraz pastyria, svidetel'stvo, sluzhenie," *Bogoslov.ru*, September 28, 2011, http://www.bogoslov.ru/text/2005170.html.

27. It was striking that at the opening ceremonies of the 2014 Winter Olympics in Sochi, references to Russia's Orthodox heritage were muted. Prominent instead were symbols from Russian fairy tales and references to Russia's military and industrial might.

28. See Patriarch Kirill's words at the opening of the 2015 Church exhibition in the Manezh, *Orthodox Rus': My History, from the Great Trauma to the Great Victory,* as reported in "Edinstvo naroda i nravstvennie orientiry," *Zhurnal Moskovskoi Patriarchii,* December 2015, 19.

29. For a classic treatment of this point, see Ernst Troeltsch, *The Social Teaching of the Christian Churches,* trans. Olive Wyon (1931; repr., Chicago: University of Chicago Press, 1981).

30. For the diversity of positions within the Church, see Papkova, *Orthodox Church*, 47–67; and Knox, *Russian Society,* 16–40. Papkova speaks of the Church's liberal, traditional, and fundamentalist wings.

31. Aleksei Peutskii, "Dozvonit do nebes," *Zhurnal Moskovskoi Patriarchii,* November 2015, 51–55.

Chapter Two. The Rebirth of Orthodoxy

1. I. I. Shagina, *Russkii narod: budni i prazdniki* (Saint Petersburg: Azbuka-klassika), 168–71.

2. See Luke 10:38–42.

3. For beautiful illustrations of the church's exterior and interior, see *Pokrovskii khram* (Moscow: Martha and Mary Monastery of Mercy, 2008).

4. See Ekaterina Malinina, *Mikhail Nesterov* (Moscow: Belyi gorod, 2001), 26–27.

5. *Pokrovskii khram*, 18. I discuss this icon in chapter 5, below.

6. Elizabeth's body was recovered and eventually brought to the Russian Orthodox church in Jerusalem. See Vladimir Vorob'ev, ed., *Postradavshie za veru i tserkov' Khristovu, 1917–1937* (Moscow: St. Tikhon's University Press, 2012), 80–87.

7. Gregory L. Freeze, "Von der Entkirchlichung zur Laisierung: Staat, Kirche und Gläubige in Russland," in *Politik und Religion: zur Diagnose der Gegenwart,* ed. Friedrich Wilhelm Graf and Heinrich Meier (Munich: Verlag C. H. Beck, 2013), 82.

8. My historical overview draws from Diedrich, "*Wohin sollen wir gehen*"; Nathaniel Davis, *A Long Walk to Church: A Contemporary History of Russian Orthodoxy* (Boulder, CO: Westview, 2003); Dmitry Pospielovsky, *The Russian Church under the Soviet Regime, 1917–1982*, 2 vols. (Crestwood, NY: St. Vladimir's Seminary Press, 1984); Marsh, *Religion and the State*, 47–147; and course lectures by Russian historian Aleksandr Mazyrin at St. Tikhon's Orthodox University (Moscow), 2011–12. See also M. V. Shkarovskii, *Russkaia Pravoslavnaia Tserkov' v XX veke* (Moscow: Lepta, 2010); Vladislav Tsipin, *Istoriia Russkoi Pravoslavnoi Tserkvi: sinodalnyi i noveishii periody (1700–2005)*, 2nd ed. (Moscow: Sretenskii Monastery, 2006); and I. V. Geras'kin, "Vzaimootnosheniia Russkoi Pravoslavnoi Tserkvi, obshchestva i vlasti v kontse 30-x–1991 gg." (PhD diss., Moscow State Pedagogical University, 2008).

9. Freeze, "Von der Entkirchlichung," 103. For the early church statistics, I am thankful to Professor Karen King of Harvard University (personal conversation, November 2011).

10. Diedrich, "*Wohin sollen wir gehen*," 147–48.

11. Freeze, "Von der Entkirchlichung," 103.

12. The statistics here and in the next paragraph are from Father Aleksandr Mazyrin's lecture, September 6, 2011; and Andrei Kostriukov, *Zhizneopisanie Arkhiepiskopa Serafima (Soboleva)* (Sophia: Podvor'e Patriarkha Moskovskogo i vsei Rusi, 2011), 111.

13. Freeze, "Von der Entkirchlichung," 106.

14. See Mariia Simonova, "Russkaia Pravoslavnaia Tserkov' i sovetskoe gosudarstvo," *Pokrov*, July 2015, 32–35.

15. Freeze, "Von der Entkirchlichung," 106–7; and Trevor Beeson, *Discretion and Valour: Religious Conditions in Russia and Eastern Europe*, rev. ed. (Philadelphia: Fortress, 1982), 70–88.

16. See Vera Shevzov, "Letting 'the People' into 'Church,'" in *Orthodox Russia: Belief and Practice under the Tsars*, ed. Valerie A. Kivelson and Robert H. Greene (University Park: Pennsylvania State University Press, 2003), 59–79. For an equally nuanced discussion in relation to medieval Catholicism, see Kevin Madigan, *Medieval Christianity: A New History* (New Haven: Yale University Press, 2015), 91–94.

17. Freeze, "Von der Entkirchlichung," 107.

18. Davis, *Long Walk*, 146.
19. Kaz'mina, *Russkaia Pravoslavnaia Tserkov'*, 57. See also Catherine Wanner, "Multiple Moralities, Multiple Secularisms," in *Multiple Moralities and Religions in Post-Soviet Russia*, ed. Jarrett Zigon (New York: Berghahn Books, 2011), 221; and Alexander Agadjanian, "Exploring Russian Religiosity as a Source of Moral Identity Today," in Zigon, *Multiple Moralities and Religions*, 16–17.
20. See also Davis, *Long Walk*, 146.
21. See Aleksei Beglov, *V poiskakh "bezgreshnykh katakomb": tserkovnoe podpol'e v SSSR* (Moscow: Arefa, 2008).
22. For a review of Soviet dissident movements, see Philip Boobbyer, *Conscience, Dissent and Reform in Soviet Russia* (New York: Routledge, 2005).
23. An example is the movement to preserve the monastery at Solovki. See Roy R. Robson, *Solovki: The Story of Russia Told through Its Most Remarkable Islands* (New Haven: Yale University Press, 2004), 256.
24. See "Russians Return to Religion, but Not to Church," *Pew Research Center: Religion and Life*, February 10, 2014, http://www.pewforum.org/2014/02/10/russians-return-to-religion-but-not-to-church/.
25. See the discussion in Dmitrii Gorevoi, "Massovoe Pravoslavie: est' ono ili net, i esli da, to, chto eto znachit?" *Sreda.org*, April 4, 2014, http://sreda.org/ru/2014/massovoe-pravoslavie-est-ono-ili-net-i-esli-da-to-chto-eto-znachit-reportazh-iz-pstgu/77324.
26. Kaz'mina, *Russkaia Pravoslavnaia Tserkov'*, 57–58.
27. Solovki again provides a good example. See Atle Staalsen, "Church, State Eye Compromise at Solovki," *Barents Observer*, January 14, 2010, http://barentsobserver.com/en/sections/articles/state-church-eye-compromise-solovki.
28. See Konstantin Akinsha and Gregory Kozlov, with Sylvia Hochfield, *The Holy Place: Architecture, Ideology, and History in Russia* (New Haven: Yale University Press, 2007), 132–33, 143–65.
29. For the total number of parishes, see "Doklad Sviateishego Patriarkha Kirilla na Arkhiereiskom Soveshchanii," *Patriarchia.ru*, February 2, 2015, http://www.patriarchia.ru/db/text/3979067.html.
30. See Mazyrin lecture, September 6, 2011; and Gorevoi, "Massovoe Pravoslavie."
31. For a description and evaluation of traditional Orthodox notions of symphonia, see Aristotle Papanikolaou, *The Mystical as Political* (Notre Dame: Notre Dame University Press, 2012), 48; and John Meyendorff, *The Byzantine Legacy in the Orthodox Church* (Crestwood, NY: St. Vladimir's Seminary Press, 2000), 48–49. For symphonia in the Russian context, see Knox, *Russian Society*, 105–31.
32. See Paul Meyendorff, *Russia, Ritual, and Reform: The Liturgical Reforms of Nikon in the 17th Century* (Crestwood, NY: St. Vladimir's Seminary Press, 1991); and Georg Bernhard Michels, *At War with the Church: Religious Dissent in Seventeenth-Century Russia* (Stanford: Stanford University Press, 1999).

33. Gregory L. Freeze, "Institutionalizing Piety: The Church and Popular Religion, 1750–1850," in *Imperial Russia: New Histories for the Empire*, ed. Jane Burbank and David L. Ransel (Bloomington: Indiana University Press, 1998), 212.

34. Ibid.; and see Vladimir Tsurikov, ed., *Philaret, Metropolitan of Moscow, 1782–1867* (Jordanville, NY: Holy Trinity Orthodox Seminary, 2003).

35. Kostriukov, *Zhizneopisanie Arkhiepiskopa Serafima*, 98–99.

36. Diedrich, "*Wohin sollen wir gehen*," 21. Other historians, however, sharply distinguish Slavophilism from a "national Orthodoxy." Many Slavophiles called for reducing centralized Church and state bureaucracies and giving more power to local councils. See Geoffrey Hosking, *Russia: People and Empire, 1552–1917* (Cambridge, MA: Harvard University Press, 1997), 271–75.

37. See Laurie Manchester, *Holy Fathers, Secular Sons: Clergy, Intelligentsia, and the Modern Self in Revolutionary Russia* (DeKalb: Northern Illinois University Press, 2008).

38. Papkova, *Orthodox Church*, 32. See also Department for External Church Relations, "The Basis of the Social Concept of the Russian Orthodox Church," August 13–16, 2000, *Mospat.ru*, http://www.mospat.ru/en/documents/social-concepts/.

39. See "Chaplin obeshchaet, chto RPTs prodolzhit sozdanie 'simfonii' s vlast'iu," November 7, 2011, *Interfax-religion.ru*, http://www.interfax.ru/russia/215578.

40. See Richters, *Post-Soviet Russian Orthodox Church*.

41. See Koesel, *Religion and Authoritarianism*.

42. See John Garrard and Carol Garrard, *Russian Orthodoxy Resurgent: Faith and Power in the New Russia* (Princeton: Princeton University Press, 2008).

43. For introductions to Orthodox worship, see Timothy [Bishop Kallistos] Ware, *The Orthodox Church*, rev. ed. (New York: Penguin, 1993), 264–306; and Alexander Schmemann, *For the Life of the World* (Crestwood, NY: St. Vladimir's Seminary Press, 1988).

44. St. Athanasius, *On the Incarnation* (Crestwood, NY: St. Vladimir's Seminary Press, 2003), 93.

45. See Ware, *Orthodox Church*, 232.

46. The theological term is *synergy*. Ibid., 221–22.

47. For an analysis of the *Missionary Concept*, see Kazmina, "The Russian Orthodox Church in a New Situation," 225.

48. *Kontseptsiia missionerskoi deiatel'nosti*, 3. Subsequent page references to this work are given parenthetically in the text.

49. For a bimonthly journal that regularly reports on these activities, see *Missionerskoe obrazovanie (ofitsial'noe izdanie Sinodal'nogo missionerskogo otdela Moskovskogo Patriarkhata Russkoi Pravoslavnoi Tserkvi)*.

50. Gabriel Bunge, *The Rublev Trinity: The Icon of the Trinity by the Monk-Painter Andrei Rublev* (Crestwood, NY: St. Vladimir's Seminary Press, 2007).

Chapter Three. Religious Education

1. Since then the building has been beautifully renovated.
2. For an overview of these activities, see Veniamin Simonov, "Besonderheiten der Evangelisierung in Russland nach der Veränderung des sozial-ökonomischen Systems 1990-er bis Anfang der 2000-er Jahre," *Una Sancta: Zeitschrift für ökumenische Begegnung* (Sonderdruck) 3 (2010): 221–27. See also the analysis in Valerii Ovchinnikov, "O pravoslavnom obrazovanii v Rossii," in *Pravoslavnaia tserkov' pri novom Patriarkhe* (Moscow: Carnegie Center and Rossiiskaia politicheskaia entsiklopediia, 2012), 261–310.
3. For general information, see the church website: http://stserafim.ru/.
4. "O religiozno-obrazovatel'nom i katekhizicheskom sluzhenii v Russkoi Pravoslavnoi Tserkvi," December 28, 2011, *Patriarchia.ru*, http://www.patriarchia.ru/db/text/1909451.html.
5. Elena Ivanova, "Pedagogika Afinskogo startsa," *Pokrov*, no. 8 (2011): 20–23.
6. For the Church's understanding of freedom, see Kristina Stoeckl, *The Russian Orthodox Church and Human Rights* (New York: Routledge, 2014), 74–75.
7. Theologians typically trace the idea of "faith seeking understanding" to Augustine of Hippo and Anselm of Canterbury. See Daniel L. Migliore, *Faith Seeking Understanding: An Introduction to Christian Theology*, 2nd ed. (Grand Rapids, MI: Eerdmans, 1991), 2.
8. Shagina, *Russkii narod*, 150–54. The Russian Orthodox Church uses the Julian (Old Style) calendar, which is thirteen days behind the Gregorian (New Style) calendar.
9. Ibid., 166.
10. See Alexander Schmemann, *The Historical Road of Eastern Orthodoxy*, trans. Lydia W. Kesich (New York: Holt, Reinhart and Winston, 1963), 300–301, as quoted in Donald Fairbairn, *Eastern Orthodoxy through Western Eyes* (Louisville: Westminster John Knox, 2002), 132; and Peter Berger, *The Sacred Canopy: Elements of a Sociological Theory of Religion* (New York: Doubleday, 1967).
11. See Alexander Schmemann, *Introduction to Liturgical Theology* (Crestwood, NY: St. Vladimir's Seminary Press, 1986).
12. Gregory L. Freeze, "The Rechristianization of Russia: The Church and Popular Religion, 1750–1850," *Studia Slavica Finlandensia* 7 (1990): 101–36.
13. See, for example, Aleksei Khomyakov, "On the Western Confessions of Faith," in *Ultimate Questions: An Anthology of Modern Russian Religious Thought*, ed. Alexander Schmemann (New York: Holt, Reinhart & Winston, 1965), 33.
14. See Hosking, *Russia*, 233–34.
15. For Brianchaninov's biography, see "Zhizneopisanie Episkopa Ignatiia Brianchaninova," in *Polnoe Sobranie Tvorenii Sviatitelia Ignatiia Brianchaninova* (Moscow: Palomnik, 2006), 1:7–72.

16. See Ware, *Orthodox Church*, 121.

17. For more on Filaret, see Tsurikov, *Philaret*.

18. Freeze, "Rechristianization of Russia," 117.

19. See Paul Valliere, *Modern Russian Theology—Bukharev, Soloviev, Bulgakov: Orthodox Theology in a New Key* (Edinburgh: T & T Clark, 2000).

20. For the important role of women in advancing religious education, see Brenda Meehan, *Holy Women of Russia* (San Francisco: HarperSanFrancisco, 1993).

21. See Beglov, "*V poiskakh bezgreshnykh katakomb*"; and Freeze, "Von der Entkirchlichung," 81–82.

22. Lidiia Kaleda and Valentin Filoian, "Moli Boga o nas: vspominaniia o sviashchenno muchenike Vladimire Ambartsumove," *Nyne i Prisno*, no. 1 (2004): 49–52.

23. For a moving portrayal of the catacomb church, see the film *Zhara* (2011), directed by Aleksandr Arkhangel'skii. For a thoughtful set of reviews, see *Td: Tat'ianin Den'*, October 28, 2011, http://www.taday.ru/text/1270975.html.

24. For similar phenomena in the countryside, see Douglas Rogers, *The Old Faith and the Russian Land: A Historical Ethnography of Ethics in the Urals* (Ithaca: Cornell University Press, 2009).

25. "Mechevskaia obshchina," June 16, 2010, *Klenniki.ru*, http://klenniki.ru/mechev-obchin. Note Mechev's personal connection to Metropolitan Filaret, who promoted Church reform and education in the nineteenth century.

26. Protoierei Pavel Khodzinskii, "Poniatie 'obshchiny' v russkoi bogoslovskoi traditsii vtoroi poloviny XIX-nachala XX vekov," *Vestnik PSTGU: bogoslovie/filosofiia* 3/41 (2012): 38–46.

27. "Mechevskaia obshchina."

28. Irina Iazykova, *So-tvorenie obraza: bogoslovie ikony* (Moscow: Izdatel'stvo BBI, 2012), 270–71.

29. For short biographical accounts of Men', see Michael Meerson, "The Life and Work of Father Aleksandr Men'," in *Seeking God: The Recovery of Religious Identity in Orthodox Russia, Ukraine, and Georgia*, ed. Stephen K. Batalden (DeKalb: Northern Illinois Press, 1993), 13–27; Michael Plekon, *Living Icons: Persons of Faith in the Eastern Church* (Notre Dame: University of Notre Dame Press, 2002), 234–60; and Irina Iazykova, "We Are Moving into an Age of Love," 2005, *Alexandermen.com*, http://www.alexandermen.com/We_are_Moving_into_an_Age_of_Love.

30. For a recent collection of his writings, see Alexander Men, *An Inner Step Toward God: Writings and Teachings on Prayer*, ed. April French (Brewster, MA: Paraclete, 2014).

31. For an analysis of holy eldership (*starchestvo*)—and especially of the roles of Ioann (Krest'iankin) and Nikolai (Gur'ianov) in Soviet Russia—see Irina Paert, *Spiritual Elders: Charisma and Tradition in Russian Orthodoxy* (DeKalb: Northern Illinois University Press, 2010), 206–13.

32. For a popular portrayal of Ioann, see Archimandrite [Bishop] Tikhon (Shevkunov), *"Nesviatye sviatye" i drugie rasskazy* (Moscow: Sretenskii Monastary, 2011), 39–73.

33. See A. A. Il'iunina, *Starets, protoierei Nikolai Gur'ianov: zhizneopisanie, vspominaniia, pis'ma* (Saint Petersburg: Iskusstvo Rossi, 2011); and Starets Nikolai (Gur'ianov), *O bogoustanovlennosti Tsarskoi samoderzhavnoi vlasti* (Moscow: Obshchestvo Svetloi Pamiati Pravednogo Nikolaia Pskovozerskogo, 2007).

34. *Kontseptsiia missionerskoi deiatel'nosti*, 6.

35. See "Mitropolit Ilarion (Alfeev) vs Dzhon Berdzhess," *Youtube.com*, April 6, 2013, https://www.youtube.com/watch?v=b7tac2SiRuQ.

36. See, for example, his popular introduction to Orthodoxy, which has been translated into English: Metropolitan Hilarion (Alfeev), *Orthodox Christianity*, 3 vols., trans. Basil Bush (Yonkers, NY: St. Vladimir's Seminary Press, 2011–14).

37. *Sviatoe Evangelie ot Marka c tolkovaniem Feofilakta Bolgarskogo* (Moscow: Nikeia, 2011), 4. The book was prepared for free distribution.

38. Episkop Vasilii (Preobrazhenskii), *Besedi na evangelie ot Marka* (Moscow: Otchii dom, 2004).

39. *Evangelie ot Marka c besedami protoiereia Alekseia Uminskogo* (Moscow: Nikeia, 2012).

40. *Evangelie ot Marka* (Moscow: Sretenskii Monastery, 2008).

41. Another Orthodox publishing house has prepared a short illustrated introduction to the *Philokalia* in an effort to make its principles accessible to a lay audience and even to children. See Ieromonakh Mitrofan (Volkodav), *Osnovy dukhovnoi zhizni po slavianskomu "Dobrotoliubiiu"* (Moscow: Olma-Press, 2002).

42. The Publications Committee issues a monthly journal, *Pravoslavnoe knizhnoe obozrenie*, which reports on book exhibits and publication events and offers reviews of new books and journals.

43. A 2009 survey determined that only 6 percent of self-identified Orthodox adherents had a priest to whom they turned for authoritative guidance. See Veniamin Simonov, "Religion und Religiosität in Russland," *Osteuropa* 59/6 (2009): 201.

44. Ieromonakh Iov (Gumerov), *Tysiacha voprosov sviashchenniku* (Moscow: Sretenskii Monastery, 2009).

45. Meyendorff, *Russia, Ritual, and Reform.*

46. Ieromonakh Iov (Gumerov) and Sviashchennik Pavel Gumerov, *Dom khristianina: traditsii i sviatyni* (Moscow: Sretenskii Monastery, 2010).

47. See Richard J. Foster, *Celebration of Discipline: The Path to Spiritual Growth* (San Francisco: Harper & Row, 1978); and Marjorie J. Thompson, *Soul Feast: An Invitation to the Christian Spiritual Life* (Louisville: Westminster John Knox, 1995).

48. According to one recent survey, more than 10 percent of Russians have experienced unfriendly encounters with priests or lay believers in Orthodox churches. See *Rossiiane—2011: rezul'taty oprosov*, 192–93.

49. The *Missionary Concept* of 2007 issues a similar warning. See *Kontseptsiia missionerskoi deiatel'nosti*, 20.

50. *Nepoznannyi mir very* (Moscow: Sretenskii Monastery, 2011), 5–6.

51. In 2011, it was already in its twelfth printing and had sold more than one hundred thousand copies.

52. For another popular introduction to Orthodoxy that is attentive to its "mystical" dimensions, see Ieromonakh Serafim (Paramanov), *Zakon liubvi: kak zhit' po-pravoslavnomu* (Moscow: Artos-Mediia, 2006). Serafim includes discussions of relics, pilgrimage, holy water, dreams, and superstition.

53. Tikhon (Shevkunov), *"Nesviatye sviatye."* Subsequent page references to this work are given parenthetically in the text. For an English translation, see Archimandrite Tikhon (Shevkunov), *Everyday Saints and Other Stories*, trans. Julian Henry Lowenfeld (Dallas: Pokrov, 2012).

54. Paul Gabel, *And God Created Lenin: Marxism vs. Religion in Russia, 1917–1929* (Amherst, NY: Prometheus Books, 2005), 159. In 1914, the Church operated 35,528 parish schools. See Diedrich, *"Wohin sollen wir gehen,"* 23.

55. For a review of some of the issues, see Koesel, *Religion and Authoritarianism*, 147–52.

56. See the discussion in Papkova, *Orthodox Church*, 93–116.

57. A. V. Kuraev, *Osnovy pravoslavnoi kul'tury* (Moscow: Prosveshchenie, 2010), 7. Subsequent page references to this work are given parenthetically in the text.

58. The textbook *Foundations of Orthodox Culture* for grade 7 in the Belgorod Region begins with an extensive discussion in "The Spiritual-Moral Foundations of Orthodoxy: The History and Theory of Orthodox Culture." Key topics include the meaning of "culture" and an Orthodox understanding of the Church, the sacraments, the Nicene Creed, and the Trinity. See *Osnovy pravoslavnoi kul'tury: uchebnoe posobie* (Belgorod: Belgorod State University Press, 2007).

59. "Peterburzhtsy men'she moskvichei khotiat izuchat' pravoslavie i islam," September 14, 2012, *Online812.ru*, http://www.online812.ru/2012/09/14/007/.

60. See "Kak pravil'no krestit'sia po novym pravilam?" *Rossiskaia gazeta*, December 29, 2011, 26.

61. *Kontseptsiia missionerskoi deiatel'nosti*, 10.

62. Ibid., 24.

63. Bishop Antonii (Cheremisov) of Krasnoiar and Enisei, "Smotrite, kako opasno khodite . . . ," July 15, 2010, *Pravmir.ru*, http://www.pravmir.ru/smotrite-kako-opasno-xodite-ef-5-15/.

64. Ibid.

65. For the ancient catechumenate, see Josef A. Jungmann, *The Early Liturgy* (South Bend: University of Notre Dame Press, 1959), 77.

66. See Valentin Kozhuharov, *Towards an Orthodox Christian Theology of Mission* (Veliko Tarnovo: Vesta, 2006), 55–56.

67. Protoierei Vladimir Vorob'ev, "Vspominanie ob o. Vsevolode Shpillere," *Pstgu.ru*, December 10, 2010, http://pstgu.ru/news/university/2010/12/10/26622/.

68. For the university's history and mission, see *Pravoslavnyi Sviato-Tikhonovskii Gumanitarnyi Universitet* (Moscow: St. Tikhon's University Press, 2009); and *Pravoslavnyi Sviato-Tikhonovskii Gumanitarnyi Universitet: 20 let, 2012* (Moscow: St. Tikhon's University Press, 2012).

69. Publicity leaflet, March 2012. See also the publicity DVD produced in conjunction with the university's twentieth anniversary celebrations: *Universitet* (2012).

70. For analyses of the 1997 law, see Witte and Bourdeaux, *Proselytism and Orthodoxy in Russia*; Papkova, *Orthodox Church*, 74–93; and Marsh, *Religion and the State*, 124–29.

71. Protoierei Maksim Kozlov, "Sravnitel'noe bogoslovie (Rimo-Katolicheskaia Tserkov')," *Pravmir.ru*, n.d., http://lib.pravmir.ru/library/readbook/2269.

72. V. N. Vasechko, "Kurs lektsii: Sravnitel'noe bogoslovie," 2000, *Pstgu.ru*, http://pstgu.ru/download/1152721799.sravnitelnoe_bogoslovie_vasechko.pdf.

73. Aleksandr Dvorkin, *Moia Amerika* (Moscow: Khristianskaia biblioteka, 2013).

74. V. A. Martinovich, *Netraditsionnaia religioznost' v Belarusi* (Minsk: Belorusskaia Pravoslavnaia Tserkov', 2010), 88–89.

75. Ibid., 141.

76. In 2012, the congress was devoted to "Education and Morality: An Issue for Church, Society, and the State." See the program book, *Prosveshchenie i nravstvennost'—zabota Tserkvi, obshchestva i gosudarstva: programma* (Moscow: Otdel Religioznogo Obrazovaniia i Katekhizatsii, 2012).

77. See "Temy k rassmotreniiu komissiiami Mezhsobornogo prisustviia v 2015–2018 godakh," *Zhurnal Moskovskoi Patriarkhii*, April 2015, 30.

78. Personal conversation, April 2012.

79. See Nadieszda Kizenko, *A Prodigal Son: Father John of Kronstadt and the Russian People* (University Park: Pennsylvania State University Press, 2000).

80. I will say more about him and his parish in chapter 6, below.

81. "Mitropolit Ilarion: Intelligentsiia nuzhna pravoslavnoi tserkvi," *Rossiiskaia gazeta*, October 24, 2011, http://rg.ru/2011/10/24/a538631.html.

82. Anastasiia Gosteva, "Liudmila Ulitskaia: Pozhalui, teper' ia na storone fariseia," *Psychologies.ru*, March 19, 2013, http://www.psychologies.ru/self-knowledge/smysl-zhizni/lyudmila-ulitskaya-pojaluy-teper-ya-na-storone-fariseya/; and Masha Gessen, "The Weight of Words: One of Russia's Most Famous Writers Confronts the State," *New Yorker*, October 6, 2014, http://www.newyorker.com/magazine/2014/10/06/weight-words.

83. Mariia Kuz'micheva, "Dogmat o Presviatoi Troitse znaiut 9% pravoslavnykh rossiian," *Sreda.org*, June 9, 2014, http://sreda.org/ru/opros/59-dogmat-o-presvyatoy-troitse-znayut-9-pravoslavnyih-rossiyan.

84. See Mchedlova, "Religioznost' rossiian," 245–46; and "Vera v astrologiiu, primety i gadaniia," *Sreda.org*, August 15, 2012, http://sreda.org/ru/opros/42-veryat-li-rossiyane-v-astrologiyu-primetyi-i-gadaniya-portret-suevernyih-rossiyan.

85. I am thankful to Dr. Igor' Riazantsev, dean of the Department of Sociological Sciences, St. Tikhon's Orthodox Humanitarian University (Moscow), for this observation. See Igor' Riazantsev, Maria Podlesnaia, and Ivan Kozlov, "I psaltir', i molitvoslov, i pravoslavnyi fleshmob, ili o traditsiiakh duchovnikh VUZov i reformakh obrazovaniia," *Bogoslov.ru*, March 28, 2016, http://www.bogoslov.ru/text/4878712.html.

86. For the multivalent meaning of Orthodox symbols, see Roy R. Robson, "The Transfiguration Polyeleos, Textbooks, and Polyphonic Learning," in *Eastern Orthodox Christianity and American Higher Education*, ed. Ann Mitsakos Bezzerides and Elizabeth H. Prodromou (South Bend: Notre Dame University Press, 2017). Robson draws on the twentieth-century Russian philosopher Mikhail Bakhtin.

Chapter Four. Social Ministry

1. For key essays on the Church's social work, see Regina Elsner, "(Des) Organisierte Nächstenliebe: Kirchliche Sozialarbeit in Russland," *OstEuropa* 59/6 (2009): 249–59; Boris Knorre, "Sotsial'noe sluzhenie sovremennoi Russkoi pravoslavnoi tserkvi kak otrazhenie povedencheskikh stereotipov tserkovnogo sotsiuma," in *Pravoslavnaia tserkov' pri novom Patriarkhe*, 69–120; and Melissa E. Caldwell, "The Politics of Rightness: Social Justice among Russia's Christian Communities," in Zigon, *Multiple Moralities and Religions*, 55, 62. See also the Russian journal *Neskuchnyi Sad*, which until it ceased publication in 2013 provided extensive coverage of the Church's social work initiatives.

2. Igumen Mefodii (Kondrat'ev), Roman Prishchenko, and Elena Rydalevskaia, *Metodologiia sotsial'noi reabilitatsii narkozavisimykh v tserkovnoi obshchine* (Moscow: Lenta Kniga, 2012), 16–17.

3. For an overview of the parish's work and Father Mefodii's approach, see "Russkaia Pravoslavnaia Tserkov' i sotsial'naia reabilitatsiia narkozavisimykh," *Zhurnal dlia tekh, kto khochet uberech' detei ot narkotikov* 1 (2012): 20–25; and the parish's website, which includes some materials in English: http://www.sgprc.ru/.

4. Leonid Vinogradov, "Igumen Mefodii (Kondrat'ev): Kak v pravoslavnoi obshchine spasaiut narkomanov," *Pravoslavie i mir*, December 27, 2013, http://www.pravmir.ru/igumen-mefodij-kondratev-o-reabilitacii-narkomanov-v-pravoslavnoj-obshhine/.

5. Igumen Mefodii (Kondrat'ev) and Elena Rydalevskaia, *Ne umru, no zhiv budu: Opyt reabilitatsii narkozavisimykh na prikhode* (Saint Petersburg: Satis Derzhava, 2006), 6–7.

6. "Kontseptsiia RPTs po reabilitatsii," draft document, 2009, shared with Father Mefodii's permission.

7. Ibid.

8. For what follows, see Mefodii (Kondrat'ev), Prishchenko, and Rydalevskaia, *Metodologiia sotsial'noi reabilitatsii,* especially 75.

9. Mefodii (Kondrat'ev) and Rydalevskaia, *Ne umru,* 3–4.

10. Mefodii (Kondrat'ev), Prishchenko, and Rydalevskaia, *Metodologiia sotsial'noi reabilitatsii,* 62.

11. "Proekt kontseptsii Russkoi Pravoslavnoi Tserkvi po reabilitatsii narkozavisimykh," *Patriarchia.ru,* September 6, 2010, http://www.patriarchia.ru/db/print/1266458.html.

12. Ibid.

13. For a general discussion of these issues, see Scott Kenworthy, "To Save the World or to Renounce It: Modes of Moral Action in Russian Orthodoxy," in *Religion, Morality, and Community in Post-Soviet Societies,* ed. Mark D. Steinberg and Catherine Wanner (Washington, DC: Woodrow Wilson Center Press / Bloomington: Indiana University Press, 2008), 21–54.

14. Mitropolit Sergii (Fomin), "Kratkii ocherk istorii sotsial'nogo sluzheniia Russkoi Pravoslavnoi Tserkvi," *Vob.ru,* n.d., http://www.vob.ru/mitropolit/trudi/science/service/sv-2.htm; and Nina Stavitskaia, " 'Detskaia tema' Ierodiakona Moiseia," *Podrostki.today,* n.d., http://podrostki.today/?page_id=39.

15. See Meehan, *Holy Women of Russia.*

16. Liubov' Miller, *Sviataia muchenitsa Rossiiskaia Velikaia Kniaginia Elizaveta Feodorovna* (Moscow: Polomnik, 2009), 180–86.

17. Inokinia Ekaterina (Pozdniakova), "Marfo-Mariinskaia Obitel': Zhizn' iznutri," *Russkaia narodnaia linia,* November 2, 2013, http://ruskline.ru/monitoring_smi/2013/11/02/marfomariinskaya_obitel_zhizn_iznutri/.

18. See the monastery website: http://www.mmom.ru/.

19. Information gleaned from a public tour of the monastery, March 21, 2012.

20. "Letopis (1996–2000)," *Obitel-minsk.by,* n.d., http://www.obitel-minsk.by/obitel-minsk_mid760.html; Ekaterina Stepanova, "Cherno-belye sestry," *Neskuchnyi Sad,* April 22, 2010, http://www.pravmir.ru/cherno-belye-sestry; *Mastirskie Sviato-Elisavetinskogo Monastyria* (Minsk: St. Elisabeth's Monastery, n.d.); Andrei Lemeshonok, "Liudiam nuzhno zhit' " (n.p., n.d.); and "Molitvami etikh liudei vy spasetes'," *Pravoslavie.ru,* August 26, 2009, http://www.pravoslavie.ru/37715.html.

21. Much of this information derives from a tour of the monastery, February 21, 2012.

22. See Lemeshonok, "Liudiam nuzhno zhit'."

23. Sergii (Fomin), "Kratkii ocherk"; and Ierodiakon Moisei (Semiannikov), "Missionerskie aspekty sotsial'no-khoziaistvennoi deiatel'nosti iosifo-volotskogo monastyria k nachalu xx-go beka i do ego zakrytiia," *Pskgu.ru,* n.d., http://inf.pskgu.ru/projects/pgu/storage/conferences/2014_01/2014-01-12.pdf.

24. Stavitskaia, "Detskaia tema." Father Moisei is currently working on a dissertation in which he discusses how children's worldview is formed. For an overview, see Moisei (Semiannikov), "Osobennosti dukhovno-nravstvennogo sostoianiia podrostkov pri raznykh usloviiakh vospitaniia: missionerskie vyvody iz pilotazhnogo issledovaniia," *Podrostki.today*, n.d., http://podrostki.today/?p=714.

25. This deficit may be related to the fact that the discipline of sociology could not develop freely during the Soviet period. As the discipline reestablishes itself today, interest in the sociology of religion is growing. See, for example, Mikhail I. Smirnov, *Sotsiologiia religii: slovar'* (Saint Petersburg: Izdatel'skii dom Sankt-Peterburgskogo Gosudarstvennogo Universiteta, 2011); and the annual conferences on religion and postmodernity sponsored by the Department of Sociology at the Belgorod State University.

26. See Kizenko, *A Prodigal Son.*

27. See Vorob'ev, *Postradavshie za veru*, 32.

28. Sergii (Fomin), "Kratkii ocherk."

29. For what follows, see the sisterhood's informational brochure: *Khram sviatogo blagovernogo tsarevicha Dimitriia v Pervoi gradskoi bol'nitse* (n.p., n.d.).

30. Information obtained from tour of the First City Hospital, November 8, 2011.

31. *Khram sviatogo blagovernogo tsarevicha Dimitriia.*

32. *Chto takoe tserkovnaia bol'nitsa: bol'nitsa sviatitelia Aleksiia, mitropolita Moskovskogo* (n.p., n.d.).

33. Ibid.

34. Tour of the First City Hospital, November 8, 2011.

35. "O printsipakh organizatsii sotsial'noi raboty v RPTs," *Patriarchia.ru*, February 4, 2011, http://www.patriarchia.ru/db/text/1401894.html.

36. Conference on Social Work, January 20, 2012. For a press release, see Stanislav Kolotvin, "Novosti universiteta: v Marfo-Mariinskoi obiteli proshel kruglyi stol posviashchennyi bogoslovskomu osmysleniiu sluzheniia miloserdiia," *Pstgu.ru*, January 20, 2012, http://pstgu.ru/news/university/2012/01/20/34956/.

37. Elsner, "(Des) Organisierte Nächstenliebe," 253.

38. See Tobias Köllner, "Built with Gold or Tears? Moral Discourses on Church Construction and the Role of Entrepreneurial Donations," in Zigon, *Multiple Moralities and Religions*, 193–95.

39. "O printsipakh organizatsii sotsial'noi raboty."

40. Conference on Social Work, January 20, 2012. See also the interview with Bishop Panteleimon (Shatov) on the occasion of the twenty-fifth anniversary of his service in the First City Hospital, *Stdimitry.ru*, n.d., http://stdimitry.ru/media-archive/orthodox-movies/536-k-25-letiyu-vtorogo-osvyashcheniya-khrama.html; and Bishop Panteleimon (Shatov), "Glavnaia zadacha gosudarstva i Tserkvi—podderzhka sem'i," *Diaconia.ru*, March 6, 2012, http://old.diaconia.ru/news/episkop-panteleimon-glavnaja-zadacha-gosudarstva-i-tserkvi-podderzhka-semi//.

41. Panteleimon (Shatov), "Kak nauchit'sia liubvi," *Obrazovanie i Pravoslavie*, September 1, 2014, http://www.orthedu.ru/news/obzor-smi/print:page,1,11034-episkop-panteleimon-shatov-kak-nauchitsya-lyubvi.html.

42. Visit to the Sisterhood of the Great Martyr Anastasia Uzoreshitelnitsa, St. Petersburg, January 30, 2012.

43. Lemeshonok, "Liudiam nuzhno zhit'," 3.

44. "O printsipakh organizatsii sotsial'noi raboty."

45. *Uchastie Russkoi Pravoslavnoi Tserkvi v bor'be s rasprostraneniem VICh/SPIDa i rabote s liud'mi, zhivushchimi s VICh/SPIDom* (Moscow: Rossiiskii kruglyi stol, 2010), 5.

46. *Khram sviatogo blagovernogo tsarevicha Dimitriia.*

47. Visit to the Sisterhood of the Great Martyr Anastasia Uzoreshitelnitsa, January 30, 2012.

48. *Uchastie Russkoi Pravoslavnoi Tserkvi v bor'be*, 9. Subsequent page references to this work are given parenthetically in the text.

Chapter Five. The New Martyrs

1. For an analysis, see Graeme Gill, *Symbolism and Regime Change in Russia* (New York: Cambridge University Press, 2013), 141–43, 210–11. For Russia's difficulty in finding a cohesive national identity, see Hosking, *Russia*.

2. Michael Birnbaum, "One Thing Is Missing from Russia's WWII Remembrance—The Allies," *Washington Post*, May 9, 2015, http://www.washingtonpost.com/world/russia-saved-europe-from-hitler-and-it-wants-you-to-remember/2015/05/09/032c606e-f33c-11e4-bca5-21b51bbdf93e_story.html.

3. See Koesel, *Religion and Authoritarianism*, 144–48. For Putin's use of Orthodox symbolic politics, see Regina Smyth and Irina Soboleva, "Looking Beyond the Economy: Pussy Riot and the Kremlin's Voting Coalition," *Post-Soviet Affairs* 30/4 (2014): 257–75.

4. For World Bank figures, see http://wdi.worldbank.org/table/4.2.

5. See Garrard and Garrard, *Russian Orthodoxy Resurgent*.

6. See, for example, the website of the Parish of the Cathedral of the New Martyrs of Podol'sk, http://neomartyrs.ru/index.php/novomucheniki/podvig-muchenichestva.

7. See Boobbyer, *Conscience, Dissent and Reform*, 210–13.

8. See Robson, *Solovki*, 256; and Anastasia Sechina, "Gosudarstvennyi muzei repressii," *Svoboda.org*, July 28, 2014, http://www.svoboda.org/content/article/25473051.html.

9. See John Sweeney, "Russian Textbooks Attempt to Rewrite History," *Times* (London), December 1, 2009, http://www.thetimes.co.uk/tto/life/article1855770.ece.

10. See Christopher Andrew and Vasilii Mitrokhin, *The Sword and the Shield: The Mitrokhin Archive and the Secret History of the KGB* (New York: Basic Books, 1999), 486–507.

11. See Archpriest John Matusiak, "Appearance of the Tikhvin Icon of the Mother of God," *Oca.org*, June 26, 2013, http://oca.org/saints/lives/2013/06/26/101821-appearance-of-the-tikhvin-icon-of-the-mother-of-god.

12. For illustrations of student work, see *Iskusstvo Tserkvi* (Moscow: St. Tikhon's University Press, 2007).

13. The Russian word that I have translated as spirituality is *dukovnost'*.

14. For his major works, see Aleksandr Mazyrin, *Vysshie ierarkhi o preemstve vlasti v Russkoi Pravoslavnoi Tserkvi* (Moscow: St. Tikhon's University Press, 2006); and Mazyrin, *Kifa, patriarshii mestobliustitel' sviashchennomuchenik Petr, Mitropolit Krutitskii (1861–1937)* (Moscow: St. Tikhon's University Press, 2012). Mazyrin was also a principal author of Vorob'ev's edited work *Postradavshie za veru*.

15. Diedrich, *"Wohin sollen wir gehen,"* 67.

16. Ibid., 63.

17. Vorob'ev, *Postradavshie za veru*, 191–92.

18. Diedrich, *"Wohin sollen wir gehen,"* 82; Vorob'ev, *Postradavshie za veru*, 117.

19. Vorob'ev, *Postradavshie za veru*, 192–200.

20. Diedrich, *"Wohin sollen wir gehen,"* 69.

21. Ibid., 81.

22. Ibid., 85; Vorob'ev, *Postradavshie za veru*, 264–65; and Ivan M. Andreev, "The Trial of Patriarch Tikhon," *Pravoslavie.ru*, October 10, 2013, http://www.pravoslavie.ru/english/print64798.htm.

23. Vorob'ev, *Postradavshie za veru*, 265–66.

24. Diedrich, *"Wohin sollen wir gehen,"* 85.

25. Vorob'ev, *Postradavshie za veru*, 269–73.

26. Ibid., 274–81.

27. See Mazyrin, *Vysshie ierarkhi*, 396–98; and Georgii Mitrofanov, *Russkaia Pravoslavnaia Tserkov' na istoricheskom pereput'e XX veka* (Moscow: Arefa-Lenta, 2011), 55–64.

28. Diedrich, *"Wohin sollen wir gehen,"* 89.

29. The phrase comes from Ephesians 4:15.

30. Acts 5:29.

31. In Orthodoxy, the sacraments are also known as "the mysteries."

32. Mazyrin, *Vysshie ierarkhi*, 397. Irina Papkova reports that Kirill, at that time head of the Church's Department of External Church Relations, was summoned to the Kremlin and asked to revise this statement. He refused. See Papkova, *Orthodox Church*, 216n25.

33. "Doklad mitropolita Krutitskogo Iuvenaliia na pervom zasedanii Tserkovno-obshchestvennogo soveta po uvekovecheniiu pamiati novomuchenikov i ispovednikov Tserkvi Russkoi," *Patriarchia.ru*, November 26, 2014, http://www.patriarchia.ru/db/print/3854970.html.

34. N. A. Krivosheeva, "Novomucheniki Russkoi Pravoslavnoi Tserkvi—chleni Pomestnogo Sobora 1917–1918 gg.," in *Proslavlenie i pochitanie Sviatykh* (Moscow: XVII International Educational Christmas Lectures, February 17, 2009), 60.

35. See the proclamation of the Holy Council of Bishops of the Russian Orthodox Church, "Of Canonization," *Holy-trinity.org*, n.d., http://www.holy-trinity.org/feasts/newmartyrs-canonization.html.

36. Vorob'ev, *Postradavshie za veru*, 46; and Krivosheeva, "Novomucheniki Russkoi Pravoslavnoi Tserkvi," 56.

37. See Boobbyer, *Conscience, Dissent and Reform*, 113.

38. For the historical debates about sobornost', see Vera Shevzov, *Russian Orthodoxy on the Eve of Revolution* (New York: Oxford University Press, 2004), 30–35. For a contemporary understanding, see Metropolitan Hilarion (Alfeev), *Orthodox Christianity: Doctrine and Teaching of the Orthodox Church*, trans. Andrew Smith (Yonkers, NY: St. Vladimir's Seminary Press, 2012), 425–35.

39. Per-Arne Bodin, "To Describe the Soviet Agonies in the Language of the Middle Ages: The Russian New Martyrs," *Communio Victorum* 47/3 (2005): 281–82.

40. For the importance of Sokolova, see Irina Yazykova, *Hidden and Triumphant: The Underground Struggle to Save Russian Iconography*, trans. Paul Grenier (Brewster, MA: Paraclete), 111–12. For the relationship of Sokolova's icon to that of the new martyrs and confessors, see *Ikona sobora novykh muchenikov i ispovednikov Rossiiskikh za Khrista postradavshikh iavlennykh i neiavlennykh* (Moscow: Russian Orthodox Church, Synodal Commission on the Canonization of Saints, 2000), http://www.wco.ru/biblio/books/novmuch1/Main.htm.

41. See Father Vitalii Glazov, "Istoriia prazdnika vsekh sviatykh, v zemle rossiiskoi prosiiavshikh," *Pravoslavie.ru*, June 23, 2006, http://www.pravoslavie.ru/put/2367.htm.

42. For the significance of the natural landscape in Orthodox iconography, see Metropolitan Hilarion (Alfeev), "Theology of Icons in the Orthodox Church," *Mospat.ru*, February 5, 2011, https://mospat.ru/en/2011/02/06/news35783/.

43. For the representation of different groups in the icon, see Kirill Emel'ianov, "Sotsial'nye aspekty sovremennikh kanonizatsii Pravoslavnoi Tserkvi," 8, which is an unpublished summary of his dissertation that he shared with me, "Kanonizatsiia sviatykh Russkoi Tserkvi kak ob'ekt sotsiologicheskogo issledovaniia" (PhD diss., Moscow State University, 2005).

44. For a list of saints in the St. Tikhon's icon, see http://www.icon-favor.ru/?page=1073. For the decanonizations, see Deacon Andrei Kuraev, "Dekanonizatsiia: gorkaia pravda," *Live Journal* (blog), December 13, 2012, http://diak-kuraev.livejournal.com/404290.html.

45. See *Kanon i akafist sviatomu Strastoterptsu Tsariu-Mucheniku Nikolaiu Vtoromu* (Moscow: Khram Sviatitelia Nikolaia v Pyzhakh, 2002), 19, 41; "Sviashchennomucheniku Sergiiu," in *Novomucheniki moskovskogo*

Novodevich'ego Monastyria (Moscow: Novodevichii Monastery, 2006), 27; and Bodin, "Describe the Soviet Agonies," 269.

46. As quoted in Bodin, "Describe the Soviet Agonies," 275–76.

47. "Kanon i akafist," 19.

48. Ibid., 44.

49. Bodin, "Describe the Soviet Agonies," 271.

50. "Kanon i akafist," 19.

51. Ibid., 46–47.

52. See Vorob'ev, *Postradavshie za veru*, 20.

53. "Sviashchennomucheniku Sergiiu," 26.

54. Elizabeth Castelli, *Martyrdom and Memory* (New York: Columbia University Press, 2004), 51, 198.

55. See Emel'ianov, "Sotsial'nye aspekty," 6; and "Chto takoe kanonizatsiia?" *Genon. ru*, October 14, 2010, http://www.genon.ru/GetAnswer.aspx?qid=111b9dd6-6797-4662-8c41-174e4e6a3144.

56. See Emel'ianov, "Sotsial'nye aspekty," 6; and "Sobor Rossiiskikh chudotvortsev, proslavlennykh na Moskovskikh Soborakh 1547 i 1549 godov," *Alchevsk pravoslavnyi. ru*, June 28, 2011, http://alchevskpravoslavniy.ru/knigi/zhitie-svyatyx/sobor-rossijskix-chudotvorcev-proslavlennyx-na-moskovskix-soborax-1547-i-1549-godov.html/.

57. See Emel'ianov, "Kanonizatsiia sviatykh," 139–43; and "Chto takoe kanonizatsiia?"

58. See Vladimir Vorob'ev, "Nekotorye problemy proslavleniia sviatykh k mestnomu i obshchetserkovnomu pochitaniiu v kontse XX–nachale XXI vekov," in *Proslavlenie i pochitanie Sviatykh* (Moscow: XVIII International Educational Christmas Lectures, January 28, 2010), 43.

59. See Emel'ianov, "Sotsial'nye aspekty," 9; and "Chto takoe kanonizatsiia?"

60. See Emel'ianov, "Sotsial'nye aspekty," 8.

61. "Sviashchennomuchenik protoierei Grigorii Serbarinov," *Bcex.ru*, n.d., http://www.bcex.ru/muzej/svyashhennomuchenik-protoierej-grigorij-serbarinov.

62. See "Istoriia khrama" at the parish website, http://hram-sofia.ru/istoriya-hrama; and "Andreev, Aleksandr Aleksandrovich," *Adamovka.ru*, n.d., http://adamovka.ru/saint/?id=160.

63. Aleksandr Mazyrin, "Mesto zhenshchin v Sobore novomuchenikov i ispovednikov Rossiiskykh," *Pstgu.ru*, October 29, 2013, http://pstgu.ru/news/life/history_rpc/2013/10/29/48859/.

64. "Prepodobnomuchenitsa Mariia (Tseitlin)," in *Novomucheniki moskovskogo Novodevich'ogo Monastyria*, 24.

65. See Igumen Damaskin (Orlovskii), "Slozhnosti izucheniia sudebno-sledstvennykh del, imeiushchego tsel'iu—vkliuchenie imeni postradavshego sviashchennos luzhitelia ili mirianina v Sobor novomuchenikov i ispovednikov Rossiiskikh," in *Proslavlenie i pochitanie sviatykh* (Moscow: XX International Educational Christmas Lectures, January 24, 2012), 14–15.

66. Kseniia Luchenko, "Uzhe nesviatye: iavochnaia dekanonizatsiia v RPTs MP," *Russkaia zhizn'*, February 18, 2013, http://www.portal-credo.ru/site/?act—onitor&id= 19584.

67. Maksim Maksimov, "Podgotovka materialov k kanonizatsii sviatykh," in *Proslavlenie i pochitanie Sviatykh* (Moscow: XVIII International Educational Christmas Lectures, January 28, 2010), 56.

68. Damaskin (Orlovskii), "Slozhnosti izucheniia sudebno-sledstvennykh del," 22–23.

69. See Ware, *Orthodox Church*, 259.

70. Luchenko, "Uzhe nesviatye."

71. Vladimir Vorob'ev, "Predislovie," in Mazyrin, *Kifa*, 5–10.

72. "Kanon i akafist," 17, 19.

73. See Kathy Rousselet, "Constructing Moralities around the Tsarist Family," in Zigon, *Multiple Moralities and Religions*, 146–67.

74. See "Mitropolit Ilarion (Alfeev) vs Dzhon Berdzhess."

75. Kathy Rousselet has argued that the veneration of the royal family is linked to nostalgia for certain "aspects of the Soviet past and for a sense of order." See "Constructing Moralities," 162.

76. Metropolitan John (Synchev), "The Life of Holy Hieromartyr Hilarion (Troitsky), Archbishop of Verey," *Pravoslavie.ru*, n.d., http://www.pravoslavie.ru/english/33316. htm.

77. Visit to Sretenskii Monastery, December 28, 2011.

78. For an analysis of changing attitudes toward women in the Russian Orthodox Church, see Briskina-Müller, "Search for a New Church Consciousness," 70–74.

79. Abbess Elisaveta (Pozdniakova), March 21, 2012.

80. For the importance of commemorative spaces in shaping public values, see Julie Buckler and Emily D. Johnson, introduction to *Rites of Place: Public Commemoration in Russia and Eastern Europe* (Evanston: Northwestern University Press, 2013), 3–9.

81. See the English-language portion of the Butovo website, *Martyr.ru*, http://www. martyr.ru/index.php?option=com_content&view=article&id=179&Itemid=27.

82. Some historians, however, are at odds with the Church over the way it interprets these events. See Neil MacFarquhar, "A Tug of War over Gulag History in Russia's North," *New York Times*, August 30, 2015.

83. See chapter 2, above, for a fuller description.

84. For an English-language description of the memorial site, see "Pages from History," *Vladimirskysobor.ru*, n.d., http://www.vladimirskysobor.ru/_mod_files/ PDF_files/buklet_levashovo_eng.pdf.

85. See "Obrashchenie Namestnika Sretenskogo Monastyria arkhimandrita Tikhona k prikhozhanam i palomnikam," a leaflet prepared by the monastery for public distribution.

86. Historians estimate that several hundred thousand people died for their faith. See chapter 2, above.

87. See Jeanne Kormina and Sergey Shtyrkov, "St. Xenia as a Patron of Female Social Suffering: An Essay on Anthropological Hagiology," in Zigon, *Multiple Moralities and Religions*, 168–90.

88. Luke's popularity is reflected in the publication of an inexpensive popular Orthodox calendar with excerpts from his sermons and letters. See *"Ia liubliu stradanie, tak udivitel'no ochishchaiushchee dushu": god so sviatitelem Lukoi Krymskim* (Moscow: Khram Sv. Dukha soshestvia na Lazarevskom kladbishche, 2013).

89. Kuraev, *Osnovi pravoslavnoi kul'tury*, 83.

90. Patriarkh Aleksii II, "Butovo — Russkaia Golgofa," *Martyr.ru*, April 28, 2012, http://www.martyr.ru/index.php?option=com_content&view=article&id=10&Itemid=1.

91. See *Novomucheniki moskovskogo Novodevich'ogo Monastyria*.

92. Patriarch Kirill, sermon preached at the Butovo memorial site, *Martyr.ru*, February 10, 2013, http://www.martyr.ru/index.php?option=com_content&view=article&id=357&Itemid=19.

93. See Aleksandr Shargunov, *Vchera i sevodnia: ot prepodobnomuchenitsy velikoi kniagini Elisavety do muchenikov i ispovednikov nashikh dnei* (Sergiev Posad: Holy Trinity–St. Sergius Monastery, 2011), 241.

94. Ibid., 10–14.

95. Mitrofanov, "My dolzhny izvlech' dukovnye uroki iz opyta novomuchenikov." For an English-language description of Mitrofanov's position, see Briskina-Müller, "Search for a New Church Consciousness," 76–77.

96. Georgii Fedotov, *Sviatye Drevnei Rusi* (Rostov-na-Donu: Feniks, 1999), 313.

97. For photographs of the new martyrs and confessors, see *Fond.ru*, n.d., http://www.fond.ru/index.php?menu_id=370&menu_parent_id=0.

Chapter Six. Parish Life

1. For recent studies of the development of parish life in the Russian Orthodox Church, see Aleksandr Agadzhanian and Katia Russele, eds., *Prikhod i obshchina v sovremennom Pravoslavii* (Moscow: Ves mir, 2011); I. P. Riazantsev, Iliia Limberger, and M. A. Podlesnaia, eds., *Prikhod Russkoi Pravoslavnoi Tserkvi* (Moscow: St. Tikhon's University Press, 2011); I. P. Riazantsev and M. A. Podlesnaia, eds., *Prikhod Russkoi Pravoslavnoi Tserkvi v Rossii i za rubezhom* (Moscow: St. Tikhon's University Press, 2013); and I. V. Zabaev et al., eds., *Nividimaia Tserkov': Sotsial'nye effekty prikhodskoi obshchiny v russkom Pravoslavii* (Moscow: St. Tikhon's University Press, 2015).

2. The following account of Father Volgin's life and work is based on extensive conversations and observations in 2011–15 as well as several websites. See Protoierei Vladimir Volgin and Aleksandra Nikiforova, "Portrety Startsev," *Pravmir.ru*, January

24, 2012, http://www.pravmir.ru/portrety-startev/; and Aleksandra Nikiforova, "Kliuch k stiazhaniiu liubvi: beseda s Protoiereem Vladimirom Volginom," *Pravoslavie.ru*, April 11, 2009, http://www.pravoslavie.ru/guest/30024.htm.

3. The Russian term is *starosta*.

4. Nikiforova, "Kliuch k stiazhaniiu liubvi."

5. For the history of the parish, see its website: http://hram-sofia.ru/.

6. "Osviashchenie krestov v sele Arkhangel'skoe," *St-catherine.ru*, February 19, 2007, http://www.st-catherine.ru/blessing_of_crosses.

7. "TV spas: o. Vladimir Volgin i Mikhail Shubin o Khrame mch Porfiriia v Teletsentre," *Youtube.com*, September 9, 2011, https://www.youtube.com/watch?v=lGIe2fx5-N4. See also "Khram," *Ostankino.ru*, n.d., http://ostankino.ru/telecenter/hram.

8. Diedrich, "*Wohin sollen wir gehen*," 23.

9. See Mchedlova, "Religioznost' rossiian," 247.

10. See Kizenko, *A Prodigal Son*.

11. See Vladimir Vorob'ev, *Ieromonakh Pavel (Troitskii)* (Moscow: St. Tikhon's University Press, 2003).

12. For Elizabeth, see Vorob'ev, *Postradavshie za veru*, 71.

13. Aleksandr Shargunov, *Pred Krestom i Evangeliem* (Moscow: Danilov Monastery, 2012).

14. *Pomni o Boge: pravoslavnyi kalendar' 2012* (Nizhnii Novgorod: Izdatel'stvo "Khristianskaia biblioteka," 2011).

15. See Nadieszda Kizenko, "Sacramental Confession in Modern Russia and Ukraine," in *State Secularism and Lived Religion in Soviet Russia and Ukraine*, ed. Catherine Wanner (Washington, DC: Woodrow Wilson Center Press / New York: Oxford University Press, 2012), 191.

16. See Alexander Schmemann, *The Eucharist: Sacrament of the Kingdom* (Crestwood, NY: St. Vladimir's Seminary Press, 1988), 229–245; and Alexander Schmemann, "Holy Things for the Holy: Some Remarks on Receiving Holy Communion," in Schmemann, *Great Lent: Journey to Pascha* (Crestwood, NY: St. Vladimir's Seminary Press, 1969), 107–33.

17. Aleksandr Filippov with Vladimir Vorob'ev, "Zhizn' khristianina dolzhna stroit'sia vokrug Evkharistii," *Pravmir.ru*, November 14, 2013, http://www.pravmir.ru/protoierej-vladimir-vorobyov-pustite-k-chashe-1/*.

18. See Metropolitan Hilarion (Alfeev), "Ispoved' ne dolzhna byt' 'biletom na prichastie,' " *Blagovest-info.ru*, October 5, 2011, http://www.blagovest-info.ru/index.php?ss=2&s=3&id=43284; and Dmitrii Karpenko, "Podgotovka k prichastiiu: kanonicheskie normy i praktika Pomestnykh Pravoslavnykh Tserkvei," *Pravmir.ru*, January 5, 2012, http://www.pravmir.ru/podgotovka-k-prichastiyu-kanonicheskie-normy-i-praktika-pomestnyx-pravoslavnyx-cerkvej/.

19. "Ob uchastii vernykh v Evkharistii," *Patriarchia.ru*, February 3, 2015, http://www.patriarchia.ru/db/print/3981166.html.

20. Filippov and Vorob'ev, "Zhizn' khristianina."

21. Diedrich, "Wohin sollen wir gehen," 212.

22. For the various Russian Orthodox attitudes toward Schmemann, see Igor' Druz', "Ideologiia sviashchennika Aleksandra Shmemena," Rusk.ru, October 7, 2008, http://rusk.ru/st.php?idar=113384; and "V Izdatel'skom Sovete sostoialas' diskussiia o nedavno opublikovannykh 'Dnevnikakh' protopresvitera Aleksandra Shmemana," Patriarchia.ru, March 30, 2006, http://www.patriarchia.ru/db/text/101061.html.

23. See Alexis Vinogradov, "Votserkovlenie Zhizni: The Churching of Life and Culture," St. Vladimir's Theological Quarterly 55/2–3 (2009): 341–51.

24. See Sergei Chapnin, "A Church of Empire," First Things, November 2015, 37–41; Chapnin, "Sovetskoe i postsovetskoe"; and Sergei Chapnin, Tserkov' v postsovetskoi Rossii: vozrozhdenie, kachestvo very, dialog s obshchestvom (Moscow: Arefa, 2013).

25. See Mchedlova, "Religioznost' rossiian," 244.

26. See Hyacinthe Destivelle, O.P., The Moscow Council (1917–1918), trans. Jerry Ryan (Notre Dame: University of Notre Dame Press, 2015), 134–36.

27. See Scott M. Kenworthy, "Russian Reformation? The Program for Religious Renovation in the Orthodox Church, 1922–1925," Modern Greek Studies Yearbook 16/17 (2000–2001): 89–130.

28. Stephen K. Batalden, "The Contemporary Politics of the Russian Bible," in Batalden, Seeking God, 241.

29. See the account in Wallace L. Daniel, The Orthodox Church and Civil Society in Russia (College Station: Texas A&M University Press, 2006), 103–7.

30. Robert Wuthnow, ed., "I Come Away Stronger": How Small Groups Are Shaping American Religion (Grand Rapids, MI: Eerdmans, 1994).

31. See Malia, The Soviet Tragedy, 83, 357.

32. See Finansovaia akademiia pri Pravitel'stve RF, kafedra statistiki, "Statisticheskii analiz dinamiki naseleniia g. Moskvy za period 2000–2005 gg.," 2007, https://referat.ru/referat/statisticheskiy-analiz-dinamiki-naseleniya-g-moskvy-za-period-2000-2005-gg-531356.

33. See I. I. Eliseeva and E. I. Gribova, eds., Sankt-Peterburg: 1703–2003, 2nd ed. (Saint Petersburg: Sudostroenie, 2003), 16–17, as quoted in "Naselenie severnoi stolitsy," Demoskop Weekly, August 1–15, 2004, http://demoscope.ru/weekly/2004/0163/tema01.php.

34. See "Istoricheskie ocherki" on the city's website, Reutov.net, n.d., http://www.reutov.net/city/history/digest/.

35. See "Khram Zhivonachal'noi Troitsy, g. Reutov," Hram-bal.ru, n.d., http://www.hram-bal.ru/temples/temple_troicireutov.php.

36. Reutov pravoslavnyi (Reutov: n.p., 2014), 34–35.

37. See Köllner, "Built with Gold or Tears?" 205.

38. Il'ia Shepelin, "Deistviia patriarkha Kirilla ne pozvoliat emu sokhranit' Ukrainskuiu tserkov': ee otdelenie — vopros neskol'kikh let," *Slon.ru*, May 28, 2014, https://slon.ru/russia/deystviya_patriarkha_kirilla_ne_pozvolyat_emu_sokhranit_ukrainskuyu_tserkov_ee_otdelenie_vopros_nesk-1105151.xhtml.

39. Leonid Vinogradov, "Prot. Vladimir Vorob'ev o rastserkovlenii molodezhi, vygoranii sviashchennikov i soblaznakh v Tserkvi," *Pravmir.ru*, April 22, 2013, http://www.pravmir.ru/prot-vladimir-vorobyov-o-rascerkovlenii-molodezhi-vygoranii-svyashhennikov-i-soblaznax-v-cerkvi/.

40. See, for example, the exchange of views in the newspaper *Za Kaluzhskoi zastavoi*, November 2011, 5; more recently, Ol'ga Trakhanova and Ol'ga Shamina, "Khramy vmesto parkov: chem zakanchivaiutsia protesty moskvichei?" *Bg,ru*, June 28, 2015, http://bg.ru/city/hramy-22905/.

41. "Russians Return to Religion, but Not to Church." Also see Evans and Northmore-Ball, "The Limits of Secularization," 800.

42. Sixty-six percent of Russians call themselves "believers." Of that number, 72 percent designate themselves as Orthodox. See Mchedlova, "Religioznost' rossiian," 244.

43. See Evans and Northmore-Ball, "The Limits of Secularization?" 795–808. They note that the overall number of frequent attenders had increased because more people identified themselves as Orthodox.

44. See "Russians Return to Religion but Not to Church"; and Mchedlova, "Religioznost' rossiian," 244.

45. "Poseshchenie sluzhb, sobliudenie posta, noshenie kresta i molitva," *Sreda.org*, August 23, 2012, http://sreda.org/opros/43-kto-iz-rossiyan-postitsya-nosit-krestik-molitsya.

46. See chapter 3, above, for surveys about belief.

47. "Poseshchenie sluzhb."

48. Mchedlova, "Religioznost' rossiian," 245.

49. "Poseshchenie sluzhb."

50. Mchedlova, "Religioznost' rossiian," 244. A 2009 survey found that 62 percent of self-identified Orthodox adherents never received Communion. See Simonov, "Religion und Religiosität in Russland," 195.

51. "Religiia v nashei zhizni," Vserossiiskii Tsentr Izucheniia Obshchestvennogo Mneniia, press release no. 789, October 11, 2007, http://wciom.ru/index.php?id=236&uid=8954.

52. Mchedlova, "Religioznost' rossiian," 245.

53. Ibid., 247. For a fuller study of this phenomenon, see Kaz'mina, *Russkaia Pravoslavnaia Tserkov'*, 261–69.

54. Chapnin, "Sovetskoe i postsovetskoe."

55. Igumen Nektarii (Morozov), *Besedy o votserkovlenii* (Saratov: Izdatel'stvo Saratovskoi eparkhii, 2010).

56. As one commentator has wryly remarked, the Church seems to believe that "votserkovlenie will solve practically every worldly problem." See Aleksei Malashenko, "Zakliuchenie," in *Pravoslavnaia tserkov' pri novom Patriarkhe*, 403.

Chapter Seven. The Future

1. See Sophia Kishkovsky, "In Russian Chill, Waiting Hours for Touch of the Holy," *New York Times*, November 23, 2011, http://www.nytimes.com/2011/11/24/world/europe/virgin-mary-belt-relic-draws-crowds-in-moscow.html?_r=0; John Sanidopoulos, "The Belt of the Virgin Mary in Russia for the First Time," *Mystagogy Resource Center* (blog), October 21, 2011, http://www.johnsanidopoulos.com/2011/10/belt-of-virgin-mary-in-russia-for-first.html; and the relevant articles in the journal *Vestnik Fonda Andreia Pervozvannogo i Tsentra natsional'noi slavy* 1/9 (2012). The tour of the belt was organized by the "Fund of St. Andrew, the First-called," which regularly brings famous relics to Russia, as well as the "holy fire" that is said to spontaneously ignite in Jerusalem's Church of the Holy Sepulcher each year during the Easter Vigil service. For an overview of the fund's activities, see A. S. Gatilin, ed., *Fond Andreia Pervozvannogo/Tsentr natsional'noi slavy: kniga-al'bom* (Moscow: Fond Andreia Pervozvannogo i Tsentra natsional'noi slavy, 2010). For a critique of the mass frenzy around these displays, see Yulia Latynina, "The False Gifts of the Magi," *Moscow Times*, January 15, 2014, http://www.themoscowtimes.com/print/article/the-false-gifts-of-the-magi/492734.html.

2. For religious symbols and rituals as sites of competing interpretation, see John Eade and Michael J. Sallnow, eds., *Contesting the Sacred: The Anthropology of Christian Pilgrimage* (New York: Routledge, 1991), 1–29.

3. Papkova, *Orthodox Church*, 47–69.

4. See Dmitrii Sokolov-Mitrich, "Ochen' malen'kaia vera," *Russkii reporter*, April 7, 2011, http://expert.ru/russian_reporter/2011/13/ochen-malenkaya-vera/.

5. See Sophia Kishkovsky, "Russian Orthodox Church Elects Outspoken Patriarch," *New York Times*, January 27, 2009, http://www.nytimes.com/2009/01/28/world/europe/28orthodox.html?_r=0.

6. See Kazmina, "The Russian Orthodox Church in a New Situation," 225.

7. See Sokolov-Mitrich, "Ochen' malen'kaia vera."

8. For a review of the events of 2011–12, see Smyth and Soboleva, "Looking Beyond the Economy."

9. "Moscow Patriarch Kiril Shows off 30,000-Euro Watch During Prayer in Kyiv," *Zik.ua*, July 30, 2009, http://zik.ua/en/photoreport/2009/07/30/190593.

10. Michael Schwirtz, "$30,000 Watch Vanishes Up Church Leader's Sleeve," *New York Times*, April 5, 2012, http://www.nytimes.com/2012/04/06/world/europe/in-russia-a-watch-vanishes-up-orthodox-leaders-sleeve.html?pagewanted=all.

11. See Protoierei Vsevolod Chaplin, "Nastaivat' na podstraivanii vsekh narodov pod zapadnuiu model' demokratii nechestno i nespravedlivo," *Pravmir.ru*, November 28, 2013, http://www.pravmir.ru/prot-vsevolod-chaplin-nastaivat-na-podstraivanii-vsex-narodov-pod-zapadnuyu-model-demokratii-nechestno-i-nespravedlivo/.

12. The Russian term for these personal services is *treby*.

13. See Vinogradov, "Prot. Vladimir Vorob'ev o rastserkovlenii molodezhi."

14. Igumen Petr (Meshcherinov), "Razmyshleniia o rastserkovlenii," *Pravmir.ru*, September 22, 2010, http://www.pravmir.ru/razmyshleniya-o-rascerkovlenii/. For a further development of these ideas, see Igumen Petr (Meshcherinov), "Sovremennoe tserkovnoe soznanie i svetskie ideologimy iz kommunisticheskogo proshlogo," in *Pravoslavnaia tserkov' pri novom Patriarkhe*, 121–40.

15. Men' is featured in a film produced with the assistance of the department. See Telekompaniia Sretenie, "Russkie Pravedniki," *Youtube.com*, February 9, 2013, https://www.youtube.com/watch?v=u5buY3oaF7k.

16. Chapnin, "Sovetskoe i postsovetskoe"; and Chapnin, *Tserkov' v postsovetskoi Rossii*.

17. Chapnin, "A Church of Empire."

18. Cyril Hovorun, "The Church in the Bloodlands," *First Things*, October 2014, 41–44.

19. For the following, see Aleksandr Sorokin, *Khram Feodorovskoi Ikony Bozhei Materi* (St. Petersburg: Khram Feodorovskoi Ikony Materi, 2013).

20. Papkova, *Orthodox Church*, 60–69.

21. For an overview of the events, see Papkova, *Orthodox Church*, 55, 147; and Daniel, *The Orthodox Church and Civil Society in Russia*, 103–7.

22. For a description of the "enchanted" Russia that existed up to the early twentieth century, see Shevzov, *Russian Orthodoxy*. For examples of recent popular Russian books that idealize the nation as Holy Rus', see Aleksandr Ananichev, *Bogom izbrannaia Rus'* (Moscow: Izdatel'stvo Moskovskoi Patriarkhii Russkoi Pravoslavnoi Tserkvi, 2012); and Sergei Perevezentsev, *Rossiia: velikaia sud'ba* (Moscow: Belyi gorod, 2009), 678–91.

23. "The Conversation of St. Serafim with Nicholas Motovilov," in *A Treasury of Russian Spirituality*, ed. George P. Fedotov (Vaduz: Bücherverstriebanstalt, 1988), 162.

24. Seventy-nine percent of self-designated Orthodox adherents in Russia have icons in their home (although only 53 percent report praying before them); 83 percent regularly light candles in front of icons in a church; and one-third of those with an automobile have an icon in it. Three-quarters bring home holy water on Kreshchenie or other days. See Simonov, "Religion und Religiosität in Russland," 209–11. The statistics are based on a Levada Center survey of 2009. A more recent survey suggests that two-thirds of all Russians have icons at home. See "Ikony v domakh u Rosiian," *Sreda.org*, January 15, 2013, http://sreda.org/ru/opros/52-kakie-ikonyi-est-v-domah-u-rossiyan.

25. Aleksandr Krupinin, interview with Protoierei Aleksandr Stepanov, *Nedelia*, January 25, 2015, http://www.grad-petrov.ru/den-za-dnem/nedelya-aleksandr-stepanov/.

26. Freeze, "Von der Entkirchlichung," 106–14. For the West more generally, see Grace Davie, *Religion in Britain since 1945: Believing Without Belonging* (Oxford: Blackwell, 1994).

27. Krupinin, interview with Stepanov.

28. Freeze, "Institutionalizing Piety," 222.

29. For critiques of the term *popular Orthodoxy*, see Eve Levin, "Dvoeverie and Popular Religion," in Batalden, *Seeking God*, 29–52; and the book reviews by Nadieszda Kizenko in *Kritika: Explorations in Russian and Eurasian History* 9 (Summer 2008): 1–14. Kizenko includes references to the most important scholarly literature.

30. For what follows, see Vasily Ivanov-Ordynsky, "Raskol'nich'ia sekta v Piterskoi oblasti (Dudachkino)," *Vk.com*, May 6, 2009, http://vk.com/topic-5551851_20629722; "Sotrudniki silovykh struktur proveli obysk vo vsekh tserkovnykh pomeshcheniiakh khrama RPTsZ(A) v Leningradskoi oblasti; nastoiatel' vyzvan v prokuraturu," *Portal-credo.ru*, October 11, 2011, http://www.portal-credo.ru/site/?act=news&id=87184; Victor Rezunkov, "Marginaly iz Dudachkino," *Svoboda.org*, August 3, 2013, http://www.svoboda.org/content/article/25065416.html; European Court of Human Rights, "Sukhov vs. Russia, Application 78116/12," *Coe.int*, November 18, 2013, http://hudoc.echr.coe.int/sites/eng/pages/search.aspx?i=001-139575; "Pozhar v pokrovskom prikhode RPTsZ derevni Dudachkino pod Sankt-Peterburgom," *Chernec 71* (blog), January 22, 2013, http://chernec71.livejournal.com/196904.html; "Prikhod RPTsZ(A) v sele Dudachkino pod Peterburgom vnov' privlek vnimanie rossiiskikh vlastei," *Portal-credo.ru*, February 25, 2014, www.portal-credo.ru/site/print.php?act=news&id=106407; and "Sviashchennik Aleksandr Sukhov: pis'mo Mitropolitu Agafangelu," *Internetsobor.org*, December 12, 2014, http://internetsobor.org/rptcz/tcerkovnye-novosti/rptcz/sviashchennik-aleksandr-sukhov-pismo-mitropolitu-agafangelu#comment-10948.

31. Bellah, "Civil Religion in America," 1–21.

32. See Robert N. Bellah, *The Broken Covenant: American Civil Religion in a Time of Trial* (New York: Seabury, 1975); and Robert N. Bellah, "The Final Word: Can Christianity Contribute to a Global Civil Religion?" in *Christianity and Human Rights*, ed. John Witte Jr. and Frank S. Alexander (New York: Cambridge University Press, 2010), 351–52.

33. For a classic treatment of the social reforming impulses of Christianity, see Troeltsch, *The Social Teaching of the Christian Churches*.

34. See, for example, Pierre Manent, *Tocqueville and the Nature of Democracy*, trans. John Waggoner (Lanham, MD: Rowman & Littlefield, 1996).

35. See Boris Makatenko, "The Difficult Birth of Civic Culture," in Aron, *Putin's Russia*, 108–26.

36. See William Gleason, "Public Health, Politics, and Cities in Late Imperial Russia," *Journal of Urban History* 16/4 (1990): 341–65.

37. I am thankful to Professor Regina Smyth, Indiana University–Bloomington, for her insights into this dynamic.

38. See Stoeckl, *Russian Orthodox Church*; and John A. McGuckin, "The Issue of Human Rights in Byzantium and the Orthodox Christian Tradition," in Witte and Alexander, *Christianity and Human Rights*, 173–90. Russian Orthodox Metropolitan Hilarion (Alfeev) has spoken passionately about defending persecuted Christian minorities and their right to religious freedom. See Metropolitan Hilarion (Alfeev), "The Voice of the Church Must Be Prophetic," address at the Tenth Assembly of the World Council of Churches, *Oikoumene.org*, November 1, 2013, https://www.oikoumene.org/en/resources/documents/assembly/2013-busan/plenary-presentations/address-by-metropolitan-hilarion-of-volokolamsk.

39. For the commitment of some nonconformist priests and laypeople to democratization in Russia, see Knox, *Russian Society*, 73–104, 187. For a cautionary word about the potential of the Church to contribute to democratic change, see Koesel, *Religion and Authoritarianism*, 179–83.

40. For these dynamics in North American culture, see David A. Hollingsworth, "After Cloven Tongues of Fire: Ecumenical Protestantism and the Modern American Encounter with Diversity," *Journal of American History* 98/1 (2011): 21–48.

41. For the song, see Archdeacon Roman Tamberg, Ansambl' dukhovenstva Iaroslavskoi Eparkhii, "Rus' nazyvaiut sviatoi," *Youtube.com*, March 7, 2013, https://www.youtube.com/watch?v=kLx3v59gUXA.

42. For the blog, see http://diak-kuraev.livejournal.com/.

INDEX

Saints, patriarchs, holy elders, monks, and nuns can be found under their religious name. Priests and deacons can generally be found under their surname, except where the author has changed their names to protect their anonymity. Page numbers typed in italics indicate illustrations.

Africa, 15
Agafangel (Preobrazhenskii), Bishop, 133, 134, 140
Aleksii II, Patriarch, 46, 51, 109, 159
Amvrosii (Mikhailov), Fr., 92
Andreev, Fr. Aleksandr, 148
angels, in the Trinity icon, 49, 50
Anna (author's friend), 55–56
anticlericalism, 21, 197–99
Antonii (Cheremisov), Bishop, 78
Anzer Island. *See* Solovki and Anzer Island
architecture of churches, 181, 204. *See also specific churches*
Arkadii (Shatov), Fr. *See* Panteleimon (Shatov), Bishop
art, religious. *See* icons; *specific artists and works*
Asia, 15–16
Athanasius, 43

baptism, 33, 35, 36, 77–79, 110, 224. *See also* Kreshchenie
beauty, divine/transcendent, 10, 18, 22, 44, 68–69, 72, 76, 100. *See also* divine, communion with the

Belikov, Fr. Maksim, 187
Bellah, Robert, 18, 217–18
bells (church), 22–23, 193
Bible, 57, 88
birch trees, 30–31
Bolsheviks: Church property dispersed, 185; Church's criticism of, 12, 45; loyalty to, 18; and martyrs, 149–50, 153; mission of, 14; monarchy eliminated, 129, 139. *See also* Communism; repression of the Church; Soviet Union
Brianchaninov, Bishop Ignatii. *See* Ignatii (Brianchaninov), Bishop
Bugoslavskaia, O., 202
Butovo church and killing field, 155–56, 159

calendar. *See* Church year
Calvinism, 3, 83, 113
canonization of saints, 138–40, 146–50, 157–58
Catherine the Great, 40
chapels, in public buildings, 9, 169
Chaplin, Fr. Vsevolod, 197, 199, 228n24
Chapnin, Sergei, 190, 202–3

children, 105–6. *See also* religious education

China, 15

Christ: communion with, 42–43, 189–90 (*see also* Eucharist); in Nesterov's paintings, 27–28, 91; Russian martyrs and, 129–30, 134–35, 142; salvific work, 54

Christendom (concept), 19

Christian community: and addiction recovery, 97–100; among followers of spiritual leaders, 61–62, 87, 183–84; Church as, 173, 178–79, 201–2; Church-state relationship and, 161–62; Dudachkino, 214–17; as entry into Church life, 46; eucharistic fellowship, 168–69, 174–75, 201; parish life and, 175–77, 183–84, 187; and social ministry, 104–5, 116; and spiritual transformation, 189–90; through friendships, 90. *See also* group study; monasteries

Christian Household: Traditions and Holy Things (Iov and Pavel Gumerov), 67–68

Christianity: in Africa, Asia, and the Middle East, 15–16; church-state relations and, 19–20; repressed under Communism, 9, 13, 21 (*see also* repression of the Church); in the West, 15, 222. *See also* Calvinism; Christian community; Orthodox Church; Orthodoxy; Protestantism; re-Christianization

Christmas, 120–21

"Christmas Educational Lectures," 85, 236n76

Christ the Savior Cathedral (Moscow), 37, 38, 42, 127–28, 138, 140, 194, 197–99, 198

church construction, 37, 184–88

Church of Cosmas and Damian (Moscow), 63, 153

Church of Sophia, the Wisdom of God (Moscow), 148, 164, 165–66, 181–82, 193. *See also* Volgin, Fr. Vladimir

Church of St. Nicholas (Klennikakh), 61–62. *See also* Mechev, Fr. Aleksei; Mechev, Fr. Sergei

Church of St. Nicholas (Kuznetsakh), 80–81. *See also* Vorob'ev, Fr. Vladimir

Church of St. Nicholas (Pyzhakh), 180, 205–6. *See also* Shargunov, Fr. Aleksandr

Church of the Protective Veil, 18, 24, 26–29. *See also* Martha and Mary Monastery

Church on the Blood (Ekaterinburg), 156

Church Slavonic, 57, 79, 88, 98, 179–81, 201

Church-state relations: and church construction, 185–86; Church's relation to politics, 135–36; in contemporary Russia (generally), 11–12, 17, 19–21, 37–38, 41–42, 199–200, 202–3, 228n24; cooperation and complementarity, 38, 143; drawbacks/dangers of, 195–96, 219, 222; God's and Church's predominance, 135–36, 143, 241n32; in the *Icon of the New Martyrs*, 143; ideal Church and, 161–62; in Mazyrin's thought, 135–37; and moral values, 35, 38, 41–42, 44; necessity of, 195–96; religious education in public schools, 17, 72–77, 117, 226n14 (*see also* religious education); social harmony as goal, 50, 76; and social ministry, 117–19 (*see also* social ministries); in the Soviet era, 33–34, 36, 41, 127, 132–35, 202 (*see also* Soviet Union); state/national interests dominant, 38, 39, 76, 117; symphonia, 17, 38–41, 50, 114, 195–96, 218, 219; in tsarist Russia, 39–41; Western vs. Russian notions of, 19, 38–39. *See also* repression of the Church; symphonia

Church year (calendar), 43, 147, 169, 201. *See also* Easter; holy days; Kreshchenie; Lent

civil religion, 18–19, 217–18

civil society, 218–19

clergy. *See* priests; *specific individuals*

communion. *See* divine, communion with the; Eucharist

Communism: canonizations under, 146–47; in China, 15; Church's understanding of its past re, 127, 129–30,

144–45; contemporary evaluation of, 124–25, 126–27; cult of leaders, 35; lingering Soviet mentality, 177; and martyrs, 149–50; and the "new Soviet man," 18, 42; Party today, 123–24. *See also* Bolsheviks; repression of the Church; Soviet Union

comparative theology, 82–83

confession: in addiction recovery, 99; during Divine Liturgy, 182; and Eucharist, 87, 173–75; in hospitals, 110, 111; for monastics, 102, 104; participation in, 32, 79, 172–73; priestly abuse, 217; priests' maturity and, 200; spiritual counselors and, 59, 171; Fr. Volgin and, 168, 170

convents. *See* monasteries

counselors. *See* spiritual fathers

cross, sign of, 39, 67

culture, Russian: Church's understanding deficient, 118; and drug rehabilitation, 96, 100; essential Orthodoxy of, 11, 12–13, 32, 74–76, 167, 207; historic buildings/traditions preserved, 36; intellectuals and, 88; Orthodox practices within, 34–35, 211 (*see also* icons; Kreshchenie); and Orthodox religious education, 53–54, 64, 73; Orthodoxy as cultural identity, 16–17, 53–54; re-Christianization and, 45–46 (*see also* re-Christianization). *See also* national identity; popular (unofficial) Orthodoxy

Damaskin (Orlovskii), Igumen, 149–50

Daniliuk, Aleksandr, 76

de-churching, 200–201

deification (divinization), 44, 45, 54–55, 100, 112, 114–16, 190. *See also* divine, communion with the; salvation; spiritual transformation

Diedrich, Hans-Christian, 40

dissidents, 20, 84, 126, 193, 202. *See also* priests: dissident

divine, communion with the: as goal, 17–18, 42–43, 45, 189–90, 208; religious education and, 54–56; through Eucharist, 42–43, 71, 168–69. *See also* beauty, divine/transcendent; deification; Eucharist; Holy Rus'; salvation; spiritual transformation

Divine Litugy. *See* liturgy of the Orthodox Church

Dmitrii and Sophia (author's friends), 223–24

Dmitrii Donskoi, Prince and St., 39, 108, 147, 150, 216

Donskoi Monastery, 33, 132

drug rehabilitation programs, 4, 12, 91, 92–100, 94, 118–21

Dudachkino community, 214–17, 218

Dvorkin, Aleksandr, 83

Easter, 4

education, 17, 33, 72–77, 117. *See also* religious education

Elena (author's friend), 174

Elisaveta (Pozdniakova), Mother, 101–2

Elizabeth Fedorovna Romanova, St., 24–29, 101, 103, 110, 138, 152, 152–54, 158, 171. *See also* Martha and Mary Monastery; St. Elizabeth's Monastery

eternal life, 42–43. *See also* salvation

Eucharist (Communion), 42–44; emphasis on, 172–73; eucharistic fellowship, 168–69, 174–75, 201; frequency of reception, 174–75, 189, 248n50; holiness through, 71; in hospitals, 108, 110; mystical nature of, 179; preparation for, 173–75 (*see also* confession); in Rublev's Trinity icon, 49, 50

Everyday Saints (Tikhon [Shevkunov]), 69–70, 79, 151, 172. *See also* Tikhon (Shevkunov), Bishop

families, 117, 176, 200

fasting, 16, 43, 44, 68, 97, 111, 169, 175, 189

Feast of All Russian Saints (icon), 143–44

Fedotov, Georgii, 161

Feodorovskii Cathedral (St. Petersburg), 203–5, 218

Feofilakt of Bolgar, 65
Filaret (Drozdov), Metropolitan, 40, 58, 233n25
Filaret (Vakhromeev), Metropolitan, 103
First City Hospital (Moscow), 108–10, 115
Foundations of Orthodox Culture (Kuraev), 74, 100, 158–59, 235n58
freedom, spiritual: Church and, 131, 134–37, 161–62, 203; illness or hardship and, 118–19; of the martyrs, 149, 154, 157
Freeze, Gregory, 39–40

Glebova, Maria, 140
Golgotha-Crucifixion Skete, 29–31, 31. *See also* Solovki and Anzer Island
Golitsyn, Dmitrii, 108
good works. *See* social ministries
Gorbachev, Mikhail, 37
Gospel of Mark, 65–66
group study, 59, 60–62, 87
Gryzlov, Boris, 204
Gulag Archipelago (Solzhenitsyn), 126. *See also* Solzhenitsyn, Alexander
Gumerov, Archmonk Iov. *See* Iov (Gumerov), Archmonk
Gumerov, Fr. Pavel, 67–68
Gur'ianov, Nikolai, Fr. *See* Nikolai (Gur'ianov), Fr.

Heat (Zhara) (2011 film), 202
Hicks, Edward, 48
Hilarion (Alfeev), Metropolitan, 65, 88, 116–17, 151, 174
Hilarion (Troitskii), Bishop, 151–52
HIV/AIDS, 116–17
holiness. *See* divine, communion with the; holy elders; Holy Rus'; salvation; spiritual transformation
holy days, 4, 37, 38, 56, 57, 120–21, 143, 209–12, 220–21. *See also* Church year
holy elders, 59–60, 61, 63, 70, 85–86, 168, 170. *See also* spiritual fathers; *specific individuals*
Holy Rus': author's experience, 4–5, 222; Christian community and, 90 (*see also* Christian community); contemporary

Russia's relationship to, 10; defined, 2–3, 5–6; *Icon of the New Martyrs* and, 144; as moral ideal, 75–76; Orthodox Church's relationship to, 13, 17–18, 22, 47–48, 72 (*see also* Orthodox Church); as political ideology, 11; promise of, 2, 208–9, 218; religious education and, 89 (*see also* religious education); visual depictions, 27–28, 48–50 (*see also* Nesterov, Mikhail). *See also* Church-state relations; divine, communion with the; renewal
Holy Rus' (Nesterov, 1905), 27, 48
Holy Rus' (The Way to Christ) (Nesterov, 1910–11), 27–28, 29, 48, 91
Holy Synod, 39–40, 57, 77, 85, 107, 137, 146
Holy Trinity–St. Sergius Lavra, 27, 33, 159–60, 165. *See also* Rublev, Andrei
hospitals, 91, 101, 107, 108–11, 115
Hovorun, Cyril, 203

Iakunin, Vladimir, 204
Icon of the New Martyrs and Confessors, 30, 31, 140–45, 141, 152, 155, 219
icons: creation of, 140; depicting prayer and service, 104; post-Communist renewal, 128; purpose, 43, 57, 140; Rublev's Trinity icon, 48–50; Sokolova and, 61–62; veneration of, 50, 68, 122, 127, 128–29, 158, 159, 250n24. *See also* Rublev, Andrei; Zinon (Teodor), Fr.; *specific icons*
ideal types, 6
Ignatii (Brianchaninov), Bishop, 58
illness, 116–17, 118–19. *See also* drug rehabilitation programs; hospitals
in-churching, 10, 13; effectiveness, 188–92, 200–202, 207; social ministries and, 97–100, 108–11, 114, 119. *See also* re-Christianization
Internet, 64–65, 66–67
Ioann (Krest'iankin), Fr., 63, 70, 85, 115, 165, 171, 191–92
Ioann (Popov), Metropolitan, 44
Iosaf (Shvetsov), Fr., 183
Iosif-Volokolamsk Monastery, 105–6

Iov (Gumerov), Archmonk, 67–69
Irina (author's friend), 2–3, 52, 80
Isaiah, book of, 48
Istnyuk, Agrippina, 109
Iuvenalii (Poiarkov), Metropolitan, 137–38,
    140, 144
Ivanova, Elena, 54–55
Ivan the Terrible, 39, 108, 206

Jesus. See Christ
John (Garklavs), Bishop, 127
John of Kronstadt, St., 86, 104, 107, 171
Joseph of Volokolamsk, St., 101, 105
Julian, Fr., 52, 80, 90

Kaleda, Gleb, 35
Kazanskii Cathedral, 37
Kaz'mina, Ol'ga, 35
KGB, 33, 34, 62
Khodyrev, Aleksandr, 186
Khrushchev, Nikita, 33, 37, 167
Kirill (Smirnov), Bishop, 133, 134, 140, 150
Kirill, Patriarch: Butovo remembrance
    sermon, 155–56; career and election,
    196–97; on Christianity in the culture,
    12–13, 14; and Church-state relations,
    199–200, 241n32; on the martyrs, 160;
    popularity, 196–97, 227n14; and public
    religious education, 73–74; and Russian
    leadership, 12, 37, 197, 199, 228n24,
    241n32; Russian liturgy proposed, 180;
    on Stalin, 21; television program, 65;
    wealth and integrity, 197–98
Klimzo, Fr. Vladimir, 64
Kochetkov, Fr. Georgii, 180
Kochurov, Fr. Ioann, 131
Kondrat'ev, Fr. Mefodii. See Mefodii
    (Kondrat'ev), Bishop
Kotkin, Stephen, 10–11
Kozlov, Fr. Maksim, 83
Kremlin, 37, 38–39
Kreshchenie (Theophany), 209–12, 220–21,
    250n24
Krest'iankin, Ioann. See Ioann
    (Krest'iankin), Fr.
Ksenia of St. Petersburg, St., 147, 158

Kuraev, Andrei, Deacon, 74–76, 89, 100,
    158–59, 224

Lavrov, Sergei, 11
Law on Freedom of Conscience and
    Religious Associations (1997), 82
lay church, 60–62
Lebedev, Sergii. See Sergii (Lebedev)
Lemeshonok, Fr. Andrei, 103, 104, 115
Lenin, Vladimir, 35, 123, 124
Lent, 4, 17, 75, 189
Levashova memorial, 156
liturgy of the Orthodox Church: beauty
    of, 44; congregational participation,
    181–83, 204; educational role, 56–57,
    59, 64, 173; intent, 43; language of,
    57, 79, 179–81, 201 (see also Church
    Slavonic); length, 182; senses engaged
    by, 43–44
Liudmila (author's friend), 51, 90
Luke (Voino-Iasenetskii), Bishop and St.,
    158–59, 245n88
Luther, Martin, and Lutheranism, 83. See
    also Protestantism

Maria (Tseitlin), 149
Mark (Arndt), Archbishop, 178
Martha and Mary Monastery, 24–29, 26, 68,
    101–2, 108, 111, 154, 158. See also Church
    of the Protective Veil; Elizabeth
    Fedorovna Romanova, St.; Nesterov,
    Mikhail; Sisters of Mercy
Martinovich, Vladimir, 84
martyrs: canonization of, 138–40, 146–50,
    157–58; commemoration and veneration
    of, 51, 129–30, 137–38, 147–48, 151–61,
    162; as examples, 150–51, 153–54, 160–63,
    206; hymns honoring, 145–46; icons and
    hagiography of, 30, 31, 140–45, 141, 152,
    155, 219; national renewal through, 124,
    126–27, 143, 145–46, 157, 160; new
    martyrs generally, 32, 128, 131, 161;
    Nicholas II and royal family as, 139–40,
    143, 145, 151, 156, 205–6, 244n75; in
    prison camps, 30; in tsarist Russia, 39,
    109. See also specific martyrs

Mary (Mother of God): icons, 8–9, 122, 127, 128–29; Protective Veil commemoration, 25; relics, 194–95, 249n1

Matrona (holy woman), 158, 206

Mazyrin, Fr. Aleksandr, 130–31, 133–36, 149

Mchedlova, Elena, 189

Mechev, Fr. Aleksei, 61, 104, 233n25

Mechev, Fr. Sergei, 61

media, 38, 58, 64–67, 167, 201. See also Ostankino broadcast center and chapel

Medvedev, Dmitrii, 10, 37–38

Mefodii (Kondrat'ev), Bishop, 93–100

Memorial (human rights organization), 126

memorial sites, 155–57. See also specific sites

Men', Fr. Aleksandr, 36, 62–63, 85, 165, 172, 179, 202–3

Middle East, 15–16

Mikhailov, Fr. Amvrosii. See Amvrosii (Mikhailov), Fr.

Mikhail Romanov, Tsar, 39

miracles, 70, 75

Missionary Concept (2007), 44–47, 77–78

missionary work, 46–47, 63, 81, 82

Mitrofa (Iurchuk), Archbishop, 175–76

Mitrofan of Voronezh, Bishop, 146

Mitrofanov, Fr. Georgii, 160–61

monasteries: Communist closure of, 128; and drug rehabilitation, 92–100; funding, 101, 103, 211; growth of, 9, 38; as invitation to Orthodox life, 192; seminaries within, 81–82; and social ministries, 79, 101, 107, 115 (see also social ministries); spiritual guidance in, 59; Tikhon (Shevkunov) on monastic life, 69–70. See also sketes; specific monasteries

Monastery of the Holy Intercession of the Mother of God (Moscow), 158

Monastery of the New Jerusalem, 39

moral values: Church rhetoric on, 117, 199; Church-state relations and, 35, 38, 41–42, 44; conservative Orthodoxy and, 206; family as source of, 189; re-Christianization and, 45, 190; societal

need for renewal, 116–17 (see also renewal)

Moscow, 8–9; church construction, 37, 185, 187–88; demonstrations in, 122, 123, 197 (see also Pussy Riot); hospitals, 108–11; the Kremlin, 37, 38–39; McDonald's in, 192–93; parish principle not followed in, 86; population, 185; public education, 73, 77; religious art, 50; sisterhoods in, 111 (see also Martha and Mary Monastery; Sisterhood of St. Dmitrii; Sisters of Mercy); as "Third Rome," 14; Virgin's Belt relics displayed, 194–95, 207, 249n1. See also Rebirth; St. Tikhon's Orthodox University; specific churches and monasteries

music, 43, 46, 96, 128, 145–46, 181

Narushev, Fr. Aleksandr, 53–54

national identity: ambivalence re, 21; in-churching and, 10, 13; national repentance, 145–46, 157, 160; Orthodox Church and, 5, 9, 11, 13–15, 20, 37, 47–48; Orthodoxy and, 5, 13–15, 19, 37, 124, 126, 153, 207; post-Communist crisis of, 18, 125–26; renewal through honoring martyrs, 124, 126–27, 143, 145–46, 157, 160 (see also martyrs); symphonia at heart of, 38–39; World War II and, 123. See also culture, Russian

nationalism, rightist, 12, 122

National Mall (Washington, D.C.), 18, 37, 217

Nektarii (Morozov), Igumen, 190

Nesterov, Mikhail, 27–28, 39, 48, 91

New Year's celebrations, 168–69

Nicene Creed, 77, 142, 181

Nicholas I, Tsar, 40

Nicholas II, Tsar, 130–34, 143, 145, 151, 156, 205–6. See also royal family

Nikolai (Gur'ianov), Fr., 63, 103, 104–5, 115, 215

Nikon, Patriarch, 39

Nontraditional Religiosity in Belarus (Martinovich), 84

nuns. *See* monasteries; *specific sisterhoods and individuals*

Old Believers, 2, 39, 67, 107
Oleg (author's friend), 18, 19
One Thousand Questions to a Priest (Iov Gumerov), 67
Orlovskii, Igumen Damaskin. *See* Damaskin (Orlovskii), Igumen
Orthodox Church: affiliation vs. participation, 10, 17–18, 36–37, 100, 170, 188–89, 207, 248nn42–43; and anticlericalism, 21, 197–99; church construction, 37, 184–88; as community, 173, 178–79 (*see also* Christian community); conservative/fundamentalist faction, 205–7; critiques of, 88, 107, 118, 144, 177, 196–203, 206, 228n24, 239n25; dealing with Soviet past, 127, 129–30, 144–45, 157; future of, 218–20; history of, 43–44; HIV/AIDS stance, 116–17; as ideal type, 6; imprimatur, 65; intelligentsia and, 35, 37, 88, 167, 172; language of, 57 (*see also* Church Slavonic); lay churches and, 60–62; leadership (*see* Aleksii II, Patriarch; Holy Synod; Kirill, Patriarch; priests; *specific individuals*); liberal wing, 195, 196; and national identity, 5, 9, 11, 13–15, 20, 37, 47–48 (*see also* national identity); not a monolith, 6; and popular Orthodoxy, 211–12; post-Communist resurgence, 2, 9–10, 36–38, 44, 128–29, 130, 165–66, 187–88; public trust in, 196–98, 227n14; re-Christianization of Russia sought, 9, 13, 40–41, 45, 117 (*see also Missionary Concept*); relationship to Holy Rus', 5–6, 13, 17–18, 22, 47–48, 72; and religious diversity, 47, 82–84; and right ritual practice, 67–68, 234n48; saints and martyrs (*see* martyrs; saints; *specific individuals*); salvific mission, 42–46; schisms, 39, 67, 214 (*see also* Old Believers); and social reform, 21–22; synodal period, 39–40; in tsarist Russia,

32, 39–41; unity of, 132–34, 135, 136; vision for Russia's place in the world, 14–15; and World War II, 32–33. *See also* Christianity; Church-state relations; in-churching; Orthodoxy; re-Christianization; religious education; social ministries
Orthodox theology. *See* comparative theology; liturgy of the Orthodox Church; priests: seminaries and education of; *specific topics*
Orthodoxy: apart from the Church, 19; author's experience of, 3–5, 220–22; as civil religion, 18–19, 217–18; and civil society, 218–19; conservative/fundamentalist faction, 205–7; as cultural identity, 16–17, 37, 53–54; cultural practices, 34–35, 211, 250n24 (*see also* culture, Russian; icons); five types, 195; folk Orthodoxy, 56; life repatterned by, 43; meaning of word, 55; moral dimensions, 75; and national identity, 5, 13–15, 19, 37, 124, 126, 153, 207 (*see also* national identity); as option among many, 207; as part of public life, 37–38, 208–9, 250n24; as personal spiritual faith/transformation, 17, 18–19; as replacement for Communism, 18; resurgence as political phenomenon, 17; right ritual practice, 67–68, 234n48 (*see also* ritual practice); of Russian culture, 11, 12–13, 32, 74–76, 167, 207; and social unity, 136; survival under Soviet regime, 12–13, 14, 32–37, 59–62, 167, 211 (*see also* repression of the Church; underground churches); in tsarist Russia, 40–41; varied definitions/understandings of, 16–17, 36–37, 45, 211–17, 223–24. *See also* Orthodox Church; popular (unofficial) Orthodoxy; re-Christianization
Ostankino broadcast center and chapel, 1–2, 6–7, 169–70

Panteleimon (Shatov), Bishop, 102, 108–9, 110, 112–14, 115, 116, 171

Papkova, Irina, 41, 195, 241n32
parishes, 164–93; charismatic priests, 86, 171–72, 183–84; church construction, 184–88; crises in parish life, 175–78; fellowship/community in, 168–69, 174–77, 183–84, 187 (*see also* Christian community); funding, 176, 186, 200, 211; growth of, 9, 89, 187–88; lay involvement, 178, 219–20; liturgical participation, 181–83; participation rates, 188–89, 200; religious education programs, 51–53, 78–79; rural vs. urban, 170–71, 185. *See also specific churches*
"Participation of the Faithful in the Eucharist" (2015), 174–75
Pavel (author's friend), 68, 223
Pavel (Shvets), Fr., 93, 120
Pavel (Troitskii), Fr., 108–9, 171
Peaceable Kingdom (Hicks paintings), 48
peace and harmony, longing for, 48–50, 72. *See also* Holy Rus'; Nesterov, Mikhail
personal relationship with God, 44–45. *See also* divine, communion with the; spiritual transformation
Peter the Great, 39–40, 88, 146
Petr (Meshcherinov), Igumen, 201
Petr (Polianskii), Bishop and patriarchal representative, 132–33, 140
Petr, Metropolitan (14th cent.), 146
Philip II, Metropolitan and St., 39, 142
Philokalia, 57–58, 234n41
Philotheus, 14
popular (unofficial) Orthodoxy, 34–37, 64, 173, 195, 209–12, 218. *See also* culture, Russian; Orthodoxy
Potapov, Fr. Boris, 166
prayer(s): and addiction recovery, 97, 98–99; daily, 43, 98–99, 102, 189; educational role, 57; intent, 43; Jesus Prayer, 58; and service, 102, 104, 115
preaching, 172. *See also* priests: charismatic; *specific individuals*
priests: as advisers/counselors, 66, 174–75, 177, 183, 234n43 (*see also* spiritual fathers); as barriers to lay participation, 200; charismatic, 86, 171–72, 183–84;

Communist persecution of, 32, 61, 62–63, 128 (*see also* repression of the Church); dissident, 36, 37, 127; gap between parishioners and, 177–78; and marriage, 223; negative encounters with, 68, 234n48; seminaries and education of, 33, 34, 44, 46–47, 58–59, 81–83, 85, 165, 172; "Soviet mentality" toward, 177; temptations of, 191–92; in the underground church, 35, 61. *See also* Orthodox Church; *specific individuals*
"Principles of Organization of Social Work in the Russian Orthodox Church," 112, 114, 115
prisoners and imprisonment, 22–23, 104–5, 197; in the Communist era, 30, 32, 51, 131, 156. *See also specific individuals*
property disputes, 185, 186, 187–88
Protestantism: and Church-state relations, 19, 54; comparative theology and, 82–83; ecumenical dialogue with, 196, 205; Orthodoxy contrasted with, 45, 57, 95, 172; outside Russia, 15–16; and ritual practices, 68; within Russia, 20, 63, 82, 95; and social ministry, 111, 113. *See also* Calvinism
Pskov-Pecherskii Monastery, 63, 70, 165, 183
psychiatric aftercare, 103–4
Pussy Riot, 41–42, 197, 228n24
Putin, Vladimir: authoritarianism of, 117, 218; baptism, 36; counselor, 72 (*see also* Tikhon [Shevkunov], Bishop); faith of, 9–10, 194; popularity, 10–11, 213; protests against, 122, 123, 197; relationship with Orthodox Church, 11–12, 21, 37–38, 124, 197, 199, 228n24; religious education program announced, 74; World War II invoked, 123

Rafail, Fr., 70–71
Rasputin, 130, 206, 216
"Reason to Doubt" (Bugoslavskaia), 202
Rebirth (exhibition), 122–23, 127–30
re-Christianization: effectiveness, 21, 188–93; and the emergence of sects, 84; identifying and measuring, 16–17,

188–90; meaning of, 222; parish growth and, 187–88; social ministries and, 112 (*see also* social ministries); sought by Church, 9, 13, 40–41, 45, 117. *See also* in-churching; *Missionary Concept*; religious education

relics: Bolsheviks' treatment of, 131, 142; and miracles, 146, 159, 214; pilgrimages to see, 87, 116, 160; veneration of, 22, 35, 72, 147, 152, 158, 159, 194–95, 249n11. *See also* Virgin's Belt

religiosity, identifying/measuring, 16–17, 31–32. *See also* popular (unofficial) Orthodoxy

religious diversity, 20, 47, 63, 82, 89, 122, 228n24

religious education, 51–90; adult classes, 51–53; "Christmas Educational Lectures," 85, 236n76; Church infrastructure, 12, 53; Church-run schools, 72–73; Church's commitment to, 63–64; as civic education, 53–54; comparative theology and sectology, 82–84; educational literature, 57–58; group study and the lay church, 59, 60–62; history of, 56–59; holy elders, spiritual fathers and, 59–60, 61–63, 70, 85–87 (*see also* holy elders); and the meaning of Holy Rus', 89; and national identity, 12; need for, 88–89; Orthodox understanding of, 54–56; Orthodox university education, 80–82; parish-based programs, 51–54, 78–79, 166; prebaptismal catechization, 77–79; of priests (*see under* priests); in public schools, 17, 72–77, 117, 226n14; and Russian culture, 53–54, 64, 73; social ministry and, 92, 97–100, 104–7; success of, 89–90; through publications and media, 58, 64–70, 167, 234nn41–42, 235nn51,58; use of contemporary art/music in, 46; writings of spiritual leaders, 61–63; young people turned off by, 223–24

religious services, as commercial relationship, 176, 200

renewal: need for, 116–17; through eucharistic fellowship, 168–69; through honoring martyrs, 124, 126–27, 143, 145–46, 157, 160. *See also* Holy Rus'; re-Christianization

Renovationists, 113, 132, 134, 151, 180

repression of the Church, 9, 24; acknowledging and remembering, 126–30, 142–45 (*see also* martyrs); memorial sites, 51, 155–57; Orthodoxy's survival, 12–13, 14, 25, 32–37, 59–62, 167, 211; present-day effects, 21; and social ministry, 113; statistics, 32, 128, 245n86; under Khrushchev and beyond, 33–34, 37, 167; under the Bolsheviks and Stalin, 32–33, 37, 58–62, 107, 126–28, 130–35, 149, 161, 167; World War II and, 32–33. *See also specific individuals*

Reutov (city), 186

rightist nationalists, 12, 122

ritual practice, 67–68, 87–88, 201, 211–12. *See also* icons; Kreshchenie; popular (unofficial) Orthodoxy; relics

Roman Catholicism, 82–83, 113, 196, 205

Romanova, Elizabeth Fedorovna. *See* Elizabeth Fedorovna Romanova, St.

Rotenberg, Arkadii, 80

royal family, 139–40, 143, 151, 244n75. *See also* Nicholas II, Tsar; tsar, restoration of

Rublev, Andrei, 37, 48–50, 50, 143, 147

Russia: benefited by Orthodox efforts, 208–9; Christianization of, 13–14; civil society in, 218–19; contemporary attitudes toward Orthodox Church in, 14; drug addiction in, 92, 94–95 (*see also* drug rehabilitation programs); economic crisis, 125; global popular culture in, 21; implications of religious rebirth in, 16; moral renewal needed, 116–17 (*see also* renewal); political protests, 122, 123, 197; re-Christianization of (*see* re-Christianization); religious pluralism in (*see* religious diversity); social work in, 113 (*see also* social ministries); tsarist, 32, 39–41, 72, 109

Russia: (*continued*)
(*see also* royal family; *specific
individuals*); urban growth, 185;
Westernization questioned, 82; Western
values in, 118. *See also* Bolsheviks;
Church-state relations; Communism;
culture, Russian; Holy Rus'; national
identity; Soviet Union; *specific leaders*
Russian language, 13. *See also* liturgy of the
Orthodox Church: language of
Russian Orthodox Church outside of
Russia (ROCOR), 138, 139, 214

saints, 43, 138–40, 146–50, 157–58. *See also*
martyrs; *specific saints*
Saltykov, Fr. Aleksandr, 140
salvation: defined, 45; focus on one's own,
192; as goal of the Church, 42–46,
189–90; in Orthodox theology, 95–96,
99; social ministry and, 113–16. *See also*
deification; spiritual transformation
samizdat (unofficial publications), 36, 126
Schmemann, Alexander, 174, 178–79
Scriptures, 57, 65–66, 88. *See also* Bible
sectology, 47, 83–84. *See also* religious
diversity
secularism and secularization: Church
struggle against, 45, 47, 118, 151, 160, 199;
negative influence of, 47, 95, 161; under
Communist rule, 21, 36, 45 (*see also*
Communism); in the West, 15
Semiannikov, Fr. Moisei, 105–6, 239n24
senses, engagement of, 43–44
Serafim (Chichagov), Bishop, 163, 163
Serafim (Sobolev), Bishop, 40
Serafim of Sarov, St., 192, 208
Serbarinov, Fr. Georgii, 148
Sergii (Lebedev), 146
Sergii (Stragorodskii), Metropolitan,
133–34, 136
Sergii, Marina, and Natasha (author's
friends), 214–16
Sergius of Radonezh, St., 27, 39, 146,
160
Shargunov, Fr. Aleksandr, 160, 171, 172,
205–6

Shatov, Fr. Arkadii. *See* Panteleimon
(Shatov), Bishop
Shchusev, Aleksei, 26
Shevkunov, Tikhon. *See* Tikhon
(Shevkunov), Bishop
Shpiller, Fr. Vsevolod, 36, 80–81
Shubin, Mikhail, 169–70
Shvets, Fr. Pavel. *See* Pavel (Shvets), Fr.
Shvetsov, Fr. Iosaf. *See* Iosaf (Shvetsov), Fr.
Siluan of Mt. Athos, St., 54–55
sin, 95–96, 116, 117, 150, 174. *See also*
confession
Sisterhood of St. Dmitrii, 108–11, 116
Sisterhood of the Great Martyr Anastasia
Uzoreshitelnitsa, 115
Sisters of Mercy, 91, 101–2, 108, 109. *See
also* Martha and Mary Monastery
sketes (semi-hermetical communities),
27–28, 29–31, 103. *See also* Golgotha-
Crucifixion Skete; monasteries
Smirnov, Fr. Dmitrii, 86, 171, 172
Sobor of the New Martyrs and Confessors
of Russia, 138–39, 142–43. *See also*
martyrs
Social Concept (2000), 41, 84, 135–36,
196
social justice, 107, 118
social ministries, 12, 91–121; Church's
purpose and motivation, 112–14, 119;
Church-state relations and, 114, 117–19;
drug rehabilitation programs, 12, 91,
92–100, 111, 118–21; history of, 107;
hospitals, 91, 101, 107, 108–11, 115;
monasteries and sisterhoods and, 25–26,
79, 101–4, 107, 108–11, 115; place of, in
Russian society, 111–12, 219; and
religious education, 104–7; and
transformation and salvation, 112,
114–16; without coercion, 99, 109
social reform, 21–22
Sokolov, Fr. Vladimir, 23
Sokolova, Maria, 61–62, 143
Soloviev, Vladimir, 58
Solovki and Anzer Island, 29–31, 31, 146,
156, 159, 212–14, 244n82
Solzhenitsyn, Alexander, 36, 76, 126

Sorokin, Fr. Aleksandr, 205
South Korea, 15
Soviet Union: Church-state relations in, 33–34, 36, 41, 127, 132–35, 202; Church suppressed (see repression of the Church); collapse of, 25, 125–26; German invasion of, 32–33 (see also World War II); Orthodoxy's survival in, 12–13, 14, 32–37, 59–62, 167, 211; religious art confiscated, 50; Solovki gulag, 30; urban growth, 185. See also Communism; Russia; Ukraine
spiritual fathers (counselors), 59–60, 70, 85–87, 97, 102, 103, 174–75. See also holy elders; specific individuals
spiritual transformation: addiction recovery and, 95–97, 100; assessing, 191; of children, 105–6; Christian life and, 189–90; illness and, 116–17; individual, 17–18, 44, 45; religious education and, 54–56; social ministry and, 112, 113–16. See also deification; Holy Rus'; in-churching; re-Christianization; salvation
Srebrianskii, Fr. Mitrofan, 28
Sretenskii Monastery, 51–53, 64–67, 70, 79–80, 90, 151–52, 156–57, 180. See also Iov (Gumerov), Archmonk; Tikhon (Shevkunov), Bishop
Stalin, Joseph: contemporary views of, 21, 123, 124, 126, 206; and the "new Soviet man," 18; and the Orthodox Church, 32, 33, 37, 127–28, 158, 198, 198–99. See also Communism; Soviet Union
St. Elizabeth's Monastery (Minsk), 102–4, 108, 111. See also Lemeshonok, Fr. Andrei
St. George's Parish (Ivanovo region), 4, 92–100, 94, 111, 118–21
St. Petersburg, 73, 77, 78, 115, 185. See also specific churches
St. Seraphim of Sarov parish (Moscow), 53–54
St. Tikhon's Orthodox University, 80–82, 128, 130, 150, 200
Sukhov, Fr. Aleksandr, 214–17

symphonia, 17, 38–41, 50, 114, 195–96, 218, 219. See also Church-state relations
Sysoev, Fr. Daniel, 47

Talshkin, Aleksei, 23
Tanya (Solovki pilgrim), 212–14
Tat'iana (author's friend), 51, 80, 90
teachers, 55, 74. See also holy elders; religious education; spiritual fathers
Teodor, Fr. Zinon. See Zinon (Teodor), Fr.
theology. See comparative theology; liturgy of the Orthodox Church; priests: seminaries and education of; specific topics
Theophany. See Kreshchenie
theosis, 43. See also deification; divine, communion with the
"Third Rome," 14
Tikhon (Shevkunov), Bishop, 69–72, 79, 86, 89, 151, 171, 172. See also Sretenskii Monastery
Tikhon, Patriarch, 80, 104, 113, 131–36, 138–40, 151, 158, 187
Tikhvin icon of the Theotokos, 122, 127, 128–29
Trinity, understanding of, 89
Trinity Church (Reutov), 186–87
Trinity icon (Rublev), 48–50, 50
Troeltsch, Ernst, 6
Troitskii, Fr. Pavel. See Pavel (Troitskii), Fr.
tsar, restoration of, 63, 124
tsarist Russia, 32, 39–41, 72, 109. See also royal family; specific individuals
Tseitlin, Maria, See Maria (Tseitlin)

Ukraine, 125, 199, 203
Ulitskaia, Liudmila, 88
Uminskii, Fr. Aleksei, 65, 86, 171
underground churches, 35, 60, 61, 179, 202
United Russia Party, 122, 123, 213
unity: of the Church, 132–34, 135, 136, 150, 160 (see also Orthodox Church: critiques of); with God, 116, 189–90 (see also divine, communion with the); social unity, 76, 136; vision of, 47–48, 50, 72 (see also Holy Rus'). See also Christian community

Unity Day, 122
universities, Orthodox. *See* St. Tikhon's Orthodox University
Unknown World of Faith, 68–69, 235n51

Vasechko, Fr. Valentin, 83
Vasilii (Preobrazhenskii), Bishop, 65, 144
Vasilii, Fr. (author's friend), 210, 220
Veniamin of Petrograd, Metropolitan, 104, 138
Virgin's Belt, 193–95, 207, 222, 249n1
Virgin's Protective Veil commemoration, 25
Vitalii (prisoner/bell ringer), 23
Vladimir (Bogoiavlenskii), Metropolitan, 131
Vladimir of Rus', Prince, 10, 44, 75, 146
Volgin, Fr. Vladimir, 1–2, 6, 85–88, 164–70, 172, 177–78, 182–84, 191–92
Volkov, Fr. Konstantin, 184
Vorob'ev, Fr. Vladimir, 80–81, 86, 88, 109, 130, 140, 171, 174, 176, 183, 200
Vyshinskii, Oleg, Deacon, 113, 114, 119

Washington, D.C. *See* National Mall
water, blessed, 209–10, 250n24. *See also* Kreshchenie

Way of a Pilgrim, 58
Way to Christ (Nesterov, 1910–11), 27–28, 29, 48, 91
West: Christianity in, 15, 222; freedom in, 136–37; and post-Communist Russia, 10–12, 125–26
Western values, 11, 19, 88, 95, 118
women: attire, 68, 197; importance to Church, 144, 148; lay sisterhoods, 26, 101, 103, 107, 111; martyrs and saints, 144, 147, 148, 149, 158 (*see also* Elizabeth Fedorovna Romanova, St.); religious education of, 51–52 (*see also* Irina; Liudmila; Tat'iana); sisterhoods and monasteries, 24, 25–26, 101–4, 108–11, 115–16. *See also specific individuals*
World Student Christian Federation, 60
World War II, 32–33, 34–35, 123, 167

Yakunin, Gleb, 36, 37
Yeltsin, Boris, 138, 205

Zinon (Teodor), Fr., 204